Pamela Sheppard MSW

Faces of the Religious Demon

Freedom Through Deliverance Counseling

Sheppard's Counseling & Publishing Center

Scripture taken from the King James Version

ISBN 978-1-84728-975-9

Published by

Sheppard's Counseling & Publishing Center
P.O.Box 356
East Greenbush, NY 12061

contact@pamsheppard.com

Other books by Pamela Sheppard MSW include:

"To Curse the Root: A Christian Alternative to 12 Steps,
ISBN 1-4259-0766-0

"Come Out of Her, God's People: Don't Receive Her Plagues"
ISBN 978-0-557-41416-1

"The Fake Jesus: Fallen Angels Among Us
ISBN 978-0-6152-1977-6

DEDICATED TO JESSIE PENN-LEWIS

As reflected also in "To Curse the Root and "Come Out of Her, God's People-, as a disciple of the Lord Jesus Christ since March 29, 1977, I am a believer who has withstood a lot of deception simply because I have walked "too comfortably" in things supernatural. For three years prior to becoming a Christian, I was deeply entrenched in New Age occultism, including but not limited to necromancy, hypnosis, telekinesis and astrology. Once I was converted and became exposed to religion, the organized church was ill equipped to advise me on how to recognize demonic deception. Therefore, I have believed that every voice that I have heard and every dream or vision that I have had was from the Lord--- a very serious mistake. Only by the grace and mercy of God, have I survived to overcome. A significant cause of my problem was that I often anchored my faith into scriptures taken out of context.

In spite of my many failures, my heart has not been hardened because much fruit has been obtained through trial and error, a godly wisdom worth more than rubies and gold. Moreover, I realize that the wisdom that I have acquired in Christ Jesus is extremely valuable in the times in which we live. However, without Jessie Penn Lewis, a woman who wrote a life changing book called "War on the Saints" almost 100 years ago , I believe that the mixtures within my own spiritual life would certainly have hindered me from the true victory of authoring this work. An incredible woman of her time, I acknowledge Jessie Penn-Lewis as having written the most life changing book that I myself have ever read. Therefore, "Faces of a Religious Demon" is dedicated to this powerful saint who wrote these words:

> "There must be more than one quantity to make a mixture; at least two. The devil mixes his lies with the truth, for he must use a truth to carry his lies. The believer must therefore discriminate, and judge all things. He must be able to see so much to be impure, and so much that he can accept. Satan is a "mixer." If in anything he finds ninety-nine percent pure, he tries to insert one percent of his poisonous stream, and this grows, if undetected, until the proportions are reversed. Where there is mixture acknowledged to be in meetings where supernatural manifestations take place, if believers are unable to discriminate, they should keep away from these "mixtures" until they are able to discern."

Although I quote "War on the Saints" throughout this book, I recommend that every reader purchase a copy of the unabridged edition for themselves. If Jesus Christ is truly your Lord and Savior and as a born again Christian you desire that your spiritual walk be free of mixtures, then you need to be aware that because of your sincerity and commitment, you are definitely a target for a religious demon. Therefore, the enemy will come at you by trying to insert a mixture, probably under the pretense of counterfeiting the Holy Spirit in order to obtain your cooperation in accepting a deadly deception. I thank the Lord for opening my eyes through the words of this great warrior, a Christian woman of tremendous fortitude and perseverance.

I thank the Lord for using Jessie Penn Lewis to open my eyes. I hope that in turn, you will be blessed by the impact that this powerful woman of God has made upon my life as revealed in these pages.

CONTENTS

INTRODUCTION

INTRODUCTION

You will be shocked to read a serious warning from a minister of more than 25 years contending that it is best that you NOT attend church in your local community. I have a pastor's heart and have functioned in the pastor's calling for about 15 of those years, and I am still a pastor. However, I personally believe that a person can grow spiritually without regularly attending an organized church. Most definitely, you should assemble with the saints, but the word of God does not lay out a detailed order of service, nor does it suggest the day you should assemble, the time or even the nature of the place or building where gathering together should take place. We live in a computerized world, where we can "assemble" 24 and 7. Simply put, I truly believe that the organized church as it now stands will be completely revamped by the Lord. Why? Because quite frankly, the traditional structures are not working. I myself have no replacements to offer, as Healing Waters is in the process of being completely revamped and reformed.

When I wrote the first 3 books, I was hopeful that repentance would bring about reformation and renewal to the organized church. However, the love of money, which is the root of ALL evil, has permeated most of the church and I seriously doubt if the Lord is going to allow it to continue to exist in its present state. Judgment is swiftly coming and I shunder at what is going to happen to church and to churchgoers. In the meantime, for those of you who feel that you need to assemble in an organized church, the following comments are provided for you to assist you in your pursuit to find a church.

Point #1: Simply stated, I personally suspect that the organized church has already been judged relatively recently, perhaps decades, maybe even a century ago. If not, then judgment is very close at hand.

It seems that Satan began to progressively establish a seat within church divisions, sects, and organizations since around the third century. Therefore, I believe that the book of Revelation was written to and for every church age. However, death has been a real blessing for the saints who have already left this earth prior to "the end." Truly, those who are alive when the Lord Jesus Christ returns for the dead and the living will face a challenge that no other church age has been required to face. I believe that we are in that hour NOW---as we live in the best of times and the worst of times. I may see the grave, maybe NOT----but my daughter and my grandson may yet be alive when He comes.

So where do we stand now?

Point #2. Well, I believe that we are in the midst of a transition.

Back in the summer of 1981, as I sat in a chair dozing,--(not asleep yet not fully awake either,) I heard the audible voice of the Lord. I didn't have to try the spirits on this one. Didn't have a chance to. He said "Pam," and my spirit caused my mouth to answer immediately--- "Yes, Lord." Then He said "I am about to do a new thing with My Church." I stirred, stretched a bit and answered, " Uh, huh." Then, in the sweetest voice I have ever heard in my life, He asked very politely, without a hint of command or demand---- "Can I use you??"

I was spiritually ignorant back then and so I answered without even thinking, "Sure Lord.

Let's start with the Roses of Hope." It took years for me to realize that "His church" was not just the local church that I was a member of. In my local church, The Roses of Hope was a money raising group who organized house parties where they had card games and sold liquor to raise money for the church. I had only been a churchgoer for two years in 1981 when the Lord called me.. Likewise, I was still as carnal as the rest of the members, but commonsense told me that there was something not quite right about THIS kind of money raising. lol. Once I mentioned the Roses of Hope, my conversation with the Lord stopped immediately and there was a deep silence. Disappointed, I thought to myself "what did I say that turned Him off?" I was such a babe.

I have heard His voice a few times since but never again quite LIKE THAT!!!

Looking back, I realize that this encounter with the Lord was one of the several ways that I received my calling 26 years ago prior to entering the ministry on Oct. 25, 1981. At that time, I did not know what a sermon was much less a calling to ministry, so it took at least 10 signs for me to finally comprehend that I was being called.

Even so, I have never forgotten the Lord's mentioning of "the new thing." What is the new thing that the Lord is going to do with "His Church?" In 26 years, I can honestly tell you that I do not yet know for sure, but there have been some signs and indications that I will share in upcoming issues.

In August 2007,--- I had yet another "conversation." There was no audible voice this time, as the communication was from " the sender of the message to my spirit and then to my mind." At the time, I was attempting to set up a conference schedule to conduct deliverance training seminars for a local church leader and I ran into a "closed door." Almost immediately, the Lord revealed to me that He was the one who closed the door.

Wondering why, I sought the Father in prayer. It didn't take long for me to be answered. In less than a week, a kind of telepathic communication took place to let me know that I was "on the wrong track". I didn't even have a chance to emotionally respond to the unexpected rejection I had recently experienced. Once I understood that it was God Himself who had "hardened her heart", I completely changed my ministerial direction and I forgot about the particular "friend" in ministry that stood in my way. I realized that God used her to "close the door.". I realize now that my ministry is not to equip or edify the traditional church on church property.

My answer came through a kind of parable. I was asked, "would you put up curtains at the windows of a condemned building?" I answered with my mind. "No." Then a kind of a speech was made that went something like this.

"A homeless person will make a home in a condemned building. To escape the elements of the weather on the outside, he will satisfy himself and "make do" with no heat, no running water, no lights, and he will share his dwelling with the occupants: the rats and the roaches." Then I was hit in the face with this statement. "If you try to edify the organized church with seminars and conferences, you will be putting up curtains at the windows of a condemned building."

Wow! I was stunned. Metaphorically speaking, it was clear to me that the condemned building was a symbol of the organized church. If this "mental conversation" was from the Holy Ghost)===== then the metaphor is suggesting that the organized church is a condemned building. Please note that I am still trying the spirits, so I am not saying "thus says the Lord" in this instance. If you have heard different, please let me know so that we can try the spirits together!!!

Condemnation suggests "judgment." The word says that "judgment will begin at the household of faith." Therefore, natural logic by simple commonsense suggests to me that "the organized church has either already been judged or will be judged very soon."

In keeping with this parable of sorts, sheep who attend church regularly are those who are afraid of the outside elements of a dangerous and sinful world, ---and rightly so-- Therefore, it makes sense to run inside church walls for protection. Yet, in keeping with the symbols, when we run inside, we find that there is no light. God is light. In Him there is no darkness at all. No light--No God!!!!! So what do we do? We "make do!!!" Reminiscing along with James from Atlanta, the church has become skilled at "making do!"

Since Jesus Christ of Nazareth is the Light and His people are referred to "as lights", the next logical thought is that He is not the Head of the organized church and very few of His people are attending church. So what of the massive, mega congregations? Same thing. No light. No God. As astutely recognized in the commentary of Michelle from Va, it's just a crowd of gatherers worshipping someone that they refer to as Jesus. To quote her exact words, "wherever the crowd gathers, there is sin crouching at the door."

In addition, there is no running water in the condemned building--- no rivers of living water---therefore, no Holy Ghost. Without the Holy Ghost, then the 7 stars are removed. The 7 stars are the angels of God.(Rev.1:20) Angels are assigned to the churches to guard and protect each flock. Without the Holy Ghost and the angels of God, it is understandable why the sheep are being spiritually damaged by the shepherds---- The RATS are the wolves in sheep's clothing---- hirelings---the so called shepherds of the flock---- countless pastors who fellowship with uncleanness, ie. the roaches.

So it stands to reason, that if this parable be from the Lord, then the leaders of the church as it now stands have fared poorly in the Lord's eyes. If this be so, then what about the sheep? Sheep need shepherds?!!! Where are the shepherds of the Lord? A condemned building can stand, maybe for years but ultimately, the beams and the walls will crumble and fall. If it doesn't fall, then the city will come along with a bulldozer and "take it down." How will the organized church come down? Read Revelation Ch. 17 and Rev. 18 about "the harlot" called Mystery Babylon.

After the fall of the towers of the World Trade Center, I thought that Rev. Ch. 18 was fulfilled for several reasons. However, one fact caused me to know that the dust fallout in NYC and the fall of "world trade" was not the complete fulfillment of this chapter. Why? Because the World Trade Center is being rebuilt. The scripture clearly states that when Babylon falls, there will be no rebuilding of her.

So I wrongly assumed that Mystery Babylon was NYC. I was born and raised in NYC. Therefore, in error, I warned everyone I knew to "come out of her." After a few years passed, I realized that NYC is NOT Babylon, nor is the USA. Any one who knows the Lord realizes that He would not command us to "come out of her, my people" (Rev. 18:4), "lest you share in her sins, lest you receive of her plagues," unless there was an actual place where we could flee to.

Where are God's people? Well, for the most part, God's people are known to be in the organized church. If Mystery Babylon were an actual city or nation, where on earth could all of God's people go in an exodus of unimaginable global proportions? Recognizing the signs of the time, a few Christians have already fled to Canada, believing that in doing so, they are going to escape the fall of America.

I say this to you. America is not Babylon because God's people are everywhere so where are His people in every nation on the planet supposed to go? To the Moon or to Mars? No. I don't know about you but I don't own a space ship. Even though severak mega-tv evangelists own personal jet planes, they don't own space ships!!! Regardless of what anybody says, America is the best country in the entire world. Meaning no disrespect to non-American readers, seekers of freedom from around the world flee their native lands all the time to find a safe harbor on American shores. There is no actual "place" that God's people can go to on this earth.

Ironically, the USA is a country founded upon the flight of spiritually oppressed people from the Old World. However, since Christopher Columbus, oppressed Americans have no earthly place that we ourselves can flee to. Think about it. Can all of God's people in the USA fit into Canada? Let's be real, here. Anyway, if America is to fall, how safe is Canada? Canada is just around the corner from us. We'd be better off in Australia or the South Pole!!!!

BUT Fear not!!! Mystery Babylon could certainly not be a physical place. In previous issues, I referred to "the Fake Jesus" and other Ascended Masters aka "fallen angels", with the two leading ones calling themselves Maitreya and Jesus Sananda Immanuel. (To read the first 6 issues on the Fake Jesus, click here.) I am not alone in my belief that Mystery Babylon is a mataphor symbolizing idolatrous religion. The "judged" church is not Mystery Babylon in its totality, but merely a part of it, Actually, there are several signs that the organized churches of today will eventually unite with all of the other false religions that relegate our Lord to a mere teacher or a prophet who they claim is a created being, "not divine".

Yet I believe that most of the true church will rise out of a righteous remnant that still remains within the organized church and others whom the Lord has touched and called who have never been church members. I realize that the outpouring of the spirit of God upon ALL flesh is coming upon "the remnant church" but clearly, the Holy Ghost will not manifest Himself in a corrupt place. The Lord will not put new wine into old wineskins. However, where the rivers will flow, I do not yet know.

Does the "new thing" require buildings to do the work of the Lord.? No, but if so, I suspect that buildings will be used on a very limited scale. The early church of the book of Acts "was not organized," as followers of the resurrected Lord assembled in each other's homes. Likewise, I don't believe that the "new thing" will be organized with boards, bishops and buildings either!!!! The only covering required is the Head Himself, Jesus Christ of Nazareth. Praise His Holy Name!!!

Nor do I believe that anyone will be able to stand in the way of "the new thing." I have perceived some signs that quietly and secretly the Holy Ghost has been taking His time over the last few decades, preparing righteous and holy shepherds--Joshuas and Calebs--- who have been refined in the fires of trial, trouble and tribulation--- leaders across the globe. There are not many of them, but like Gideon's army, there will be enough to do the job.

So what should we do in the meantime? Well, we should "watch, pray and wait. " Some of God's people have already heeded the call and we have "come out of her." Others of you may have to stay within the condemned building for a time or at least on its periphery, until you too "hear the call."

It is not my job to "call you out." This is not my intention. Some people are addicted to church and if they were to "come out" without the proper care and support systems in place, additional spiritual damage might be incurred. As withdrawal from alcohol without medical supervision is life threatening, so too, an exodus from the organized church at the present moment may be too shocking to the spiritual system of longterm "churchaholics."

Actually, it is wise NOT to come out until you hear the Holy Ghost for yourself. The problem is that most sheep within church walls for a considerable length of time are so deaf and so blind that they simply cannot hear and they cannot see. Moreover, the enemy has built up a formidable stronghold by seducing them to heed and believe false doctrines or to become emotionally attached to pastors, buildings, church traditions, choir members, etc.. The god of this world has blinded them, almost beyond repair. (II Cor 4:3,4) Only God Himself can release the prey of the mighty and set free the lawfully captive. (Isaiah 49:24-26) In each case of spiritual blindness, prayer should beseech the Father based upon His mercy, grace and pardon.

My job is simple. I preach righteousness and truth, both by mouth and on the printed page. That's all I have to do. The Lord does His work of deliverance, and from time to time, allows me to share in His power. I commit to sending you the truth through each and every issue and let the Spirit of Truth --aka- the Holy Ghost open your spiritual ears to hear, to understand and to obey Him when He calls you out of Mystery Babylon. By His grace anad mercy, I believe that He will restore your spiritual hearing and your spiritual sight, if the condition of your heart is sincere, meek and upright. You yourself have an unction from God to see and if you hunger and thirst after righteousness, I strongly believe that when the time is right, you will hear His call.

To simplify matters, here is a general overview of the organized church of today.

There are two main sects of Christians: Catholics and Protestants. Within Protestantism, there are three main branches: the denominations, the non-denominations, and the word of faith/charismatic movement. The church of James from Atlanta's youth falls under the category of a denomination, the Baptist Church. The second church that James and Michelle both describe is what is categorized as a word of faith, non-denominational charismatic church.

There are many denominations. There are a few denominations that are charismatic, ie. the pentecostal churches. There is one denomination that calls itself "full gospel baptist."

It should be pointed out that every non-denominational church is not necessarily charismatic or word of faith. However, practically ALL word of faith churches are charismatic and therefore they have much in common with some denominational pentecostal churches.

So where should you attend church while you "watch and wait" for the Lord's "new thing?" Good question. Everyone is not like me. As a watchman, I was actually called to stand alone. So this is just my opinion for those who have a different calling. My advice may be of some value to you, as it is based upon decades of experience with the denominational and the non-denominational, charismatic word of faith movement.

Point #3 In truth, I personally believe that the best option---the wisest choice--is to stay out of the organized church entirely, especially if you are a babe in Christ or one who is lost, but seeking Him.

However, if you a churchgoer and you are still attached or even addicted to "church", then know this. By far, if you are attending a charismatic church, be it Pentecostal, or word of faith---

you are not in a safe place.

section I

wiles and strategies

Chapter 1:"The house is burning!!!"

Only second to preaching the gospel in His Great Commission, the Lord Jesus Christ instructed His disciples to go forth and cast out demons in His Name by the power of the Holy Ghost. (Mark 16:17) In the Lord's day and time, this was a rather simple instruction. During His ministry, Jesus did not have to teach, defend or explain the existence of the unseen world because the people grasped the reality of demons without difficulty. In fact, both natural and spiritual discernment of evil spirits was commonplace. For example, when a woman of Canaan came to Jesus on behalf of her daughter, He did not have to convince or persuade her that her daughter was demonized. This Canaanite mother was certainly not ignorant as she cried out to Jesus "my daughter is severely vexed with a devil." It is obvious from the scripture that she understood what demonic oppression entailed. (Matthew 15:2)

Yet, almost two thousand years later, the ignorance of bible toting people of God concerning the powers of darkness has caused "Faces of the Religious Demon" to be both vital and necessary. In truth, Satan has been extremely successful over the centuries to not only keep the church in the dark about himself and his devices, but the religious demon has actually been able to manipulate the organized church to even promote Satan's sinister agenda. Almost one hundred years ago, Jessie Penn-Lewis, in collaboration with Evangelist Evan Roberts wrote a life-saving and life changing book entitled "War on the Saints." As indicated in my dedication, this book has no competition or comparison. Simply put, the pain of opening my blind eyes to how the religious demon had deceived me palled to the astounding joy that truth brings. "War on the Saints" literally set me free, equipped me to serve and inspired the contents of this book.

One hundred years ago, Sister Lewis and Brother Evans saw evidence in their time that the church of their day had been restored to a good measure of the Pentecostal power and authority of the early church. Therefore, "War on the Saints" was written as a kind of textbook to the church of the early 1900's. These two brave spiritual warriors were compelled to warn their contemporaries of the special onslaught of an army of deceiving spirits unleashed upon the organized church of their day:

> "Through lack of knowledge, the majority of even the most spiritual people, do not carry out a full and perpetual war upon this army of wicked spirits; and many are shrinking from the subject, and the call to war against them, saying that if Christ is preached it is not necessary to give prominence to the existence of the devil, nor to enter into direct conflict with him, and his hosts. Yet large numbers of the children of God are becoming a prey to the enemy for lack of this very knowledge, and through the silence of teachers on this vital truth, the Church of Christ is passing on into the peril of the closing days of the age, unprepared to meet the onslaught of the foe. On account of this, and in view of the plainly given prophetic warnings of the Scriptures; the already manifest influx of the evil hosts of Satan among the children of God; and the many signs that we are actually in the 'later time' referred to by the Apostle; all believers should welcome such knowledge about the powers of darkness, as will enable them to pass through the fiery trial of these days, without being ensnared by the foe." (War on the Saints, 9th edition, pg. 2)

Unfortunately, from the spiritual workshop of my own ministerial experience within the organized church, I have perceived that this warning certainly has not been heeded and the perilous prediction of "War on the Saints" has been virtually ignored for almost a century. In this present hour, I sense that the organized house of God is burning and the man-made institutional programs and structures themselves are headed toward ever increasing worldly compromise. As the institution of "church" moves toward becoming "Mystery Babylon," the blind lead the blind. Since the publication of "War on the Saints," the 20th century has come and gone. How pathetic it would be if we who live in the 21st century allowed ourselves to be destroyed for a lack of knowledge of the wiles of the devil, when we are the unique recipients of a computerized age, unprecedented within human history for the availability of knowledge and information.

I myself wonder if the wiles and strategies of the religious demon within the organized church have been overlooked for too many decades. Is it possible that the revival and restoration of its former glory may not be resurrected, no matter how hard the faithful pray ? At this point in time, I can honestly declare, "I don't know." Too often I hear in the spirit the Lord's voice cry out to those who remain in Mystery Babylon, "Come out of her, My people, that ye be not partakers of her sins, and that ye receive not of her plagues." (Revelation 18:4) Those whom the Lord would call "my people", could He be referring to traditional churchgoers? I suspect so.

Therefore, I call the discerning to rise up out of the burning house and arm yourself with knowledge concerning how to extinguish the fires that are tormenting and ultimately destroying God's people for a lack of knowledge of the truths that are in this book. I call those in the true church, the Body of the Lord Jesus Christ, to be baptized with the powerful waters of the Holy Ghost, waters that heal. As long as I live I will never forget the day--- January 8, 1983---that the spirit of prophecy overshadowed a 9 year old girl in my living room when this young child cried out "the waters of heaven shall flow down upon the house of the minister and the minister's daughter. These waters shall heal the city. Great miracles shall flow from this house." Then, 7 months later, the first trickle of deliverance water that flowed from our spiritual house materialized when my daughter at 14 years old and I faced a demon for the first time, and together, we cast it out.

For many years I believed that this prophecy about miracles flowing from the outpouring of "waters that heal" was yet unfulfilled, completely overlooking the words of Jesus Himself when He revealed that the casting out of demons is, in itself , a miracle. (Mark 9:39). God's prophetic announcement is not empty or void of power but it will bring forth what it boldly commands. Most certainly yet rather unobtrusively, I have been casting out demons from professing Christians since 1983 yet not once within the approval or even the concern of any organized church. In truth, to operate this ministry openly and without hindrance, the Lord chose to call me out of the African Methodist Episcopal Zion denomination in June 2004. He showed me in a dream that I was like a light that was hidden under a mattress. The Holy Ghost made it very clear to me that He would not perform miracles in my ministry if I remained in a dark, dry, defamed place. Therefore, I moved out of the dark and dry into the light and wetness of "healing waters."

Could it be that the destructive fire within countless denominational, and non-denominational churches of the 21st century may be too out of control to extinguish?

Could it be that the parable of the kingdom of God, where Jesus described how a mustard seed grew to monstrous proportions---a huge tree where the birds of the air came and lodged in its branches is symbolic of the organized church in our times? Moreover, are the birds a metaphorical depiction of the religious demons that now lodged in the organized church's many branches or denominations and sects? (Matthew 13:31) It is rather clear in the beginning of Matthew Ch. 13 verses 4 and 18 that Jesus opened the parable with "birds" as symbolic of demons or of "the evil one." Consequently, I don't believe that within the very same teaching, the Lord would not maintain the same symbolism for birds throughout Chapter 13 of Matthew's gospel.

There are those who are feverishly trying to save the institutional house through evangelistic programs and revivals, church reformation attempts, mass media marketing campaigns, and ecumenical collaborations and compromises. These are those who believe that emphasis should be placed on saving the institution of the organized church. However, I believe the Lord's declaration of the prevailing power of the church was not referring to her as an institution, but as a spiritual body of believers who, by not denying His name and keeping the faith, would remain His. The question is not whether or not the burning house SHOULD be saved. No, the question goes a lot deeper. The question is "CAN the burning house be saved? Quite frankly, sin and deception has permeated the house so deeply, that only a profound, deep move of repentance and contrition can save the organized church. As Jesus declared to the 7 churches in the book of Revelation, "Remember therefore, from whence thou art fallen, and REPENT, and do the first works, or else I will come unto thee quickly, and will remove thy candlestick from his place, except thou REPENT." (Revelation 2:5) Since He clearly states that the candlestick is a metaphor for the church, it is apparent that Jesus Himself will bring down various organized church systems.

Therefore, "Faces of the Religious Demon" is a work of love to those who remain in the true spiritual house without walls--- His Body---a house that cannot and will not burn. The destructive fire of deception that emanates from the gates of hell may have already prevailed against the institutional buildings of stain glass, brick and mortar. I don't know. However, of one thing, I am certain. Satan's army will never win against the true Body of Christ. As such, with this book, I am steadfastly committed to fighting to win freedom for souls who are in bondage to religion. As a spiritual fire-fighter, my job is to rescue the perishing. Perhaps various readers will recognize that they are bound by perceiving a reflexion of themselves in either one case or in bits and pieces from other profiles. If you are among believers in Jesus Christ, non-believers in Him and even among agnostics who happen to be tired of the superficial, the unfruitful and the religious, then reading this book is worth your while. In fact, if one reader receives light that penetrates his or her darkness, I count it as the ultimate success. I pray that you will have an open mind to face the truth and seek help.

Endnotes:

1.Iaking of a Prophet: A Spiritual Indictment to the Organized Church." Also published by Author House and Healing Waters Counseling Center, (ISBN 1-4208-4725-2) this book will be an eyeopener regarding how a religious demon has infiltrated a historic African American denominational church over a 200 year period.
2.If you would like to officially register in our deliverance training program called "The SEW Program", then email us at thesewprogram@yahoo.com , expressing your desire to

register.
If you seek deliverance counseling by telephone, then contact us at hwccdeliverance@yahoo.com or call our toll free number at 1-866-492-2409

Chapter 2 Exposing Counterfeits

When I consider the Lord's parable concerning the five foolish virgins and the five wise virgins, my attention is drawn to His last words of admonition---"watch therefore." (Matthew 25:13) My understanding of the symbols in this particular last days parable is that the five foolish virgins are born again believers within the spiritual house who will be ill prepared to recognize the signs of the times and the Lord's soon return. Some have considered that since the foolish virgins were "without oil," that this is a sign that they were not saved in the first place and therefore represented nominal, unsaved churchgoers. I disagree with that interpretation.   Metaphorically, a virgin symbolizes purity in the natural. Since a parable is a natural story that highlights a spiritual truth, virginity is akin to sinlessness or righteousness from a spiritual perspective. How can an unsaved person be symbolized as clean and untainted? Therefore, I believe that all 10 of the virgins in this parable symbolize the elect of God , with the five foolish among them falling to the deception of counterfeits, mainly because "they were not watching."

To watch is to keep awake, attentive and alert as the epitome of vigilance. Watching involves caution, discretion and an emotional detachment from every factor that would distract one's attention from the primary issues at hand in a particular situation. The best watching is an observation that maintains a certain distance from those obstacles that are distracting , because obstructions of this kind draw our attention away from what is crucial to discern. I suspect that Peter the Apostle remembered the words of the Lord's prediction concerning how he would deny the Lord three times. Peter neglected to be vigilant to guard himself from the influence of the religious demon on the day the Lord was crucified, a factor that provided a doorway for the lying spirit and the demon of fear. Although Peter did not heed the Lord's warning that Satan desired to sift him like wheat, the prayers of Jesus kept Peter's faith from failing him. (Luke 22:31) With the hard lessons of Satan's wiles well learned, Peter was well equipped by his own failure, truly capable of warning the Christians of his day through first hand experience:

> Be sober, be vigilant; because your adversary the   devil, as a roaring lion, walketh about, seeking whom he may devour: Whom resist steadfast in   the   faith, knowing that the same afflictions are accomplished in your brethren that are in the   world.   (I   Peter 5:8,9)

To this equation of watching, the Lord Jesus also added prayer. (Mark 14:38)   In teaching His disciples to pray, the Lord provided His followers in every generation that followed with the reason why prayer is mandatory. Simply put, God's will is not being done on earth as it is in heaven. We watch to know how to pray and what to pray. I myself take every new counterfeit exposed by alert and purposeful watching as the meat of my prayer life. Today my prayers stop demons in their tracks before they can even initiate a deception. By maintaining an attitude of watching as a strategy of resisting the enemy, my continual prayer is that the Lord will allow the Holy Spirit to enlighten my path.   In this regard, I have found that prayer involves making a commitment to refuse all ground to demons and taking back all that we ever gave to them by our mistakes and ignorance, surrendering ALL to Jesus Christ.

Although not   terminology directly used in the bible, a synonymous term for the religious demon in the New Testament is   the spirit of the Antichrist (I John 2:18) The spirit of the Antichrist will cleverly infiltrate the church and use religion to both deny and defy Christ very sneakily. The Apostle Paul also warned Timothy about seducing spirits that teach false religious doctrine (I Timothy 4:1-4) as well as those who have a form of godliness but who deny the power. (II Timothy 3:5). Paul also warned the church of a class of demons that could transform themselves into beings of light,--- false apostles and deceitful workers hidden within human vessels, within a clever masquerade of   genuine apostles of Christ. (II Corinthians 11:13-15) The Catholic deification of the Lord's mother Mary is yet a very clever device of the spirit of the Antichrist.   A classic example is evident within Catholicism, where followers not only pray to Mary , but teach that she herself was immaculately conceived. Truly, the deification of the Lord's mother is a subtle, though outright   denial of the Lord's sole divinity. It is true that Mary was a virgin when she conceived Jesus, but she did not remain a virgin. She became the mother of James and the Lord's other brothers and sisters, children conceived through carnal knowledge.

If you are a Roman Catholic, I will tell you the truth in love. It is true that Mary was a virgin when Jesus was born but she did not remain a virgin throughout her lifespan. Furthermore, in scripture, one could surmise that there was some friction between Jesus and His family during the course of His three year ministry. This is why when they sought to speak with Him and Jesus was told that his family was waiting outside, Jesus practically retorted, "my mother and my brothers are those who hear the word of God and obey it." In other words, the implication was that his natural family were not obeying the word of God, and that would include Mary. Mary was at the cross, and John took care of her for her remaining years. She was a saint in the same way that all who follow the Lord Jesus Christ are called "saints." That means you , if you are born again. In short, Mary is dead, her spirit is with God but her body is in the grave with the rest of the saints. Only the saints who were dead at the Lord's crucifixion have been raised. (Matthew 27:51-53) Since Mary was not among the dead at that time, she too is waiting for the return of her Son to obtain a bodily resurrection of the saints along with the rest of those that have departed in Him.

The Lord Jesus Christ is merciful and full of grace. For centuries, He has tolerated a unholy competition with the false image the Roman Catholic Church has created of His birth mother. In his Internet article entitled "The Truth About Roman Catholicism" by M.H.   Reynolds,   you   will   find   these words:(http://catholic.cephasministry.com/the_truth_about_catholicism.html)

> "The place accorded Mary in the Roman Catholic Church is not scriptural nor is it new, but it cannot be denied that, during the last one hundred years, veneration of Mary has dramatically increased....note that the exaltation of Mary and the term, Mother of God, became official Catholic dogma in 431 AD with prayers to her proclaimed in 600 A.D. But, note also that the Immaculate Conception of the Virgin Mary was not proclaimed until 1854; her 'Assumption' not until 1950; and her title 'Mother of the Church" 'not until as recently as 1965."

In the Bible, the word fornication and idolatry were connected. In heathen nations like Ephesus for example, prostitutes would have sex with men right in the temple to appease the goddess Diana. Throughout the old testament, God would speak to His people through the prophets and call them harlots because they followed after or worshiped other gods of neighboring heathen nations. In the Book of Revelation, when Jesus addresses the church at Thyatira, He expresses indignation at a local false prophetess that he surnamed "Jezebel." I believe the Lord is saying to the church at Thyatira, "you have created a goddess out of a woman to worship her. In this way you have committed fornication or idolatry and have broken My commandment which says that you shall have no other gods but Me!" Along these same lines, I believe that Roman Catholicism has created "a Jezebel" out of the Lord's mother Mary.

Therefore, in keeping with the spirit of Mary, another synonym for the religious demon is "the spirit of Jezebel," imputed by the Lord with both an old and a new testament influence. (Revelation 2:20) The spirit of Jezebel will be defined in more detail in later chapters, but simply and generally defined, the spirit of Jezebel is a demon with two interconnected facets: religion and witchcraft. As a false prophetess and a religious goddess, these two demons also function separately but they work together in the spirit of Jezebel.

I also believe that unseen force behind old testament Babylon, the building of the tower of Babel and several other forms of pre-Christian idolatry are in themselves "religious." The first time I personally heard the term "religious spirit" or "religious demon" was in a prophecy that I received in 1983. In this word, I was given a spiritual warfare assignment against 7 high ranking demons that I began to refer to as "the Seven Walls", with the religious demon as wall number 5 in the list: alcohol and drugs, homosexuality, prostitution, witchcraft, the religious demon, prejudice and poverty. Years later, I was surprised to learn that the term "religious demon" was actually being used by well known Christian writers like Derek Prince, Rick Joyner and others.

What has astounded and simultaneously humbled me the most in my personal contact with the deception of the religious demon is that like Jesus, religious demons were assigned to me from the very foundation of my ministry. As Jesus was driven into the wilderness to be tempted of Satan at the beginning of His ministry, I too was confronted on the day that I preached my first sermon. To memorialize the occasion, a picture was taken of me on October 25, 1981 at the conclusion of the worship service. To my amazement, the face of a gargoyle is quite distinguishable in the background, outlined in green on the photograph, with its green eyebrow positioned slightly across the forefinger of my left hand. The religious demon has been my unseen watchdog for decades,--- sending me false dreams, false healing, ministerial enemies and counterfeits of all kinds, particularly pretenders sent to befriend me as ministerial helpers.

Yes, I have been surrounded by Judas Iscariot types, a few as betrayers but most of these religious demons have used counterfeit professors of faith in Jesus Christ, disguised as believers. Planted within my ministry to try to derail me from my divine purpose, it has taken years for some of them to be exposed.1 As Judas' betrayal of Jesus was crucial to the Lord's fulfillment of His destiny at the cross and as Peter who denied Him was used as a vessel to start and build the New Covenant church upon the rock of the Lord's victory, religious demons sent to me within various proclaimers of faith have also served me well. As no spiritual experience is ever wasted for those who are in Christ Jesus, these counterfeits and hypocrites were also used by the Lord to bring forth the truths revealed in this book. The spiritual fruit that is presented within these pages is the conclusive evidence that the evil inflicted by the enemy to a true child of God will work together for good to those who love God and are called according to His purpose. (Romans 8:28)

In the final analysis, my love for the Lord Jesus Christ is upheld in my relentless search for and commitment to truth. Therefore, I can look back over almost 3 decades in the Lord and declare that no weapon that the enemy formed against me prospered. From members in churches that I have pastored to church leaders of all ranks and positions, to friends and even men who became my husbands, the religious demon either in the form of the spirit of Judas, Jezebel or the Anti-Christ was each exposed before major damage was inflicted upon me. What was covered has been uncovered, and what was hid has been made known. What I have learned in the dark, is now manifested in the light. Birthed out of much trial, tribulation and trouble, the persecution, the wiles and the strategies of this many faceted demonic trio of the spirits of Judas, Jezebel and the Anti-Christ have been progressively unmasked over time. In truth, I am a rebel with a cause---my cause is complete deliverance for the captives in spirit, soul and body. As a revolutionary, I personally concur with the words of George Barna in his book entitled "Revolution":

> "Get used to the fact that your life is lived in the context of warfare. Every breath you take is an act of war. To survive and thrive in the midst of the spiritual battle in which you live, seek a faith context and experience that will enhance your capacity to be Christ-like. This mission demands single-minded commitment and a disregard for the criticisms of those who lack the same dedication to the cause of Christ. You answer to only one Commander in Chief, and only you will give an explanation for your choices. Do whatever you have to do to prove that you fear God, you love Him, and you serve Him---yes, that you live only for Him. That is the commitment of a Revolutionary." "(Revolution, pg. 26,27) 2

I myself am so committed. In view of the fact that I have dedicated this book to Jessie Penn-Lewis, a woman who, in my estimation, is one of the most outstanding spiritual revolutionaries of the 19th and 20th centuries, I believe that it is important to point out to her critics from the outset that I do not personally believe that a demon can enter into the spirit of a born again person. Jessie has been misquoted and therein misunderstood. I believe that the regenerate spirit is the exclusive domain of the Holy Spirit, where light and darkness have no fellowship or concord. (I Corinthians 6:9). Even so, it is clear that demons of sickness and infirmity are capable of residing in various parts of a true Christian's body. Demons may also seduce, vex, torment and confuse the human soul, but I personally believe that the newborn spirit of the bona fide Christian is demon free.

Moreover, I believe that the deception surrounding whether or not demons can possess a Christian,--- spirit, soul and body--- is caused by the fact that there are many professing believers in the organized church who are not really saved and therefore any apparent possession is rooted in a counterfeit salvation experience. A deeper treatment of this subject can be found in Chapter 4 entitled "Counterfeit Births."Sister Jessie maintained that any ground obtained by a demon, no matter how small or seemingly insignificant, is "ground possessed," even though the captive himself may have no obvious manifestation of total possession. I myself happen to agree with her point of view.

It is important to note that a powerful tool of the enemy is to cause believers to argue and contend over the concept of Christian possession, a clever device to divert attention away from the real issues. In my mind, even though the term "possessed Christian" is an oxymoron, even the slightest of ground claimed by the enemy can be so debilitating and even toxic to spiritual growth and empowerment, that "what's the point of quibbling over terms and inches?!!" I have found that if a demon has only one inch of territory, it will seem like a mile to a tormented captive. Once the Body of Christ clearly "gets the picture" of the existence of an unseen host of evil spirit-beings actively engaged in deceiving and misleading every human being, only then will we be able to trace and track their operations in the lives of others and especially within our own lives.

The main purpose of this book is to unmask the true nature of the warfare as it pertains to exposing religious counterfeits. Counterfeits come disguised like faces covered with various masks. Each face of the religious demon offers new insights and new challenges because of the various façades that human beings unconsciously employ as defense mechanisms in order to maintain pretenses. Since the flesh is naturally adept at self deception, demons use human innate weaknesses as an entrance or "doorway" to mix their own brand of deception with the self deception of the captive. Consequently, the demonic face hides behind the captives own persona, making exposure problematic. The lust of the flesh, the lust of the eyes and the pride of life within the captive's natural carnality provides a convenient cover to the unseen forces where demons will hide within.

As the pride system wavers, I have found that the captive will begin to get a better view of his real self. As he starts to feel his own feelings, to recognize his own desires, to gain his freedom of choice, to make his own decisions, the opposing forces line themselves up to keep the captive bound. With increasing clarity, the captive's real self begins to emerge and his soul senses the difference between his real image or "face" and the mask of the religious demon. Yet, he has become accustomed to passivity. This inner conflict of great dimensions is astutely explained in "War on the Saints:"

> "Passivity! How many have fallen into it, little knowing their state! Through the passivity of their faculties much time is lost in dependence upon the help of outward circumstances, and environment. In the lives of so many there is much 'doing,' with so little accomplished, many beginnings, and few endings. How familiar we are with the words 'Yes, I can do that,' and the impulse is moved by the time the need for action has come, the passive man has lost his momentary interest. This is the key to much of the lamented 'apathy,' and the dulled sympathy of Christians to really spiritual things, whilst they are keenly alive to the social, or worldly elements around them. The worldling can be stirred in the acutest feeling for the sufferings of others, but many of the children of God have, unknowingly, opened themselves to a supernatural power which has dulled them in thought, and mind and sympathy. Ever craving for comfort and happiness and peace in spiritual things, they have sung themselves into a 'passivity'---i.e., a passive state of 'rest,' 'peace' and 'joy'---which has given opportunity to the powers of darkness to lock them up in the prison of themselves, and thus make them almost incapable of acutely understanding the needs of a suffering world." (War on the Saints, 9th edition, pg. 84) 3

The subtle inroads of passivity are hard to travel. However, once the captive commits himself to walk in the light as opposed to continued darkness, the counterfeits become progressively clearer to the open-minded believer in Christ Jesus. The many devices of the religious demon become clear once the searchlight of truth begins to shine on those areas that the captive's pride system had trained him to ignore, justify or minimize. For example, as the captive learns the difference between the presence of God and the Person of God, he will understand the counterfeits of the religious demon. When the captive learns that both the Father and the Holy Spirit will never usurp or even minimize the Son's place within the godhead, the captive will begin to see how counterfeits were able to fool him once he began to pray directly to the Holy Spirit or to the Father without mentioning the name of Jesus.

SPIRIT AND SOUL ARE NOT THE SAME!

Various strategies of the religious demon are presented in these pages so as to prepare the elect not to fall to deception in the latter days. Therefore, in order to understand how a person becomes demonized, it is important that the reader understands himself as a triune being: spirit, soul and body. In summary, the spirit is that part of man's nature that receives communication from God and learns to understand Him. The soul acts as the conductor or mediator to the spirit. Man's soul includes his personality, his intellect, his emotions and his will. All people have such a soul, and the different elements of the soul can either serve God or be yielded to sin. Man's spirit is a higher faculty in man that comes alive when a person becomes a Christian, as Paul had written in Romans 8:10, "If Christ is in you, although your bodies are dead because of sin, your spirits are alive because of righteousness."

Therefore, the spirit of a person is that part of him or her that most directly worships and prays to God (John 4:24, Phil 3:3). New Testament writers identify the 'body',--- a person's physical being,--- as distinct from one's soul and spirit. Since the spirit is the exclusive domain of a born again person, I believe that the demons that afflict the saved reside in either the soul or some internal organ of the body. The stomach and the brain seem to be the most likely location of the precise place where the demons take residence in the body of a saved person. When in the soul, demons most often inhabit the mind, the emotions and the human will.

In Greek literature, the word 'flesh' usually meant nothing more than the human body. It was also used this way in the New Testament (John 1:14, Rev 17:16; 19:18, 21). However, Paul often used the word 'flesh' to denote the entire fallen human being, not just the sinful body but the entire being, as affected by sin. When the unbeliever "walks in the spirit", he can only experience the dark side of the occult and even when he believes that he is walking in the light, he is still in darkness. Since witchcraft is a work of the flesh, no one but a saved person can truly "walk in the spirit." However, the believer can also live in the flesh or in his carnal nature. Paul repeatedly encourages the believers to overcome the deeds of the flesh by living in the spirit. In Galatians 5:17, Paul writes "For the flesh lusts against the spirit, and the spirit against the flesh; and these are contrary to one another, so that you do not do the things that you wish."

From this verse, we note that the potential of the flesh energized by Satan in the life of the Christian should not be underestimated. Given free rein, the flesh will direct our choices, making us do what we know we should not do. This inner conflict between the flesh with his human spirit is very real, but there is considerable disagreement as to its precise meaning. Some believe that 'flesh' here refers to a 'sinful nature' continuing after salvation, while others view it as simply the physical flesh and its natural tendencies. Still others focus on the 'fleshly' or 'worldly' habits and patterns that continue after justification. Although the precise meaning of 'flesh' (in this verse) is unclear, Paul's intent is plain. The desires of our flesh are at odds with what the Holy Spirit desires for us, which is to be free from sin.

When the Bible refers to the "flesh" in connection to human nature, it does not mean the body. Flesh on the body consists of muscle, fat, skin, etc. However, the term "flesh" in the word of God is referring to our carnal nature. The flesh, or the carnal nature, is a mixture between the soul and the spirit and the soul and the body. Carnal Christians are said to be "flesh oriented." The flesh masquerades as "spiritual." Those who are in "the flesh", cannot please God. (Romans 8:8) I don't believe that this scripture is referring to the physical body but rather to human nature that has not been subjected to the cross of Christ. When the flesh has not been broken by God, it is controlled by its earthly humanity. Human nature has the capacity for "good works" that can appear to be "spiritual" and therefore, it must be crucified and rendered "dead in Christ." The good not only "die young," but good people also die and on the other side, they find themselves in hell because they never knew Jesus. Once the good side of human nature is crucified along with the sinful side, only then can we walk in the spirit and not fulfill the lust of our flesh.

In 1 Thessalonians 5:23, Paul writes: "Now may the God of peace Himself sanctify you completely; and may your whole spirit, soul, and body be preserved blameless at the coming of our Lord Jesus Christ." Notice the particular order of 'spirit', 'soul' and 'body' in this verse. As this verse indicates, God works from the inside out, sanctifying our entire being so that we can live with Him forever. Consequently, the process of a person's salvation does not begin with the soul. At rebirth, the spirit is immediately changed; from within our new garment or wine skin, the process of sanctification begins in the regenerated spirits where the Holy Spirit has taken residence. Even so, our souls are incrementally changed on a daily basis over the length of our remaining years on earth. As we submit to the leading of the Holy Spirit by presenting our entire being,--- spirit, soul and body--- to the triune God as a living sacrifice, our transformation into the image of Jesus Christ will be in motion and continue throughout our lifetime, as long as we don't grieve the Holy Ghost by being conformed to this world. (Romans 12: 1,2)

The true meaning of obtaining eternal life is to allow the Son to reveal the Father and the Holy Spirit to reveal the Son. One of the main reasons for Jesus coming to earth was to be a living symbol of the Father to mankind. This is because God is a Spirit. The spirit is difficult to understand without a living or natural symbol. Therefore, Jesus on earth is the living, human symbol Who is also divine. When we look in the face of Jesus in the gospels, we are able to see the Father and as we watch and study Jesus in the gospels, we can perceive the character of the triune God.

Just as the Father, the Son and the Holy Ghost are One, so to is the trinity of each human being who is also "one"--- yet with separate and distinct functions, abilities and manifestations. The soul is the agent that links the spirit world and the body. Man could not exist without the soul. The spirit can leave the body and travel a certain distance and return. However, once the soul has left, the body is "brain dead" or deceased. The soul also receives, evaluates, discards and or accepts messages between the spirit and the body, as it makes decisions through human will power. Besides man's will, the soul consists of the mind, the emotions, feelings, perceptions, and personality. The body is only aware of earth consciousness----what it can sense in the physical world. It cannot communicate to the spirit directly without the help of the mind, located not only in the brain,but within the human soul. The soul within the body is aware of the physical world. For example, the mind knows when the body is in pain.

To project a more precise picture of how the 3 parts interact with each other, consider the example of feeling the sensation to urinate. While you are awake, the sensation tells the brain who enlightens the mind that you need to find a bathroom. No problem. Yet, just go to sleep. Upon receiving the same sensation, while the soul is sleeping, the spirit will create a bathroom in your dream in a rather imaginative way. You will actually see yourself going to the bathroom, yet since your soul has been inactive, your body has not taken any action. As you continue to sleep, your spirit caused your mind to believe that you have already urinated but your body is still having the sensation. Ultimately, the body will take charge by increasing the sensation, wake up the soul, and then you will get up out of the bed and find the bathroom. In some cases, the body will override the soul as in the case of bed wetters. However, most often, it is the soul who supervised the entire action. Without the soul's involvement, no action will take place. In this particular example, while the soul was asleep, the spirit tried to help out, but any bathroom that the spirit created was only imaginary. The soul is the glue that connects two different planes of existence.

Furthermore, the soul is immortal. As such, after death, the soul will not only store emotional memory, but the souls of those who do not die in Jesus will have memory of pain beyond the grave.(Luke 16: 19-31) Therefore, the soul is connected to both the physical and spiritual realms. It has the power of free will and is responsible for the eternal welfare of the person. Before Adamic sin, I believe the spirit controlled the whole person as Adam and Eve spoke with God face to face. After the fall, the soul became dominant, often yielding to the pressures of the body. As it now stands, for the spirit to govern, the soul must give its consent. In the bible, man is compared to a building. In fact, Jesus referred to man as a house in Matthew 12. Man is also called "a temple." As the temple of God, we are like the tabernacle of the children of Israel in the Old Testament. The courtyard is akin to our body, the holy place is like our soul. The Holy of Holies is compared to our spirit, where God in the person of the HOLY SPIRIT resides, once we are born again.

A part of the soul's renewal is brokenness followed by restoration. Brokenness is extremely important to deliverance because the Lord requires us to be "crucified" before we can be used. Brokenness is that time in life when we are emptied of self, ready for nothing but the Lord. It is the time when God can make us who He wants us to be. Brokenness often feels like someone came into the room of our lives and suddenly turned the light switch off. Jesus revealed that unless a seed falls to the ground and dies, it cannot become what it was destined to be.(John 12:24) The same thing is true for us. Unless we are willing to humble ourselves and walk through the valley of brokenness, we are too rigid and hard to be molded in the hand of God. But once we've walked through the corridors of loneliness, heartache, insecurity and helplessness, we become like clay in the hand of God,--- ready to be shaped, formed and used for His great purpose in the fulfillment of His high calling.

Consider Psalm 34:18, "The Lord is near to those who have a broken heart, and saves such as have a contrite spirit". This scripture suggests that brokenness is the essential condition for deliverance. Being broken requires us to surrender. Once surrendered, there is no longer any rebellion to the works of God in our lives. More than just simply being powerless before God, being broken means also being made to see our sins as God sees them. No more adopting the standard that society uses to measure sins. Instead, we come to the realization that our sins hurt God as much as or even more than they will eventually hurt us. Only then, can God's deliverance take place. Brokenness often involves a series of failures in life where everything we lay our hands on turns to dust. It was as if God wants us to learn to rely and depend only on Him, not on our own strength and intelligence, our financial resources, our networking contacts, or our talents. Through brokenness, God may actually expose us to ridicule, isolation and contempt from those in the world.

As in the case of Job, the Lord will often use the enemy to cause it to seem like there is no light at the end of the tunnel, where everything seems to be rising around us, or something is causing us to sink, causing us to drown. A time of darkness, a time of turmoil, a time of despair. In both of my previous books, I call the breaking "the dark night of the soul." Through this process of brokenness, the Holy Spirit refines us to be vessels ready for His purposes. Through the dark corridors of failure, rejection, insecurity and helplessness, we become like clay in the hand of God--- ready to be shaped, formed and used as a vessel of honor. The work of brokenness is complete when we come to the place where we no longer fear death, where to die is gain and to live is to no longer be an obstacle to the work of the Lord, fully dedicated to the coming of the Lord's kingdom. A broken vessel is detached from the pleasures and the seductions of the world.

Jesus made a statement to the woman at the well that I don't believe has been fully understood by the organized church when He declared that since the Father is Himself "a Spirit", those who worship the Father must worship Him in spirit and in truth.1 Considering that man is a soul, who has a spirit that lives in his body, my understanding of the Lord's words is that worship of the Father is not to be centered in the soul. In this regard, I have come to understand that true worship is neither emotionalism nor intellectualism. God is worshiped only through the spirit and not by the flesh. Since the soul represents the self of man, it is the seat of sin within us, even for those who have become saved. The soul cannot discern the things of God without the help of the born again spirit. Since the spirit and the body merge in the soul, the soul is very powerful. Therefore, the soul must be RENEWED.

It is important to note that carnal worshipers are key targets for demonic infestation because of one main fact that led to Lucifer's fall from heaven: Satan has always desired worship from God's creatures, with little regard to its form, motive or its cause. Even though he openly receives worship from those who practice the religion of Satanism, it satisfies the demonic world even more for Satan to receive adoration from the deceived and the unsuspecting. For example, while the Lord seeks worship and service in cooperation with human free will, religious witchcraft under the domain of the spirit of Jezebel seeks to control, dominate, intimidate and manipulate its religious converts. In direct opposition to the Lord's way, the religious demon's goal is to overtake the human will through deception and coercion. Nevertheless, witchcraft is rarely without religious overtones. A rare case myself, I was one of a very few atheists who practiced witchcraft back in the early 70's. Deceived by New Age occultism, I knew nothing of religion, nor did

I seek it. As I look back 3 decades, I believe that the reason why I was able to instantly be delivered from the spirit of divination and sorcery on the day that I was born again, is that I was not dually possessed by a spirit of religion.

The handwriting of ordinances that were against all sinners was nailed to the cross of Jesus the Christ, the Son of the Living God. Therefore, I believe that once we become "born again" or "saved," our victory over demons is possible, probable, but decidedly not automatic. Clearly, Satan was defeated at the cross by Jesus Himself so we are not called to defeat Satan. What we are called to do is to unmask Satan's unseen army where they are under cover, set captives free as we rescue the perishing. Consequently, victory over deception is our daily challenge in spiritual warfare and deliverance. Moreover, it has been my experience as a disciple of Jesus Christ and as a professional therapist that victory over deception can be substantially assured. Once bona fide believers become self educated to the wiles, methods and strategies of the demonic system, and learn how not to give the enemy any additional ground, the spiritual foe is defeated.

The reality is that even though a saved person has been translated out of the kingdom of darkness into the kingdom of light, spiritual ignorance can serve as a dark cloud that blocks out the light of the Holy Ghost from penetrating our spirits. If we do not learn how to walk in the light as He is in the light, we give the demonic army an advantage. In this regard, even though our position in Christ is of one of light, it is a huge mistake to think that focusing on light alone is sufficient.   Therefore, my goal is to enlighten and to expose darkness, particularly as it operates within a religious system. As such, it is crucial for the reader of these pages to understand that darkness is not always gross despicable sin.

For those who know Christ, darkness can be vague, obscure, gloomy and confusing---a wisdom that does not come from the Father of lights—a folly that is sensual, yet subtly demonic. (James 3:15) Darkness can also be suggestive of concealment, like a cloud that blocks the sunlight and creates a gloomy day, or a thick curtain that keeps a room dark, even though the sun is shining right outside in all of its brightness. To walk in darkness is to give the religious demon an unholy advantage where he will enter into both spiritual and man-made temples, and through a blasphemous masquerade, attempt to exalt himself as God. When the religious demon has been able to enter into a Christian temple of either flesh or brick and subsequently obtain worship for itself through fraudulence and deceit, this is truly an abomination of desolation. (Daniel 11:36)

As an obstruction to truth, darkness can also manifest itself within the lives of Christians as hidden obstacles and hindrances, where all of the religious demons' wiles, tricks and devices are set in motion to keep us in the dark, even about our own spiritual condition. Walking in darkness after Jesus Christ has translated us into His kingdom is certainly a spiritual affront to the Holy Ghost. Particularly, if we say that we have fellowship with Jesus yet we continue to walk in darkness, we lie and we do not practice the truth, ignorantly making ourselves collaborators with the father of lies. (I John 1:5,6) Almost a century ago, Jessie Penn-Lewis succinctly described this dilemma faced by the ignorant believer:

> "When a counterfeit presence, or influence, is accepted, then they
> go on to counterfeit a "Person" as one of the Persons of the Trinity, adapted
> to the ideals or desires of the victim...Here lies the danger point which first
> opens the door to Satan. The working upon the senses in the religious

realm, has long been Satan's special mode of deceiving men throughout the whole world, of which he is the god and prince. He knows how to soothe and move, and work in every possible way, and in every form of religion ever known, deceiving unregenerate men with the form of godliness whilst denying the power. Among the truly converted, and even sanctified believers, the senses are still his way of approach. Let the soul admit a craving for beautiful emotions, happy feelings, overwhelming joy, and the conception that manifestations, or 'signs' are necessary to prove the presence of God, especially in the Baptism of the Spirit, and the way is open for Satan's lying spirits to deceive."(War on the Saints, 9th Edition, pg. 105-106) 4

Also known as the spirit of truth, the primary job of the Holy Ghost is to manifest the light of truth in our lives, as believers are conformed into the image of Jesus Christ. How sad and unfortunate it is for those who have been set free to remain in bondage because their flesh is in love with religion rather than with the Savior. Even though demons know them to be free, they will do whatever they can to cloud the issue and continue to bind them illegally through deception. In reality, the irony is that bound believers will find themselves entrapped within a self imposed passivity. In truth, the hidden cause of their captivity is spiritual blindness. Spiritual blindness is the inability to perceive God's truth. As a naturally blind man cannot give himself sight, a spiritual sight comes only from the Holy Ghost. Unfortunately, he will not be able to perceive and understand the truth if he does not receive divine enlightenment. Yet because his spiritual blindness has grieved and quenched the Spirit of Truth, he himself has blocked the unction within them to help him to "help himself."

As a case in point, I received a telephone call from a professing Christian woman who I will call Daisy. Daisy claimed that a former pastor with roots in the Caribbean had her bound by placing a verbal spell on her. In fact, according to Daisy, this man actually planted verbal seeds in her mind by openly declaring that she was under the spell of his demonic power. Through their sexual contact, a demonic soul tie was formed, where Daisy believed that every minor ache or pain in her body was being sent to her by this witchcraft practicing minister. So when she called me, I cast the demon from her over the telephone. I knew in the spirit that the demon left her. I even heard it leave like the sound of a fading echo. Yet a week later, Daisy called me complaining, "I feel a pain in my knee and so the minister is at it again, and I can't restrain myself from sending him some money." This is a classic example of how passivity of mind can use the captive as his or her own jailer and even casting out a demon will not set the captive free.

Passivity also operates on the collective mind. Even though the 21st century is characterized by religious deception, believers in Christ Jesus today seem content to passively sit back and allow a select group of mega ministers and other Christian Hollywood types to identify the signs of the times for them, rather than be watchful themselves. For example, with every less than noteworthy newspaper report, particularly in the middle east, various apocalyptic watchmen have professionalized the reporting of these occurrences around the world with such a sophisticated, scholarly and authoritative application that I personally find much too confusing for the average believer to monitor and determine its accuracy.

In truth, I do not believe that Jesus intended for any one who follows Him to lower their spiritual guard by relying on others to watch on his behalf. Just as we don't need a weather man to tell us that spring is coming, we also don't need people to complicate the obvious. Case in point. If the Anti-Christ is actually a human being, then it is clear to me that he shall come forth out of Christianity for a very simple reason. Satan has had a seat in the organized church for centuries. There is no better place for the devil to conceal, prepare and empower his son of evil and destruction than within a worldly Christian system.

The word of God clearly testifies not only to the fact that demons were operating during the Lord's earthly ministry, but that renewed demonic activity will manifest in the latter days. (I Timothy Ch:4:1-4) Paul's warning to Timothy does not merely relate to new manifestations of evil in the world but to an ever increasing apostasy in the professing church, a cult promoted by seducing spirits of a highly sensitive spirituality. In spite of this infiltration by demons into the organized church, it is not my personal intent to disparage the local church or to suggest that all local churches need to be closed down. I myself pastor a local assembly as well as an international Internet body of believers. However, the organized church is an institution created by man, not even described or promoted by the Word of God:

> "There is nothing inherently wrong with being involved in a local church. But realize that being part of a group that calls itself a "church" does not make you saved, holy, righteous, or godly any more than being in Yankee Stadium makes you a professional baseball player. Participating in church-based activities does not necessarily draw you closer to God or prepare you for a life that satisfies Him or enhances your existence....Sadly, many people will label this view 'blasphemy.'. However, you should realize that the Bible neither describes nor promotes the local church as we know it today. Many centuries ago religious leaders created the prevalent form of 'church' that is so widespread in our society to help people be better followers of Christ. But the local church many have come to cherish---the services, offices, programs, buildings, ceremonies---is neither biblical nor un-biblical. It is a-biblical--- that is, such an organization is not addressed in the Bible." (Revolution, pg. 37) 5

Therefore, since the church model of modern times is neither promoted nor discredited in the Word of God, I believe that it's viability should be determined by some very wise and practical applications:

1. In terms of its structure, is it an episcopal denomination or an independent body? Quite frankly, if it is a connected church, then even though it may be uncorrupted at the local level, linked to an ungodly authority or "Mother Church" will eventually spoil or damage the spiritual fruits throughout the entire system. By nature of its organization, a religious demon will have a seat in high places. The complicated, political form of an episcopal church with a connected governing body should be avoided primarily due to its structure. Consequently, its bishops and leaders will be prone to cover-ups, particularly where improprieties and outright sin may be involved among its various charges. In my second book, I describe this dilemma:

> "A Bishop's power lies in his ability to appoint a pastor and fill a pulpit. Since pastors in full time ministry are totally dependent each year

upon whether or not the Bishop chooses to favor them with an appointment to a church that will be lucrative enough to continue to provide for themselves and their families, a conflict of interest automatically inherent within the Episcopal form of church government will ultimately manifest." (The Making of A Prophet, pg. 84) 6

Dealing with sin in such a structure is like trying to eliminate roaches from a city block where all of the buildings are erected side by side and are therefore "connected". If you bomb one apartment with a pesticide, or even exterminate an entire building, the roaches will simply run upstairs, downstairs or to the building next door. Regardless of how clean you keep your apartment, you will not be able to contain the roaches, especially after dark. Just go in the kitchen and turn on your lights and hundreds of them will be flying around as if they had wings!!! Every connected building has to be bombed from one corner to the other on the entire street, or the roaches will soon return. So is the fate of the connected churches. The leaven of the Pharisees is impossible to contain without a complete annihilation.

2. Where an independent church is concerned, the issue is not so much its structure but whether or not it has a system in place to avoid spiritual neglect or abuse. Within a small assembly or a mega church, every sheep in that church should have someone who personally knows him and who ministers to his personal needs. If members are compelled to go outside of their local church to receive competent counseling, deliverance, healing and recovery, then I suspect that the primary benefit experienced in church is merely a soothing of their flesh as as a by-product of the worship experience of song and praise. Moreover, congregations of this kind provide a social environment for family members. In my opinion, social contacts with Christians can be obtained at a Christian concert and family activities are available at the local YMCA. If your spiritual needs are not being met at your local church, then you are just involved in a social club and your local church has no real spiritual value.

3. The independent churches that can be very dangerous include those that call themselves "deliverance churches." In some of these assemblies, the religious demon and the witchcraft spirit are running rampant with counterfeits in worship, doctrine, prayer and other strange practices including a heavy emphasis on being slain in the spirit.

> "A demonstration of real power is not falling slain. We see a lot of this phenomena in the ministries of TV evangelists, particularly in the Pentecostal and non-denominational churches. Demonstration of God's power would be after you have fallen out in the spirit, what condition were you in when you got to your feet?!!! Where you healed? Were you delivered? Did God speak to you a word in due season concerning a special problem you have been challenged with? Or did you just pass out because everybody else was passing out!? (The Making of a Prophet, pg. 199) 7

4. I agree with Dr. Rebecca Brown's warning concerning various counterfeits manifested through the speaking in other tongues, primarily among word of faith, pentecostal and Charismatic Catholic churches:

> "Christians have made the terrible mistake of assuming that ALL tongues are from God. How wrong they are!...It is well known that many

occultic rituals are done in tongues....The fact that Catholics speak in tongues is not proof that they are filled with the Holy Spirit. Too many of these precious Catholic souls assume that because they are speaking in tongues, they are saved. How can the Holy Spirit be operative and manifesting in a system of idolatry? Those involved in the Catholic Charismatic movement who really start reading and studying the Bible soon realize they must separate themselves from the idolatrous Roman Catholic Church if they are going to serve the true Jesus of the Bible." (Prepare for War, pgs. 182,183) 8

5.However, the crucial factors of your assessment of a local church actually relate to the security of your eternal life,which is truly where the rubber meets the road. Why go to church if, in the final analysis, you do not escape damnation by traveling the narrow way to eternal life? Assuredly, you should examine how and with what regularity the doctrines of repentance, resurrection and rebirth are being preached and taught? A church with a Jezebel influence will minimize or overlook the importance of these "3 R's" through excessive tradition, polity and other less important priorities of doctrine.

6.If a local church minimizes the need to learn the devices of the devil or does not even recognize the existence and the workings of demonic forces in these times, then it is in a low condition of spiritual life and power. I believe that such a church should be avoided like the plague. In fact, such ignorance on the part of a congregation's leadership is an indication to demons of the leaders' accommodation to them through fear, an open door to demonic influence. According to Jessie Penn-Lewis:

> "A perspective view of the ages covered by the history in Bible records, shows that the rise and fall in spiritual power of the people of God, was marked by the recognition of the existence of the demoniacal host of evil. When the Church of God in the old and new dispensations was at the highest point of spiritual power, the leaders recognized, and drastically dealt with, the invisible forces of Satan and when at the lowest, they were ignored, or allowed to have free course, among the people." (War on the Saints, 9th edition, pg.27)

Consequently, if there is no emphasis in the local church on spiritual warfare and deliverance, that church is without spiritual power.

7.The emphasis upon the Word of God in a church should and could be a good sign; Nevertheless, it is misleading and immaterial to base your assessment of a church solely upon evidence that all its members carry bibles, yellow markers and recite scriptures. For when leadership doe not rightly divide the word, then heresies posing as revelation truths give place to the doctrines of devils that Paul warned Timothy about (I Timothy 4:1): the prosperity gospel, dominion teaching, "name it and claim it", pre-tribulation rapture, submission to authority, eternal security, no ordination for women, and other doctrines too numerous to mention even in one book.

False doctrines of this kind are skillfully birthed by teaching demons to deceive and exploit the people. If the devil had nerve enough to get "religious" by reciting scripture out of its context to tempt the Lord Jesus Himself, then he has trained his demonic army to do likewise to us. (Matthew 4:1-11) "Out of context" preaching tends to draw those who have not truly repented and nor been converted, but who are enticed to come to church by the excitement that scriptural hype can produce. Such preaching and teaching draws people, places and things to the building.---those who seek blessings to get their needs met or to fulfill their dreams---but they have not really been drawn to Christ.

8.A church after the Lord's heart is the church of Philadelphia: those who do not deny His name and who have kept His word.(Revelation 3:7-13) This is a church that will not compromise the truth, either for the favor of the world or for unity with other churches. Since we all see through a glass darkly, a good pastor is one who continually examines if he is rightly dividing the word. When errors and contradictions are uncovered, then a good pastor openly and publicly admits to his or her mistakes, correcting any inaccurate teachings without hesitation. The Lord declared that the church of Philadelphia was of little strength, so it is clear that His assessment was not based upon numbers of members, wealth or resources. I believe that a major part of keeping His word is to go forth and cast out demons. A good church is about building people so that they can confront the demonic influences to expel the darkness in their own environment, equipping the sheep to be living stones, holy vessels for the Spirit of the Lord to dwell in.

In this regard, without reservation, I share deliverance counseling methods that have worked for me as well as my mistakes, so that you can gain a more comprehensive grasp of the complex issues associated with the religious demon's wiles and deceptions. Various strategies have been designed to uncover the cause, apply the blood of Jesus against it, and to fortify the captives' salvation with faith, truth, righteousness, peace and the word of God. My goal is to ensure that the unction of the Holy Ghost will be released to flow with ease. Various fictionalized cases studies derived from my own personal, pastoral and professional experience are presented throughout the book in order to expose the faces of the religious demon. I have also included samples from the the SEW Program, my training model for deliverance counselors and workers in the Appendix. Also sharing from various intimate details of the manifestations of the religious demon in my own personal life, I have left no holes barred.

Where general deliverance is concerned, I have found that once Christian captives have been armed with self knowledge, with clear understanding as to who they are in Christ and finally with the wiles and tricks that the enemy generally employs on their own particular brand of carnality, virtually all demons have left on their own accord, without the need to even cast them out in some cases. Some personal testimonies from captives who were set free are also presented in the Appendix. Predominately, I have been able to conduct deliverance counseling by telephone all over the country and even abroad. Divided into four stages, the average length of counseling is about 4 months. Labeled "a brief therapy," Spiritual Bootcamp Sessions (SBS) fall under 4 stages: ASSESSMENT, PRE-DELIVERANCE, DELIVERANCE AND POST DELIVERANCE.

Emphasis is placed on two inter-connected demons that work together as the spirit of Jezebel: the religious demon and the witchcraft demon. In comparison to other demons,this duo puts up a formidable fight. Where the religious demon is concerned, my hands have been tied unless through counseling, the captives have been brought to a place where they have humbled themselves to the fact that their spiritual experience has been filled with deception. Unless their pride is broken in this area, the religious demon will keep them bound. For this very reason, faces or profiles of this demon are presented throughout this book. Therefore, in the ensuing chapters, you will find an interconnected experience taken from several chapters of my life interacting with the lives of others. We wrestle not against flesh and blood and so it is not my intent to reveal the faces of people but of the unseen demonic forces that secretly entrap all susceptible human beings.

It is my personal view   that the deliverance counselor should serve as a front line intercessor--- a corner man in a spiritual boxing ring of combat where the captive and the demons go to blows.   As "a corner man", I have carefully examined specific cases mentioned in the word of God as well. Studying the opponent, finding his weaknesses, and developing new strategies and techniques are but a few of the responsibilities of "the corner man." Like a fighter in a boxing ring, ultimately its the captive's responsibility to stand and fight the good fight of faith, armored with weapons that are not carnal, but mighty through God to the pulling down of strongholds. (II Corinthians 10:4-6)

Endnotes

1.(I suggest that you read Luke 16 concerning the rich man who died, whose soul could feel the burning of the flames in hell)

2.George Barna, Revolution, Tyndale House Publishers, 2005
Barna defines a revolutionary as one who doesn't "go along to get along." This is a believer that does not "go to church" but who IS the church, ready to risk resources, image, comfort and security to devote themselves to a zealous pursuit of intimacy with Jesus Christ., pleasing God and blessing people. In my own words, those who close the doors to the religiosity of the religious demon. According to such a definition, then I am comfortable to be labeled a revolutionary, as I have defined myself as a "rebel with a cause," committed to remain an "un-churched Christian."
3. Jessie Penn-Lewis, War on the Saints, 9th edition, Thomas E. Lowe Ltd, NY, 1973, Originally published in 1916, pg. 84
War on the Saints is frequently quoted in this book. Every other quotation taken from either the abridged or unabridged versions of the book by Jessie Penn Lewis, "War on the Saints" originally published in 1916.   The abridged version is published by CLC publications, printed in 2004. The unabridged, hardcover version is in its 9th edition, published by Thomas E. Lowe in 1973. Throughout the book, each quote will indicate whether it be from the abridged or the unabridged editions.

3.Ibid, pg. 105-106

4.Barner, pg. 37

5.Rev. Pamela Sheppard LMSW, The Making of A Prophet: A Spiritual Indictment to the Organized Church, Author House,2005

6.Ibid, pg 199

7.Dr. Rebecca Brown, Prepare for War, pgs. 182-183

Chapter 3: Wheat or Tares?

In these end-times, the true remnant church of Jesus Christ consists of believers everywhere, whether denominational or non-denominational, whether assemblies of thousands or storefront churches of ten. If you are a church of thousands, I believe that you should employ one pastor to shepherd no more than 100 members, for a pastor must have the capability to leave the 99 to seek after the more serious needs of the one. Each pastor should also concentrate on training assistant pastors so that no sheep is isolated or overlooked. Those who comprise the true church are soldiers for the Lord Jesus Christ --- warriors who have not sold out to the devil by allowing the religious demon to have dominion in either the pulpit or the pew. These are the ones that the Lord Himself commended in His word to the church at Philadelphia---those who have kept the faith and have not denied His Name by preaching a flawed gospel. (Revelation 3:8) If you are among this remnant of God through whom the Lord's kingdom will completely come, I believe that He will use you---not only by the preaching of the gospel but also by preparing you to the cast out demons.

Actually, the preaching of the gospel has already been done. For two millennium, the word of God has been preached from one end of the world to the other since the Day of Pentecost. The gospel is a very simple message: Jesus coming out of heaven to earth, born of a virgin, crucified for our sins, died and was raised from the dead, was seen of many, ascended and, praise God, He is coming back. Therefore, part one of the Great Commission is practically accomplished. This is the gospel in a nutshell, a word that is published every Christmas and every Easter, in spite of Santa Claus and the Bunny. I am a clear example of an atheist who had never heard the word preached from a pulpit or from a TV evangelist, never even handed a tract nor had I ever opened a bible. If an atheist could be drawn to Jesus just based upon the word that was preached through the holidays of Christmas and Easter, ANYONE CAN BE!!! This is the reason why the enemy is taking a strong stand against keeping Jesus as the reason for both seasons.

It is not surprising that I believe that the church is in the pitiful condition that it is in today because of a gross neglect of part two of the Great Commission which is "go forth and cast out demons!" Therefore, I write to the faithful of the church at Philadelphia, and exhort you to remember the words of Paul to Timothy: "In the last days, some shall depart from the faith, giving heed to seducing spirits and doctrines of devils." (I Timothy 4:1) As the word of God has foreshadowed in various scriptures, seducing spirits are thriving in the organizational church today in the form of the religious demon. So beware, oh, precious ones! Beware of demons that will come in your midst and try to hide in your sheepfolds, whose mission is to bring down the true Body of Christ. To be successful, Satan must be very deceptive. In one of His parables, the Lord announced that in the midst of His planting wheat in His field, an enemy came along and planted imitation wheat called "tares" or weeds. Consequently, the Lord declared that toward the end of the age, there would come a point in time when the imitation wheat and the true wheat would look identical. (Matthew 13:37-43)

Stated in Chapter 2 but restated here, Satan has always wanted to be worshiped. It truly satisfies the demonic world ---delicious for Satan to be worshiped by the deceived and the unsuspecting. It may surprise you to comprehend that religious demons are involved in every aspect of worship,--- masquerading as the gifts of the Spirit, speaking in tongues, falling slain in the spirit, healing and even in the ministry of casting out of demons. The religious demon is also the evil spirit behind every false doctrine that uses the word of God out of context. Although Satan knows that Jesus defeated him at the cross, he is like a dethroned ruler---a Hitler type---who fights to the bitter end, even though he knows that he has already lost the war. People still died in battle unnecessarily in World War Two, even though the war was actually over.

Warfare tactics from a defeated leader can be very untrustworthy and crafty. For example, in various ways, the religious demon and the witchcraft demon seem to overlap in their functions, and then at other times, seem to be in opposition to each other. There are times when Satan appears to fight against himself with these two demons, but this tactic is merely a smoke screen. When these two demons appear to work at odds with each other, it is only because they can obtain a more widespread advantage. The practice of witchcraft is itself a false religion that boldly denies the divinity of Jesus Christ through Satanism while the religious demon may or may not deny that Jesus is Lord. The religious demon's primary target is the church, while the witchcraft demon focuses on secular humanists, atheists, and intellectuals who are attracted to the "broad way." The common purpose of both the religious and the witchcraft demons is to subvert worship away from the triune God and divert it to the world, the flesh and the devil. Although covert and secretive, the goals of Satanism are clear. Satanists openly defy God and seek worship for Lucifer. In an unholy trinity of man, the Anti-Christ and the devil, Satanists perform their ritualism through the practice of witchcraft. While the Lord seeks worship in cooperation with our free will, witchcraft seeks to control, dominate, intimidate and manipulate its converts. Its primary goal is to overtake the human will through deception and coercion.

Where the religious demon and the witchcraft demon primarily differ is in the domain and nature of power. The religious demon's power is sustained simply because its captives do not have a love for the truth and are therefore spiritually blind. Jesus declared that if we know the truth, the truth will set us free. I believe that freedom comes when we are able to nullify the enemy's plans. To nullify is to deprive of effect, to neutralize or to render his plans illegal. It is clear that Satan is allowed to continue to operate as an outlaw until Jesus Himself jails him upon His second coming. Even so, we can "jail" Satan's demons--- rendering them prisoners of war--- by pulling the cover off of their deception with our love for the truth. It should also be noted that when the religious demon and the witchcraft spirit combine their efforts in the spirit of Jezebel, they are a formidable team, as discussed in upcoming chapters.

So be warned that those who do not love the truth are in serious spiritual danger. I believe that we are now living in an era when the Lord will turn over those with a religious demon to a reprobate mind. At that moment, the captive's thoughts will be permanently darkened to the degree that he becomes incapable of receiving the truth. (Hebrews 6:1-8)Without the mercy and grace of God, a captive with a reprobate mind will remain deceived, thereby providing a permanent home to the religious demon. If the truly wise Christian would simply develop objectivity, neutrality, and perceptiveness, he would enhance his powers of spiritual discernment almost immediately. Then if willing to face his own character defects of the soul, repent, forgive and humbly receive correction, the religious demon would flee from him on its own accord. The strength of this demon lies in the fact that the captive's flesh is gratified by counterfeit supernatural experiences that are a mixture of lies with truth. So it is imperative that those who are zealous in religion test and examine themselves, to see if they be in the faith. (II Corinthians 13:5)

Even in the face of complete truth, the witchcraft demon will fight to maintain its ground based upon its own perceived "squatter's rights." In other words, the oaths, marks (tattoos) and vows that are often a pivotal component of ritualistic meetings and worship services support the witchcraft demon's refusal to "leave it's house." Imagine that the witchcraft demon is waiving a lease, declaring, "I have a right to be here and you can't evict me, not even with the Name of Jesus." This is why it is imperative to have the captive disavow all oaths and vows, cover all markings and tattoos, and remove from the home all books, jewelry and other articles that are connected to the witchcraft demon. I have even discovered that captives will on occasion have to disavow the deeds of their parents or ancestors from previous generations, without breaking the commandment that requires the honoring of parents.

Sometimes the religious demon's strategy is to deny supernatural power while in other situations, it will manifest a supernatural power that is counterfeit, masquerading as an imitator of the 9 supernatural gifts of the Holy Ghost. Wherein some faces of this demon will call the true manifestations of the anointing of the Name of Jesus as "of the devil", yet another face of the religious demon also attracts those who seek signs and miracles with manifestations of counterfeit power. Imitations of God's true power are covertly worked for evil, using Satan's original anointing in reverse. Those who hunger for physical manifestations are particularly vulnerable. In such instances, God's people are destroyed for a lack of knowledge of the true presence of God. Aptly put in "War on the Saints" , "What believer is there that does not long for the 'conscious' presence of God, and would not give up all to obtain it?" (J.P.-Lewis, pg. 106, 9th edition.)

Moreover, there are those who are unsaved who are practicing idolatry without knowing it because they belong to a church that proclaims to be based upon the bible. Many of these people are practicing a false religion. Any religion that does not have Jesus Christ as Lord and Savior is an idolatrous one, including Judaism without Christ as the Messiah. Any religion that has added another book to the bible is a false religion, including Mormonism (Latter Day Saints), Jehovah Witnesses, and others. Because of its various idolatrous practices, Catholicism can be added to this list. Religious demons in conjunction with the witchcraft demon are behind such groups as the Freemasons, the Eastern Star and other secret societies.

There are also religious demons that are involved in the occult, the New Age Movement, hypnotism, yoga, tarot cards, Ouija boards, color therapy, astrology, ---this is a long list, where old practices with new names are added to it daily. Furthermore, witchcraft and religion coincide within the spirit of Jezebel, along with the spirit of drug and sex addictions. Within the witchcraft branch of sorcery, hallucinatory drugs like opium and peyote have maintained an integral part of long standing within various indigenous religious systems. Therefore, it stands to reasons that drug addicted captives would also be attracted to religiosity. In this regard, I have encountered several captives under the influence of Jezebel, who enter the revolving door of drug addiction, lasciviousness, and religiosity. Within various pagan religions, sex plays an important role in the appeasement of the Gods and therefore, the sexual gratification of coitus is connected to spiritual ecstasy and intimacy with the gods.

With so many faces, methods and strategies, how can a person with a religious demon be generally identified? The answer in a nutshell is that a person with a religious demon is without power to bare real fruit for Jesus Christ. He or she will have "a form of godliness that denies the power thereof".(II Timothy 3:5) Some of them are extremely obvious in society. For example, there are the "Jesus Freaks" that have stickers all over their cars and Jesus written all over their persons. The religious demon causes them to be especially weird in order to turn the unsaved not TOWARD Christ, but AWAY from Him. Simply put, the lost will say to themselves "if I have to act like this freak, I don't want no parts of Jesus Christ!" The other obvious group are those who end up on mental health medication, many of them even declaring that they themselves are the Christ. Demons of fear and anxiety often join up with the religious demon to cause a person to fear the destruction of the earth and the final judgment. Several of these persons will also require mental health medication.

However, the ones who are the most dangerous are the ones that are the most difficult to discern. Countless of this kind may have big grins on their faces and tell you that Jesus loves you and invite you to their church. Generally though, a person with a religious demon who is a consistent churchgoer is usually out of balance in some way. For example, they cannot receive correction, they are rigid in their interpretation of scripture, often taking scripture out of context to put the brethren in bondage, their emotions are unstable---they are either reaching for the stars filled with ecstasy at the glory of God or they are in the deepest valley of despair and depression. Some of these people will leave you long sermons on their telephone answering machines, can not say a sentence without saying "amen, praise the Lord, I'm blessed, love you". Some will appear to enjoy being passive and victimized, as they believe that they are "suffering for the Lord." Then there are those who operate like witches or psychic mediums, never without "an alleged prophetic word from the Lord", even holding meetings where they perform what is called "spiritual readings."

Here are some obvious signs that raise my spiritual eyebrow:

1.ALWAYS the most noticeable in a worship service---dancing, shouting, wailing, falling slain in the spirit, doing the "holy dance"--- yet there is known, repetitive sin in their lives. In truth, their Christian walk does not manifest the 9 fruits of the Spirit. Jesus said "you shall know them by their fruit." Although they may be intelligent and successful, the fruits of holiness: love, joy, peace, longsuffering, goodness, gentleness, faith, self control, and meekness are not apparent. It has been my experience that those who have an addiction history are also susceptible to the religious demon. For example, I have known several recovering addicts to be an active, public voice in expressing their belief in Christ, yet their repetitive relapses into drug abuse spawns barefaced and degrading sins. The demon then uses their ineffectual religiosity among onlookers in the church and in the world to publicly shame Jesus Christ and deny Him as the only eternal power of God by whom the world can be saved.

2.Some professing Christians can be extremely NARROWMINDED, CRITICAL, JUDGEMENTAL,AND LEGALISTIC. They are skillful at keeping in bondage those "less spiritual" than themselves. These kinds of people can be found in any church, but they tend to infiltrate pentecostal settings, particularly because of their "waiting meetings." (War on the Saints, pg. 63)

3.They love worship and church more than they are concerned about saving souls. This demon will persistently divert attention away from the Great Commission with "too much church!" Then there are those who are so overwhelmed with thoughts of revival and the needs of others, that they are blind to their own condition.

4.They do not want to hear about Satan, demons, or deliverance. Their actions are often based upon a great fear of this subject. If demons are "in" them, the demons will fear that someone with faith may cast them out and so the captive will be negatively affected by the demon's fear of being unseated.

5.The most outstanding character trait in a person who may have a religious demon is PRIDE. These are often people who cannot take correction or ever admit to being wrong.

6.They are more concerned about growth in numbers than about the spiritual growth in Christ of each babe in Christ.

7.They are preaching a prosperity gospel. It should also be noted that even people who are good tithers may have a religious demon, particularly with the advent of the devilish doctrine of prosperity and materialism. I am referring to the "plant a seed and reap a hundredfold harvest" believers. In short, the best religious demon is a "wolf in sheep's clothing." Sheep praise the Lord, they tithe, they support the pastor, they pray for the sick and shut ins. To recognize a wolf, one needs the Lord to reveal him or her to you, as well as bless you with the wisdom to know how to handle the situation, once the wolf has been identified. How does a religious demon manifest itself? Well, if my words have penetrated your mind by now, you will not be surprised to realize that the answer to this question is that its manifestations are limitless.

8.I have come upon a new breed---those who have grown up in word of faith churches or who may even be the offspring of preachers, who claim to have gotten saved when they were toddlers or prior to the age of 12. When they reach adulthood, they are practiced in religiosity and Christian platitudes but will have no real fruit of salvation. They are like word of faith robots, yet there comes a point in time when they realize that what they thought was faith was really habituated learning, akin to reciting the Pledge of Allegiance or singing the Star Spangled Banner. They memorized and recited words without real intellectual or affective understanding of the scripture's significance. At some point in their adulthood, these "church trained" young people realize that "something is missing." Some will continue with the religiosity because their pride keeps them from embracing the truth, others will rebel and seek worldly pleasures, while others will be convicted and seek to know what is blocking them from true salvation.

Captive to Christian Cults

A woman I call "Irene" wrote to me and sought prayer for her 10 year old daughter who was diagnosed with a rare form of cancer. Since Irene believed that her daughter's disease was demonic in its origin and also considered that it might be caused by an ancestral curse, I conducted an assessment through a telephone interview. Irene appeared to be a committed, dedicated believer. However, the assessment revealed prior occult involvement. The most outstanding insight into the root cause of the problem was the fact that Irene and particularly her husband belonged to an African American religion that I had never heard of before called "the Coptic" faith. According to standard procedure, I searched the web to learn more about this religion.   I did not have to study the Coptics in any great detail to know immediately that this was a false "Christian" church. I discovered that this religion originated in Egypt, its trademark being the exaltation of black people as a "superior" race. The Coptics glorify the elders of the church by calling them queens, kings, princes and princesses. With this limited knowledge, the pursuit of a deeper study of this religion was unnecessary, as its darkness was clearly discernible.

In the course of the initial interview, Irene revealed that during a special prayer and fasting vigil conducted by the members of her Coptic church for her daughter's healing, hundreds of mice broke forth throughout the church. The members ran screaming from the sanctuary as the splashing sounds of mice could be heard throughout the building, as mice were crushed underfoot. NEEDLESS TO SAY, THIS WAS NOT A GOOD SIGN. Mice in the old testament are symbolic of tumors or in other words, cancer. A knowledge of the symbolic language of the scriptures as well as the scriptural references in the word of God that declare that there are no distinctions in Christ, caused me to recognize immediately that Irene and her entire family were under the influence of a religious demon.

Early in our interaction, I became convinced that Irene's daughter's cancer was connected to her parents' attachment to the collaboration of both the religious and the witchcraft demons that evidently rule the Coptics. As an aside, although Irene did not deny my assessment, she indicated that for her to pull herself and her daughter out of the Coptic Church would be devastating on all aspects of her life, particularly because her pastor was her father in-law. Such a step would bring about a family discord that Irene admitted that she was not prepared to confront. I sympathized with her, not underrating or trivializing the impact of her decision to remain a member of the Coptic Church, even though she herself had deep reservations about it prior to contacting me. Unfortunately, I was placed in a position to have to refuse to participate in her case any further. All I could do was to ask the Lord to continue to reveal and expose this idolatry to Irene, her husband and the rest of the family. I have learned from experience that I would have put myself in jeopardy when those with knowledge and parental authority refuse to obey the Lord.

As Jesus warned in Matthew 10, HE DID NOT COME TO BRING PEACE, BUT A SWORD! IF YOU LOVE FAMILY MORE THAN YOU LOVE JESUS, THEN YOU ARE NOT WORTHY OF THE LORD!! (Matthew 10:34-39) Some may disagree, but since Irene knows the truth yet refuses to obey, she is not worthy for me to stand in the gap for her daughter to receive her healing. In addition, I would be risking myself to a counterattack if I attempted to stand with Irene while she is in open rebellion. Taken as a case in point, I believe that rather than attempt to study darkness in detail, my contact with false religions and the like is limited yet purposeful. Therefore, I suggest that a deliverance worker should study the overall strategies and devices of darkness as they relate to each captive's personality traits and qualities of the soul that cause him to be vulnerable. Since light will overpower darkness when light is "turned on", so too both the counselor and the captive should not just study the light but practice walking in the light without failing to find out just enough about the darkness that pertains to the particular situation.

Prayer is definitely the answer in most cases. The prayer must be purposeful, seeking the Lord to reveal and expose the unknown and the invisible. My own personal testimony is a clear example of how fervent and effectual prayer exposed me to the light. Although the witchcraft demon lost the power to use me as a medium when I got born again, I was still confused because I had no pastor or teacher. The confusion centered in my belief that occult practices that yet remained a significant part of my spirituality were the reason why

I got saved. I reasoned, "how could communicating with the spirits of the dead be so bad when the experience drew me to the Lord?" I did not understand that it was "in spite of" those practices that I became born again. Either an angel or the Holy Spirit Himself reached into the occult world and snatched me out of darkness. My confusion remained for about 4 years because of the very limited knowledge of the word of God that I had acquired as a babe in Christ. In fact, it has taken all of my 29 years in Christ for me to completely eradicate every single occult influence of my 3 year walk on the dark side. Furthermore, those within the Christian community who had contact with me in the early years were also not grounded in the word or in deliverance ministry. Today, spiritual blindness is even more pervasive.

Once I got saved, I carried over into Christianity some of the false teachings I had received as a result of my New Age practices. This is typical experience, particularly for converts who have left the occult. Consequently, I was a true believer who for four years looked like the lost. I believe that my personal testimony to captives in bondage to either a religious demon or a witchcraft spirit clearly demonstrates that the Lord can send someone to them whose spiritual knowledge and experience these captives will respect. Simon the sorcerer in the word of God is a biblical example. (Acts 8:9-24) In my case, the word of God helped me to discard reincarnation. After all, it was easy to see that if many earthly lives were required to reach salvation, what would be the purpose of the cross? Therefore, I could easily understand that "it is appointed unto man once to die, and then the judgment." (Hebrews 9:27) However, as a babe in Christ, I still had an affinity for communication with "my spirits of the dead." I did not know that these spirits were not the dead, but that they were demons.

No Christian that I knew in the late 70's early 80's could persuade me otherwise. I had a spirit of divination and I was practicing necromancy, a term that was not even in my vocabulary in those days. I thought that "my spirits" had led me to Christ and not even my bible study teacher, Steve , could convince me otherwise. Most of those who claimed to know the word among my Christian associates in 1981 could not recognize that I was a believer, and so I was considered by them to still be a witch. As I faithfully attended Steve's bible study, he was the one wise man who could discern that I was a child of God. Although he admitted that he was afraid of me, Steve prayed for me, "that the Lord would send someone in my life whom I would receive to rightly divide truth to me." In my second book, "the Making of a Prophet: A Spiritual Indictment to the Organized Church", the impact of Steve's prayer for me is concisely described:

> "Within two weeks, Steve's prayer was answered and I met Matte Elan, a born again Asian martial arts expert. Matte Elan is the first and only human being to ever call me a prophet. He declared 'I used to be able to kick a door and turn it into sawdust by the power of the devil. I am not a minister, but I know enough to tell you that Satan is masquerading as God in your life because he know who you are. Satan knows more about you then you know about yourself. You see, sister, the Lord has called you to be one of His prophets. You are a prophet of God!'

> This was a shocking eye opener. That very day, as soon as I got home, I burned all of my occult books. Matte also told me to get baptized---completely immersed---and so I called a local church and made a special appointment for baptism." (P. Sheppard, 2005) 1

I also ran to a little church and had them baptize me, immerse me that very day. I can't remember how I knew to do that---whether Matte told me or if I just knew it in my spirit. Several Christians had been trying to reveal truth to me, but I would only hear it through someone who had also "been there, done that"---someone who had experienced demonic power first hand. Likewise, I believe the most powerful, effectual prayer for a captive in bondage to a witchcraft demon is to seek the Lord to visit the captive in a personal, supernatural way, in order to shock the captive to remove the blinders from his own spiritual eyes. Once this happens, then the demon will flee of its own accord. Only truth will cast the religious demon out and that truth may need to come through either a human vessel whose knowledge and spirituality the captive respects or if the captive has a personal confrontation with the Lord Himself.

The Victory is Already Won!

In spite of the power of the religious demon, I believe that the revelations of spiritual warfare and deliverance within these pages attest to the greatest irony: that even though man was created a little lower than the angels, that the triune God has brought forth a fallen race of sons and daughters who will obtain complete victory in the invisible war over spiritual entities that have mighty powers. In the words of the late Donald Grey Barnhouse:

> "War has been declared. The great, governing cherub had become the malignant enemy. Our God was neither surprised nor astonished, for, of course, He knew before it happened that it would happen, and He had His perfect plan ready to put into effect. Although the Lord had the power to destroy Satan with a breath, He did not do so. It was as though an edict had been proclaimed in heaven: 'We shall give this rebellion a thorough trial. We shall permit it to run its full course. The universe shall see what a creature, though he be the highest creature ever to spring from God's Word, can do apart from Him. We shall watch this experiment, and permit the universe of creatures to watch it, during this brief interlude between eternity past and eternity future called time. In it, the spirit of independence shall be allowed to expand to the utmost. And the wreck and ruin which shall result will demonstrate to the universe, and forever, that there is no life, no joy, no peace apart from a complete dependence upon the Most High God, Possessor of heaven and earth."(The Invisible War, 1969) 2

Even though our victory is assured, the Lord's present day warriors within the remnant church should be prepared to fight in cold blood. (War on the Saints,, pg. 197-198, abridged edition) To fight in cold blood is to always be prepared to fight, both in season and out of season. By now, the contents of this book should have sufficiently opened your eyes to the reality that the true Bride of Christ is about to enter her season once judgment has fully begun within the household of faith. Therefore, we need to be able to recognize conflict that exists within "a cold war." During a cold war, on the surface, it appears not to be any conflict. Nevertheless, we must always be prepared to fight, even when a demonic attack has diminished. Let's face the facts. Demonic onslaught against the true church of Jesus Christ will not fully cease until the Lord Himself returns to earth.

I believe that when the two-edged sword falls on the harlot church and her hirelings, the spiritually damaged and captive sheep will have no place to run but to those of His servants who have kept the faith by righteousness--- believers who have not denied His name with idolatry. Consequently, the church of Philadelphia is being prepared to be the spiritual hospital for those who have been abused by the traditional organized church. The primary battleground to restore the sheep is of course within each individual captive's mind. As the mind is renewed by the word of God, the deliverance worker or counselor must also teach the sheep who have been damaged how to cast down imaginations and every high thought that would exalt itself above the knowledge of Christ, and to bring each thought into the captivity of the obedience of The Lord Jesus Christ. (II Corinthians 10:4,5)

COUNTERFEIT GIFTS

Of the 9 gifts of the Holy Ghost, there is not one gift that the religious demon has not been successful at imitating, capable of fooling even the very elect. These 9 supernatural gifts can be grouped into 3 categories: The power gifts of healing, miracles and faith; the "seeing" or revelation gifts of discerning of spirits, the word of knowledge and the word of wisdom; and the utterance gifts of prophecy, tongues, and interpretation of tongues. More than one book could be written about this particular facet of the religious demon's repertoire. Generally speaking, since the counterfeits are innumerable, every supernatural manifestation must be tried, to see if it be of God. Sometimes, the only thing that you can do is wait. For example, I received a highly developed, well conceived vision by email of impending world wide doom which was to have occurred on January 23, 2006. Today is May 17, 2006 and we are all "still here." Here are some excerpts from this email of impending destruction:

> I saw the Sky and suddenly out of the Sky airplanes where falling everywhere. it was like ripples, there where ripples in the sky, like there is in water. These ripples where like sound waves or electronic disturbance directed from the ground against this airplanes which made them fall out of the sky. This is scalar electromagnetic waves, which the Russians have perfected. This weapon will bring down aircraft, missiles, nations, etc.

> In the next vision, I saw many warehouses and then the ocean with a harbor appeared, in the harbor was a cruise ship which was on fire and is sinking. I was in the water outside the ship, I could see many animals in the water around the ship, they started moving and they must be somehow crocodiles or what ever, they were there eating up those who try to jump into the water escaping the fire on the ship. I tried to tell them don't jump, I was screaming and screaming but it was useless, they didn't listen they jumped anyway. (The great eagle of Babylon, the party ship of the U.S., will begin to burn through many judgments. As the Medes and Persians fought against Babylon and eventually took it so it will be for the U.S. in the day of the Lord. We are told that those who jump ship will also die at the hands of these beasts. {Isa.13:13} Therefore I will make the heavens to tremble, and the earth shall be shaken out of its place, in the wrath of Jehovah of hosts, and in the day of his fierce anger. {14} And it shall come to pass, that as the chased roe, and as sheep that no man gathereth, they shall turn every man to his own people, and shall flee every man to his own land. {15} Every one

that is found shall be thrust through; and every one that is taken shall fall by the sword. ... {17} Behold, I will stir up the Medes against them...Â {18} And [their] bows shall dash the young men in pieces; and they shall have no pity on the fruit of the womb; their eye shall not spare children. These are the same people, whose symbol was the bear, that fight against the modern day eagle. The modern day bear, Russia, will join with them to eventually defeat   the   eagle   as   history   repeats.)

In the third vision, suddenly I was in the water (somehow in the harbor area in New York) I could see people floating in the water and all kinds of things and I was shocked and moved back as I looked down I saw the head of the statue of Liberty in the water next to me, then suddenly a big hole was blown out in the midst of the skyscrapers. People where melting like wax. nuclear explosion. Then in addition to this explosion, suddenly I saw flat across the map of the United States and saw the following names jumping up, I heard the names of the cities as I saw them raise up off the map somehow I knew that these cities would be attacked at the same time: Cincinnati, San Francisco, Montreal, Atlanta, Dallas and Washington D.C

In the fourth vision, I saw Mexico City there were three planes trying to land at the same time came in from three different directions and crashed mid- air...Then came Hawaii and I saw some tragedies, must be through some type of big wave, like Tsunami wave. Tragic, wiped out I believe the islands were sunk....then at the end I saw written: "CAN NOT BE   OVERRIDDEN"
Then about two days later, the vision about New York came back very strong. I was again under the water, the statue of Liberty was in the water with me, I said Lord take me out of the water, take me out, now, praise God I was cold, it was so real, and I saw again the hole which was blown into the skyscrapers. It seemed that it was important for me to be under in/under the water, vantage point, I saw something, so suddenly I saw and a submarine coming to the surface and then after this there were many, it was like a fleet, and they were Russian, which was important for me to see. They all came to the surface in the Harbor, with the hole in the buildings , looked to me like the inside of the hole was coming out around the hole like it had been shot from the North to the South, Russia....I saw black Helicopters everywhere and men coming out on ropes and invasions of a sort... (This may be U.S. special forces but the shot from the north could come from a sub because there are many waters north of NY.) I saw another fleet of ships going towards the disaster and t hen I saw a ship compass and the compass was in the direction of Southwest. (The Russian invasion fleet from the northeast.)

After this we prayed specifically to receive an indication about timing. So as we prayed, the Lord gave me a vision about a boat which wrote in the water 23 (it came from top to down) in the spirit I knew this was January.... (1-23) and then the boat came again and wrote 2006 from the left to the right. (This date may be the beginning of these judgments which will end in the future invasion of the U.S. in the day of the Lord. The Bible code spoke of an all out nuclear war between the U.S., Russia, and China in 2006 but it also showed that it is delayed. It is delayed until the day of the Lord when the sun and the moon are darkened after the tribulation [Mt.24:29] and the earth is shaken out of its place when all nations are gathered against Babylon [Isa.13:4,6,9-13]. A possible confirmation to the 1-23-06 date is below.)

Included with these four visions were "confirmations" from several others who had similar dreams and visions. I wonder if those who had these visions rationalized another scenario to relieve them of the embarrassment they must have faced on January 24, 2006 once they realized that the Statue of Liberty was "still standing." According to Jessie Penn-Lewis:

> "Visions may come from one of three sources. The Divine, from God; the human, such as hallucinations and illusions because of disease, and the Satanic, which are false. 'Visions' given by evil spirits, also describe anything supernatural presented to and seen by the mind or imagination, from outside; such as terrible pictures of the 'future'; flashing of texts as if they were lit up; 'visions' of widespread 'movements,' all counterfeiting either the true vision of the Holy Spirit given to the action of the imagination. The Church is thus often made a whirlpool of division through believers relying upon 'texts' for guiding their decisions, instead of the principle of right and wrong set forth in God's word." (War on the Saints,9th edition, pg. 150)

I was emailed these four visions of disaster on 1/21, just two days before the predicted "day of doom." Consequently, I did not have long to wait to try the spirits. To the person who sent these visions by email to me, I wrote:

> "With a disaster such as described by this visionary , there is no preparation that we can undertake other than to pray and prepare our hearts to die and be with Jesus or to be supernaturally delivered by Him. Even though I am one of the elect , no one will survive other than by a miraculous "Red Sea" type of rescue, I will do as Jesus has declared and "take heed that no one deceives me" and I will "fear not." However, if this vision be divine, then in His own words "but for the sake of the elect, those days will be shortened." (Matthew 24:22) Since I am one of the elect, this is my prayer in such a case. 'Let the days be shortened for the sake of the elect who are on earth at the time of the disaster.' This is truly the only way that I can prepare for a holocaust of this nature."

It is amazing that people who seem to know the word of God continue to overlook the very clear admonition of the Lord, not recognizing that visions such as these are in contradiction to the Lord's own words, that "But of that day and hour NO ONE KNOWS, not even the angels of heaven, but My Father only." (Matthew 24:36) Since pride goes before a fall, I personally believe that anyone who thinks that God chose to give to them an exact date that neither Jesus nor the angels of God have been made privy to, is of a most high minded, haughty spirit indeed. They are probably among those with religious demons that Jesus warned the elect about who would say that they have seen Jesus. We must keep our Lord's words in mind: "therefore if they say to you 'Look, He is in the desert! Do not go out; or 'Look, He is in the inner rooms!' do not believe it." (Matthew 24:26)

Since it is clear that a religious demon is the author of these visions, what would be its motive to spread these lies? Besides promoting widespread fear, there are several interconnected motives, only one of which is the embarrassment of the visionary. Moreover, the religious demon's goal is to chisel away at the integrity of the prophetic gift, in order to cause people to disregard or minimize a truly divine prophetic utterance in the near future. A visionary myself, I can look back now and assess that several of my own dreams and visions over the last two decades were sent to me by a religious demon in order to lift up my pride as well as to diminish my faith, once the visions and dreams did not come to pass. For example, the religious demon knows that I am called to a ministry that includes the power gifts of healing, faith and miracles and therefore, he has sent me several counterfeit messages so as to cause me to lust after power "for power's sake."

Through personal experience with his symbolic and spiritual "thorn in the flesh", Paul the Apostle's testimony is that power and pride go hand in hand. Likewise, those who move in the power gifts must also be tried through the fires of refinement because there is no good thing in the flesh. (II Corinthians 12:1-10) My testimony is that on more than one occasion in the early 80's, the religious demon has tried to exalt me. For example, I saw myself in dreams, standing before congregations of thousands, commanding cut off limbs to grow back, and even raising the dead. Since it has been more than 20 years since I had such visions, today I remain "neutral", as I cannot say for sure whether or not these messages were from God or from the religious demon. I suspect that such visions emanated from the religious demon. To take advantage of the pride of life that was in my soul over the years, it is not difficult for me to perceive how the religious demon could be the source of these dreams and visions. Unclean motives can produce unclean prophecies.

In this regard, those who are called to operate in the power of the Holy Ghost must examine their own hearts to see if they remain under the sway of a lust for greatness. As I have watched various ministers on television demonstrate a need for spiritual heart surgery, one particular example comes to mind. I believe it was a Sunday at 7pm EST in the month of August of 2002, that a TV program was aired when mega-preacher,Bishop Clarence McClendon, began to utter a so-called word of knowledge or prophecy about a person he believed to be present in the congregation that very night. Since I recorded the program, I was able to transcribe his words:

"I don't want to embarrass anybody, but I MUST obey God. There is a man here. You have given your life to God. You WERE a drug dealer. There are people who are trying to pull you back." Then with a complementary grin and a chuckle, the Prophet crooned, "and you were verrrrrrrrry good!"

In short, the Prophet's body language, facial expressions and remarks clearly suggested that he was stroking or complimenting a former drug dealer who had once been very successful at his illegal trade.

The Prophet continued.

"This has been your question. You've said 'God, I've made a lot of money. I know that is wrong.' You have feel that because of what you have, that God is against you and he's going to take it all away from you. And you're wondering if you should sell just a little to keep things going."

Then the Prophet responded to what he had just predicted is this drug dealers question and emphatically shouted, "NO! The Spirit of God is going to take the gift that you have, anoint that gift and prosper you on a whole new dimension." By now, the congregation is clapping and shouting. Then the Prophet continued reading the drug dealers thoughts with "and you've been wondering if you can use this money you've made dealing drugs."

Suddenly, the Prophet made an outburst as an answer to this the drug dealers second imaginary question about the use of his illegally gained profits:

"Absolutely, man!!! Money is neither good nor evil. Its whose hands its in. Now that you are a sanctified son of God, all you need to do is turn it over to Him. The word of the Lord is that this gift in you is going to be anointed tonight. I need to lay hands on you. That is the word of the Lord, whoever you are, come forward!"

Not once did the Prophet call for this drug dealer to repent of his sin. Nor did he explain what he meant about "the gift" in the former drug dealer. I suspect that he was referring to leadership skills and business acumen. However, the epitome of success for a drug dealer would be to not get shot or murdered, to stay out of prison and to avoid becoming a drug addict himself! Yet, it also takes a lot more than that! It takes an unhealthy lust for money that is the root of the drug dealer's hardness of heart and willingness to accept the entire spectrum of criminality and anti-social behavior that comes with that underground life.

Now to everyone's amazement, a man is brought forth by one of the members of the Prophet's congregation. This man is crying and weeping. It is clear from his clothing and his demeanor that this could not be the slick, successful former drug dealer who had been born again for awhile and who was considering that perhaps he will have to give an account to God for the wealth that he obtained illegally. In fact, this particular man is obviously struggling with poverty. Sobbing his way to the altar, the man is sincerely repenting. He is brought to the front and stands in front of the Prophet.

When the microphone is put to the Prophet's mouth, he can be heard saying "I'm sorry. I'm sorry." The Prophet begins to question him and asks "what are you feeling?" The man answers, "I feel the Spirit. I feel free!!" Then the Prophet questions the church member that had ushered the man to the front. It turns out that this particular member had JUST led this young man to Christ in the back of the church. Once the man was saved, he revealed that he had been dealing with addiction and that he had just started selling drugs the previous Friday. That particular morning, this young man woke up and he indicated that the Lord had impressed upon him to come to the service and be saved.

It should have been very obvious to any one with good common sense, that this young man, a novice who tried to sell drugs just one time, was not a successful drug dealer who was wondering what was going to become of all of his money and material possessions. Then the Prophet began to engage the crowd and expeditiously flow with what was happening, convincing the onlookers that the slumped over, weeping, poorly dressed addict barely standing before him was indeed the successful drug dealer that he had just prophesied about.

> "Now, I didn't know you before, isn't that right? I've never seen you before and I know nothing about your life. Praise the Lord! Let me bless you and lay my hands on you. I've never met you. There is no way I would know that you were here. Let me ask you. What made you want to come to Jesus?" The man answered, "I got tired. I got tired of everything."

Ignoring the fact that the Holy Spirit had already drawn the man to Christ BEFORE he came to that service, that the man declared that he felt the Spirit and that the Lord had already set him free, the Prophet screamed at the devil, "let him go! Spirit of addiction, come out of him." Then he hit the man in his stomach, and the man collapsed to the ground. While he lay there, the Prophet stared into the TV screen and dramatically declared: "the Holy Spirit is filling him now. I was pregnant with this. I see 20 drug addicts getting delivered." Then his face filled the camera in a close up angle. Glaring into the TV, the Prophet shouted "I want every ex-drug dealer to know that you are welcome in THIS house. There is deliverance in this house."

To observe the sheep not carefully try the spirits to see if they be of God is of particular concern to me. In light of the information that was presented, I have to question the circumstances surrounding this particular occurrence. Could it be that what actually happened is that perhaps one of the Prophet's close confidants revealed to him that a wealthy former drug dealer was in attendance in the service? And hoping to encourage the man to donate a sizable offering to his ministry, it appeared that the Prophet may have attempted to placate the former drug dealer. Through a subtle inference, without directly speaking the words, it appeared that the Prophet implied that if the prosperous drug dealer put some big bucks into the collection plate, the Lord would allow the drug dealer to keep the balance of his money and worldly goods. If this supposition could be verified and proved true, then of course the Prophet's integrity would be no different from that of a carnival psychic who plays mind games with his audience.

A less accusatory scenario is that perhaps the Prophet merely got caught up in his prophetic ministry, and did not try the spirits himself. When ministers, including myself, move in the supernatural gifts of the Spirit, we may mis-judge a particular manifestation because we are eager to see our special anointing confirmed and verified. Countless times, I myself have been too hasty in accepting a manifestation as from the Lord. However, when I have not properly discerned the spirit, I have come forth as soon as possible and informed my congregation, "that was NOT the Lord!" There are other times when I have been compelled to report, " Sorry, but that wasn't God like I thought. It was the devil." In all fairness, I admit that I do not have the pressures of national television to contend with as does Bishop McClendon." However, I DO have the WEB and I am an author! So believe me, if I ever write or preach ANYTHING on the Web or in my books that I discover to be incorrect, I will publicly correct myself as soon as conceivably possible!!! We ALL see through a glass darkly! These are the last days and we all need to be cautious and careful.

The bottom line here, is that it was clear to me that the man who came to the altar was not the prosperous drug dealer that the Prophet had described in his prophetic utterance. Little did he know that at the same time that he was calling forth the drug dealer of either his own imagination, invention , or intention, the Lord saved a hopeless, poor addict and set him free from the spirit of addiction without the Prophet's foreknowledge. This is truly the ministry that we all should be about! The saving of a lost soul, praise God! The minister's job is certainly not to placate church members who have prospered by corrupt and illegal means to share their wealth with the church.

There was a time that I myself was very attracted to this particular prophet's ministry. A charismatic, rather handsome young man, his manner of articulation suggested intelligence and breeding. With a certain flair and bravado to his personality, it was easy for me to discern his apparent ambition towards glory in his quest to become a mega preacher of great renown. As for me, it took almost 20 years of trial, tribulation and trouble to burn out the dross of ambition and striving for greatness within my own soul and so I can touch that same quality in others as a former personal counterpart. Accordingly, my own experience has enhanced my spiritual discernment to recognize what I perceive to be the spirit of pride and ambition in others,--- an open doorway to demonic deception. To me, nothing is more important than setting free the sheep, one captive at a time. Once again, Jessie Penn-Lewis prophetically put the spiritual nail on the head almost 100 years ago in her assessment of the religious demon's overall motive:

> "Many a believer has left his path of 'grain of wheat multiplication,' caught by a vision of 'world-wide' sweeping in of souls, given by Satan, whose malignant hatred, and ceaseless antagonism is directed against the true seed of Jesus Christ, which in union with Him, will bruise the serpent's head. To delay the birth, (John3:3,5), and growth of the Holy Seed (Isaiah 6:10), is the devil's aim. To this end, he will foster any widespread surface work of the believer, knowing it will not really touch his kingdom, nor hasten the full birth into the Throne-life of the conquering seed of Christ. The safe path for believers at the close of the age is one of tenacious faith in the written Word as the sword of the Spirit, to cut the way through all the interferences and tactics of the forces of darkness, to the end." (War on the Saints, 9th edition, pg. 151) 3

Consequently, trying the spirits to see if they be of God is no simple task. Furthermore, the New Testament offers no unequivocal instructions on how to determine whether or not a supernatural experience is from the Lord or from the devil other than what we read in the book of Hebrews: "But strong meat belongeth to them that are of full age, even those who by reason of use have their senses exercised to discern both good and evil." (Hebrews 5:14) Simply put, we learn how to uncover the source of supernatural manifestations by frequent "use." Spiritual exercise translates into practice by systematic application or exertion through the blood, sweat and tears of our own spiritual brow---where we learn to discern by trial and error. One of the fallacies that has been exposed to me through trial and error is the faulty assumption that if an occurrence supernaturally foreseen comes to pass, then it must be a message from God. On the contrary, God makes it very clear in Deuteronomy that a prophet or a dreamer can receive a word or sign that does come to pass, and use that word to draw people away from Him:

> "If there arise among you a prophet, or a dreamer of dreams, and giveth thee a sign or a wonder, and the sign or the wonder, COME TO PASS, wherefore, he spake unto thee, saying "Let us go after other gods, which thou hast not known and let us serve them; Thou shalt not hearken unto the words of that prophet, or that dreamer of dreams: for the Lord

your God proveth you, to know whether you love the Lord your God with all your heart and with all your soul." (Deuteronomy 13:1-5)

In fact, one of my first experiences of a spiritual counterfeit was presented in a prophetic dream that I received in 1979. The intent of that dream was to draw me into a sinful relationship with an AME Zion minister. At that time, I had barely left the occult and I was totally unaware of the fact that I was called to ministry. This particular dream set me up to fall into a trap that would scar my ministry even before I knew that I was called. Still a babe in Christ, I had a supernatural dream that pointed me in the direction of this sinful minister whse name I have changed to   Rev. George Bernard Charles. Without the prophetic nature of that dream, I would not have been attracted to Rev. Charles. Subsequently , when every element of the dream came to pass   in one day about two weeks later, I assumed that the dream was from the Lord.   I write about the dream and the subsequent occurrences in "the Making of a Prophet:"

> "One night I had a dream that I saw a man standing beside the church with a minister's robe over his arm. He was wearing a navy blue Sears and Roebuck suit and blue suede shoes. With a smile on his face, this man whom I had never before seen, spoke to me in this dream by chuckling, "Girl, I'm gonna marry you!...This was the first of several prophetic dreams inspired by demons to seduce me into fornication." (pg. 48)

In the chapter called "Demonic Soul Ties," the strategy of the religious demon to entrap women to be driven by the need to seek to serve the Lord as co-pastor with a husband as "senior pastor" is explored in more detail.   However, in this instance, I approach this subject from the standpoint of how the religious demon will employ a prophetic dream or vision that actually comes to pass in its attempt to prove to the Lord God that you can be drawn away from Him through the lust of your flesh. As I look back, the religious demon's motive is clear. He wanted to make my transition into ministry as difficult as possible, so that I would believe that I could not effectively minister without co-pastoring with a spouse:

> "When I responded to the Lord's call in 1981, I had no idea of what my acceptance of His call would mean on a denominational level. I had no idea that regionally I would become a member of a cadre of 70 or so ministers in Western New York, where it turned out that I was the only woman among them. My first 'wake up' call was that I was literally doomed to rise within the denomination before I even got started because of the affair that I had engaged in prior to my calling with Rev. Charles. As a result of my past indiscretion, Rev. John Carpenter, one of the regional directors called 'presiding elders,' had become a formidable enemy. Before he left the area for the last time, Rev. Charles had revealed that Elder Carpenter was trying to seduce him and was therefore jealously furious of me. In fact, Elder Carpenter blamed me as the reason why the Bishop sent Rev. Charles to Kansas City. So when he saw me come before him to gain entrance into the ministry, Elder Carpenter was determined that it would not happen, not so long as he was presiding elder." (The Making of a Prophet, pg. 63)

Elder Carpenter was not against women in ministry and so I am convinced that had I not fallen into sin with Rev. Charles, Elder Carpenter would have treated me fairly and supported my ministry as I have witnessed him do for many others over the years, both women as well as men. Since I was in no way attracted to Rev. Charles, the religious demon tempted me into sin based upon my sincere yet impure desire to please God. My faulty assumption that the coming to pass of a prophetic dream was an indication that it was a word from God led to the next faulty assumption--- that Rev. Charles was the Lord's divine choice of my future husband. The demon orchestrated this dream by having Rev. Charles declare that I was to be his wife. Nevertheless, the Lord still used this turn of events to have His own way. Since Jesus had no intention for me to be embraced by the AME Zion Church, the Holy Spirit used Rev. Carpenter's twenty-two year hostility to keep me from rising to prominence in a sinful place. So it all worked out by the grace of God, and the victory is still mine.

ENDNOTES

1.Taken from my second book, "The Making of a Prophet: A Spiritual Indictment to the Organized Church, Author House, 2005, pg. 55

2.Donald Grey Barnhouse, "Invisible War: The Panorama of the Continuing Conflict between Good and Evil," Zondervan , 1965. Although Barnhouse is in disagreement with Jessie Penn Lewis regarding Christians having demons "in them", there is much in his book worth reading. As for Jessie, he wrote:"We put forth categorically in spite of the works of the English group known as the Overcomers, whose bible is frequently Mrs. Penn-Lewis's book, "War on the Saints." We know of no more insalubrious idea than that which would turn Christians to introspection, looking for attacks of Satan within....There is no fellowship between righteousness and unrighteousness. There is no communion between light and darkness. There is no concord between Christ and the devil...pg. 166." It is obvious that Barnhouse does not believe that a Christian can have a demon "inside" of him. It may seem contradictory, but I agree with both Lewis and Barnhouse. This obvious disagreement is more one of perception and language then of actual substance. And where I believe that both of them "miss it" is that there are many professing Christians who have demons "in them", primarily because they never got saved in the first place. This subject is explored in the next chapter.

CHAPTER 4 : Counterfeit Births

I am concerned, and even appalled to have come across in the last few years an extremely serious condition that may be of epidemic proportions within the organized church. The problem was first brought to my attention in the lives of those who sought deliverance from demonic torment and other professing Christians. At first I believed that their primary misconception was a lack of understanding about repentance. However, now I have found that the issue goes even deeper. My recent work with clients has brought my attention to the alarming trend that most captives do not understand resurrection and therefore are not saved or "reborn." Without the resurrection there can be no new birth.

As recorded in 1st John, the spirit of the anti-Christ will deny that Jesus has "come in the flesh." Since the spirit of the anti-Christ is the biblical name for the religious demon, I believe that it his handiwork that causes people to not understand the Lord's BODILY resurrection.   The religious demon's primary intent is to deny that the Holy Spirit raised Jesus Christ from the dead. Therefore, anyone who does not believe in the BODILY resurrection of Jesus Christ is still in his or her sins, according to Paul's first letter to believers in Corinth. (I Corinthians 15: 13-19) If a person is still in his sins, then of course, he is not saved. If he is not saved, then the spiritual weapons will not work for him.

What I try to encourage within the heart of each captive is to create a fighting spirit. One who has a fighting spirit must believe in the weapons of his warfare, which are not carnal. However, without a belief in the resurrection the correct way, the captive is without sufficient power to withstand the fight. Demons can be cast out of anyone, saved or unsaved. However, the one set free will not be able to stand if he is defenseless. Therefore, his condition could worsen. Without a belief on the BODILY resurrection of the Lord, the one who has been set free will become meat for as many as 7 additional demons. (Matthew 12: 43-45) Since faith cannot stand without the resurrection, it is clear that without a belief in the BODILY resurrection of the Lord Jesus Christ, no man can be saved.

Furthermore, without the shield of faith, the captive will not be able to escape the fiery darts of demons. When Jesus Himself cast out devils from captives who were so bound that they did not have a will of their own, once delivered, it was an easy thing to believe on the one who delivered them. However, once Jesus ascended and left the work of deliverance up to the elect of God, it is crucial that the captive believe that Jesus arose not "in spirit" only but in His material body. If Jesus did not arise in His body, then the Christian faith is no different from any other religion. This is why the religious demon is so against the resurrection. The religious demon's strategy is to remove "the power" by denying the major foundational truth of the faith ---which is that on the 3rd day, the Lord arose from the dead IN HIS BODY, never to die again. If Jesus did not arise from the dead, then this means that Jesus did not defeat death in the flesh.

The irony is that repentance and resurrection are considered to be among the most elementary of the foundational principles of Christianity. (Hebrews 6:1,2) Therefore, it is evident that the strategy of the religious demon for centuries has been to penetrate the organized church with various customs and polity that will effectuate a counterfeit religious experience. For example, the tradition of the altar call invitation as well as various professions of faith, particularly the repeating of the sinner's prayer may, by their very nature, block a true salvation experience. According to Dr. Rebecca Brown, the altar call invitation and the various professions of faith fall into this category:

> "This is a common practice in most churches, especially the fundamentalistic ones. In this practice, people desiring to become church members go forward to the front and repeat a profession of faith. Any satanist can easily repeat a profession of faith. I consider this practice a dangerous one for two reasons: First, as I said above, any satanist can repeat or read a profession of faith. Secondly, any unsaved person can do the same. If a person cannot, without any prompting, state clearly why he believes he is saved, then he probably doesn't understand the concept well enough to be saved in the first place. Jesus said that if we are ashamed of Him before men that He would be ashamed of us before His Father. Anyone wanting to become a church member should be able to clearly state his faith, in his own words, before the congregation. If he cannot do this small thing before other Christians, how can he ever stand against our enemy or witness to the lost world?"(R. Brown, pg. 188) 1

I answer Dr. Brown's rhetorical question without hesitation. HE CANNOT! It seems that the central issue that has been diluted in the preaching of the gospel within the organized church is the meaning of sin for every human being. In short, sin must be punished. Jesus paid a debt that He did not owe, the sinner owed a debt that he could not pay, and he needs someone to pay that debt for Him. The sacrifice that Jesus made as Our Substitute involved more than the pain of being nailed to the cross and being whipped and beaten. The worst of the Lord's suffering was emotional in that after He became sin, He was separated from His Father who had to forsake Him. The godly sorrow of repentance as inspired by the leading of the Holy Ghost should cause a sinner under conviction to feel sorrow not only because of his own personal sin nature, but also because of what the Lord went through for his or her sake.

Certainly, the sinner may not necessarily comprehend the depth of the Lord's agony, but he should at least be aware of the fact that the Lord's suffering was for him or her, in particular. It is important to note here that there are those who know that they are sinners but they are not saved because the gospel has not been preached in a manner that causes them to see Jesus in His substitutionary role for each one of them individually. Moreover, in order to be saved or "found", one needs to know that he is lost. Therefore, I believe that it is crucial to salvation that sinners understand with their minds and feel in their emotions the essence of their alienation,--- separated from God with Satan playing the role as their father. (Ephesians 2:5, Colossians 1:21) Taken from "The Making of a Prophet," the following words succinctly depict the problem:

> "In the non-denominational church, they respond at the altar to a 'believe, confess and receive' gospel, Romans 10:8---that if you confess the Lord Jesus with your mouth and believe in your heart that God has raised Him from the dead, you shall be saved.' In the old line Pentecostal denominations, they have come to the altar seeking the Holy Ghost and the speaking in tongues without having repented for sin and they too are in a mess today. Not to say that there are not countless people in the traditional

denominations that are not saved. After 22 years serving in such a denomination, I have witnessed the dire need for an invitation that will bring conviction of sin and repentance. However, my experience is that because the unsaved in denominational churches are not open to the invisible world of the spirit, they generally do not have the added problem of becoming demon oppressed." Sheppard, p. 128, 129)

Furthermore, those who speak in tongues within a charismatic, pentecostal, or word of faith church have reasoned that since tongues is a sign of the infilling of the Holy Ghost, and that this infilling is subsequent to salvation, therefore the one who utters MUST be saved.   It is my belief that the only true evidence of salvation is not tongues, but the fruits of the Spirit as manifested primarily as "love for the brethren." We know that we have passed from death unto life, because we love the brethren is the true barometer. (I John 3:7-14;John 2:8-11),   Not only have I known countless tongue speakers who manifested a lack of love for the brethren, but most of the captives I have ministered to have spoken in tongues. Therefore, as a result of counseling several people who have spoken in tongues yet who do not understand either repentance or resurrection, I myself conclude that persons who are not saved can also speak in a tongue which raises the question "what is the source of their tongue speaking?" The obvious answer is that it is a counterfeit manifestation, emanating from the religious demon.

I further believe that the traditional congregation's invitation, of "opening the doors of the church," has ushered in   countless demons. The AME Zion Church has a superior practice of placing those who seek to escape the wrath that is to come on a probationary membership status. The founding fathers of Methodism were wise enough to not only create a procedure to ensure a bona fide salvation but also to protect the body from fellowship with unbelievers. However, over time, the full enforcement of this practice became ineffective, as people were brought into permanent church status without having manifested fruits of salvation. I personally believe that when converts can demonstrate that they are truly disciples of the Lord, then I can fellowship with them as brethren, and not before.

Yet another open door to the religious demon is the coined spiritual phrase, a Christian idiom most frequently expressed is "the Lord led me." In a book called "Unholy Devotion," the author aptly warns of the danger of spiritualizing:

> "At first glance the phrase sounds quite spiritual, but a close examination of Scripture reveals that it is not always biblical. On several occasions the phrase is used by or to describe false prophets or deceptive people. Jacob deceived his father by spiritualizing issues. Esau, Jacob's brother, had just gone hunting. Too quickly, it seemed, Jacob, claiming to be Esau, brought the killed game to his father. "How did you find game so quickly?" Isaac asked. Having usurped Esau's place, Jacob lied to his sick, blind father. But notice Jacob's very 'spiritual' response: 'The Lord your God gave me success." (Gen27:20) Jacob was playing dangerous games, spiritualizing in order to manipulate someone he knew would believe such words. Jacob wasn't a false cult leader or prophet; he was God's own chosen servant".

"Christians often think that the seeds of heresy are found only in cults and in off-beat sects of Christianity. But John, in his first letter, and Paul, in his letter to the Ephesians, reminded us that heretical teachers are often found within the church itself. Jesus notes that the dormant seeds of heresy can be buried in the lawns of the church. In Matthew 13, Jesus tells a parable of the kingdom of heaven: The enemy sowed sees within this kingdom. In our desire to discover and understand the doctrines of cults, we may forget that potential gardens of heresy lie within our own walls. Remember: Sun Myung Moon was raised a Presbyterian; David Berg, founder of the Children of God, was once an Evangelical pastor; Jim Jones pastored a Christian church; many leaders in the People's Temple and Jonestown were former members of Nazarene, Roman Catholic, Baptist, Methodist and Assemblies of God Churches." 1 (HL Bussell, pg.111)

Besides the altar call, the invitation to Christian discipleship, and the various professions of faith, there are other coined religious platitudes and phrases like "Jesus, come into my heart" and "I accepted Jesus into my life" that could lead to counterfeit births. I myself have not been able to find any scriptures in the bible that suggest that we should ask Jesus to come into our hearts. I believe that when the Lord says that we must abide in Him, He means that we must stay in Him without wavering, in other words,---- to continue, to dwell, to be present, to remain. This is the essence of the Greek word, that was translated "abide" in John 15. Accordingly, baring fruit in Christ is a manifestation of a believer continuing and remaining in Him.

Another term or expression that I believe is wrongfully applied within the organized church is the re-dedication of the backslider. In truth, there is no such word in the New Testament to depict a backslider. To say the least, the term "backslider" is an oxymoron or a misnomer. Most assuredly, my understanding of the word of God is that those who walk away from the faith were probably never truly among the elect in the first place and if the truly saved were to depart from the faith, there would be no chance for a re-dedication anyway. (Hebrews 6:1-6) I believe that there are those who are under the sway of the Judas spirit, the spirit of Jezebel as well as the spirit of the anti-Christ--- many even born into a religious, churchgoing family, yet their hearts were never touched by the gospel. The words of the Apostle John ring true regarding the spirit of the anti-Christ, the religious demon:

"Little Children, it is the lat time: and as ye have heard that Antichrist shall come, even now are there many anti-Christs; whereby we know that it is the last time. They went out from us, but they were not of us; for if they had been of us, they would no doubt have continued with us; but they went out, that they might be made manifest that they were not all of us. (I John 2: 18- 19)

I myself am a product of such a family. My late grandfather, Cyril Oscar Sheppard Sr., a bishop in a Greek Orthodox African Caribbean Church originally founded in Antigua, raised 7 children in the church he founded, along with his wife Gretta. Of his 7 children, only one son remained an active churchgoer, a faithful member of his father's church for the remainder of his life. As I write these words, 4 of my deceased father's siblings are now over 80, and as in the case of my late father, they remain non-churchgoing to this day. Though born into the organized church and pastored by their own father until they became adults, the preached and taught word never produced a rebirth in their hardened hearts toward Christ. Grandpa Cyril did not live to witness in the flesh that his seed of devotion toward the Lord was not fully cut off, by virtue of the fact that the one whom Grandma Gretta often called "a heathen", ended up among the elect, a minister of the gospel of Jesus Christ. My grandfather died when I was 17 years old and Grandma Gretta died in May, 1976, less than a year before I became born again.

In terms of my own salvation experience, I thank the Lord that I was not hindered by church polity. I am truly grateful to God that no one ever gave me a tract, nor did anyone invite me to church as an adult. Sent to church as a child, my maternal family never discovered even unto this day that I stayed on the ghetto streets of Harlem, never entering the church doors at St. Phillip's Episcopal Church on 133 Street in New York City, except once. Although my maternal relatives were religious, they were not churchgoers either, so they had no idea that I didn't go when sent. In truth, I rejected church polity like the plague. I recall clearly that the very first day that I was sent to Sunday School, the teaching was about the Trinity. I wondered to myself , "how can 3 Gods be One God?" Since I didn't understand, I never went back. It is amazing that they still confirmed me even though I was never there. I was probably about 8 or 10 years old.

On my father's side, Grandpa Cyril, though a minister, left me alone but I stood against Grandma Gretta countless Sundays, refusing to attend their church that was on the second floor of their huge brownstone in New York City—a house where I spent many weekends as a child. Grandma Gretta was right. I was as heathen as heathen can get. As a child, I didn't even believe in Santa Claus. Since my mother and father were separated, my father enforced his legal right of custody, and I was in his care most weekends. Since he was often working either running numbers or tending bar, he saw me intermittently and I was really in the care of his parents, who were zealous churchgoers. Every Sunday morning without fail, Grandma Gretta woke me with a poke in the side with her cane, until I finally jumped up and finished my sleep underneath the bed. She would bend down, poke that cane under the bed, until in utter frustration, she would give up and shout out loud, "Pam, ya be a heathen!!!! You got no trainin at all, ya little wretch, ya!!"

By the time the Holy Spirit drew me to the cross, all I knew of the gospel as an adult was what I had learned from the holidays of Christmas and Easter. I have often wondered why my testimony is so graphic. I understand today that it was purposefully so, in order that I would be able to fully understand the salvation experience. The Lord needed someone like me to help those who were raised in church to recognize that you don't have to be a rocket scientist to get saved. I don't expect everyone's rebirth day to be as sensational as what occurred to me on March 29 1977!! However, I DO expect that every one born into the kingdom of God should feel the joy of their salvation and the blessed assurance of knowing that Jesus belongs to them. The joy that I experienced in coming to Jesus had nothing to do with escaping the wrath that is to come. At the time, I had no idea that without Jesus I had been destined for hell and that once saved, I didn't have to go. I knew of heaven and hell conceptually, yet if my rebirth can be considered a model, fearing eternity in hell or even desiring to go to heaven are not necessary to becoming "born again."

As previously stated, I cannot repeat it enough that sinners are often sorry for their sins, but sorrow for sin alone doesn't get them saved. That is because such sorrow is merely a manifestation of self pity and not really a demonstration or an awareness of how their own personal sin has hurt God Himself. The scripture refers to "godly sorrow" that bares the fruit of salvation. (IICorinthians 7:10)I believe that another way to put that would be "sorry for God." I remember very clearly that when I got saved, I continued to cry and I couldn't stop. Now don't get me wrong. Everyone who cries is not saved either. My tears had begun for myself. As I progressively came to terms with the darkness that was within me, I had to face the contradictions in my soul---a heavy undertaking for a person who thought herself to be so basically good, so right.

Yet my sorrow noticeably changed and I couldn't put my finger on it. I continued to cry, without knowing why I was crying. I was on the telephone with a friend who gave me a nudge with "you know why you are crying" and I replied "No Vivian, I do not know." This went back and forth between us that way when suddenly, I threw my head back and life changing words burst forth from my mouth: "I'm crying for what they did to Jesus." With that outcry, I knew in a split second that everything I had heard about Jesus was true---that He died for my sins and that He was raised from the dead.   Since I had been an atheist from a child, this was quite a shock to me.

All of a sudden, with the phone still in my left hand, I went into travail, like I was giving birth to a baby, but the contractions were not in my womb. They were in my chest, in my spirit. Yet, I didn't know what a spirit was. However, I could see in the spirit something like the hand of God go inside of me. I had about 3 or 4 strong contractions within, and then viola. I felt like I had just been born and I was 33 years old. Then the Holy Spirit used my friend on the phone to say this: You have just given birth to your new spirit in Christ Jesus. Go run some water in your bathtub and baptize yourself in the Name of the Father, the Son and the Holy Ghost. And I did.

The feelings in all of this are hard to describe. There are few words to express what I felt. Joy!!! Newness. Clean. Giddy. Forgiving. Light---like I could run through a troop and leap over a wall. There were these three little boys---neighbors who went to school with my daughter, who used to pick on my daughter Zonnita and call her "nigger." I could not stand those kids. A few minutes after I got born again, the school bus dropped off the children. So when I opened my door for Zonnita, the little boys were in the hallway. I remember I swooped them up and hugged all three of them, asking them if they wanted a cookie. I can't remember if they took the cookies. All I know is that they looked at me with real suspicion in their faces like they were saying to themselves, "has this lady lost her mind?!" These boys as well as Zonnita had come home from school and found me in this condition. She looked at me strange also. In fact, I spent most of the day laughing and crying at the same time. The next day was equally strange but oh so joyous. I have been saved now for 29 years and I have had some great times with the Lord. But this was the DAY of DAYS!!!!

I had bought a bible a few days before I came to Jesus because of a dream that I had that was clearly about Him. It was a rather shocking dream. I dreamed that I gave birth to a baby and forgot about the baby for 3 weeks, as I was partying, and having myself a ball. Then all of a sudden, I remembered the baby. Rather than thinking that the baby had to be dead, all I could think about was that I had not changed the babies diaper in three weeks. So I went into the adjacent room. It was a very serene place and the baby was laying on his back, looking up, with a bright glowing light about him. He was alive and very peaceful looking, brown, with straight black hair and dark, big bright eyes. I opened up the baby's diaper and he was clean but there was a wound on his side that was healed. I thought to myself "must have been the diaper pin stuck him." In those days there was no such thing as pampers without pins. As I was about to close His diaper, the baby spoke quietly "May I have my cross please?"

Still asleep, I remember that I was in a state of shock,--- me---a zealous unbeliever. It never even dawned on me while dreaming that a newborn baby should not be talking or that a baby who had no nourishment or water in three weeks would be dead. My sole focus of concentration was intrigued by what the baby spoke to me concerning the cross. So while yet asleep, I tried to make the dream straighten itself out. I began to reason with myself. "He didn't ask me for a cross. He asked me for a pillow. I'll go get the baby a pillow so he can lay on it." There was a pillow in the room, so I picked it up. But the pillow turned into a cross in my hand.

When I awoke, I was a bit nervous, to say the least!!! Since I was an unbeliever, I simply didn't understand this spiritual contradiction and so I went and purchased a bible. I had not yet really begun to read it until the day I got born again, a few days after I had obtained it. When I opened the bible, it opened to John 3---that which is flesh is flesh and that which is spirit is spirit. Again I say, you must be born again. After what had just happened to me a few moments before, I understood spiritual rebirth completely. I was able to view my natural experience with spiritual accuracy. I myself in the flesh was born 33 years before but now I was born again, not in flesh,but in spirit this time. Four years later, when I preached my first sermon, It was from John 3, "you must be born again. That was on October 25, 1981. My life has never been the same. In truth, old things have passed away and every thing that has happened in my life in the last 29 years have been new.

When I have judged and examined my rather unusual rebirth experience, I have asked myself "since the witchcraft demon already had me, why would a religious demon lead me to Jesus?" My response to my own question was "perhaps he wanted me to infiltrate the church with witchcraft." So I reasoned, if I myself am not saved, then the religious demon has made a serious error. The history of human strivings to know the future through divination would fill many shelves of books. When I was sent to the African Episcopal Zion Church in 1979, it was already filled with divination and all kinds of spiritual counterfeits. In fact, my very first pastor was a West Indian witchcraft practitioner. (See Chapter 2 in "The Making of a Prophet.") Since this book is my effort to expose spiritual deception, I would have to concur that if my own rebirth experience was itself counterfeit to lead me into the church's doors, the fruit of my efforts in this hour bares witness of the failure of the religious demon to use me to spread more witchcraft within the organized church.

To expose a counterfeit birth, we must remain humble, obedient and wise--- following Paul's advice to the Corinthians in his second letter: "Examine yourselves, whether ye be in the faith, prove your own selves. Know ye not your own selves, how that Jesus Christ is in you, except ye be reprobate?" (13:5) According to this scripture, I have personally found through experience that the Holy Spirit will reveal to the captive himself whether or not he is truly saved. Consequently , I believe that an important point to emphasize regarding the way to handle the religious demon in the remnant church is that as ministers and leaders, we must remember that it is not our job to attempt to separate the saved from the unsaved. For if we were to contend with the religious demon in carnal ways, the Lord warns us that we might endanger or even damage some of His true wheat in the process. Therefore, in cases where salvation is not obvious, I warn you to proceed with caution and with the wisdom of God. Sometimes the saved looks like the sinner and sometimes the sinner looks like the saved.

Of course, the one who is in most danger is the sinner who looks like the saved because he is in jeopardy of being eternally lost. So if demons are cast out under the assumption that the sinner is already saved, then we can expect that the demons will return and the captive will be bound even tighter. In situations such as these, praying for the gift of discernment of spirits is definitely appropriate and in order. However, our most important tool is to assure that the sheep understand repentance, resurrection and rebirth, the three essentials of the gospel. Whether deluded or conniving, it is important to determine whether or not a captive to the Jezebel demon is completely surrendered and committed to it or merely seduced by it, for I believe that only the deceived can be helped.

Although covert and secretive within the organized church, the goals of the spirit of the Anti-Christ are clear. Its primary agenda is to defy God by receiving worship within an unholy trinity of man, the Anti-Christ and the devil. While Satanist openly defy the Lord and seek worship for Lucifer through ritualistic practices, the religious demon as the spirit of the Anti-Christ employs deception and counterfeit spirituality within the souls of professing believers in Jesus Christ. Unlike the witchcraft demon, the religious demon takes pleasure in deceiving those who openly worship Jesus Christ by using their unsaved vessels to provide covert worship for Lucifer. A carnal or soulish worshiper is one who has not really repented of his sinful nature. Consequently, I believe that people who may have been raised in church yet who never learned how to worship in spirit and in truth have become captive to the religious demon. Since the primary strategy of the religious demon is to overtake the human will through deception, the amount of unsaved people who are regular church worshipers is astounding.

The faces of the religious demon are countless and diversified and it would take several books of this nature to describe them all, primarily because they adapt themselves to the personalities of their captives. For example, there are those who are unsaved who are practicing idolatry without knowing it. Many of these people are practicing a false religion. Any religion that does not have Jesus Christ as Lord and Savior is an idolatrous one, including Judaism without Christ as the Messiah. Any religion professing to be "Christian" that has added another book to the bible is a false religion Mormonism (Latter Day Saints), Jehovah Witnesses, and others are of this sort. Legalistic religions like Seventh Day Adventist also fall into this category. Because of its various idolatrous practices, Catholicism can also be added to the list. Religious demons in conjunction with the witchcraft demon are also behind such groups as the Freemasons, the Eastern Star and other secret societies.

There are also witchcraft demons with a religious focus under the government of Jezebel that are involved in the occult, the New Age Movement, hypnotism, yoga, tarot cards, Ouija boards, color therapy, astrology, ---this is a long list, where old practices with new names added to them daily, including bionics and psionics. On a rather basic level, today there are multitudes who guide their lives by reading horoscopes and consulting the spirits by ouija boards, automatic writing and other means. Remember the words of Paul to Timothy: "In the last days, some shall depart from the faith, giving heed to seducing spirits and doctrines of devils." Finally, religious demons are in both of the two categories of churches on earth today: the charismatics or non-denominational ones and the traditional or the denominational churches.

How can a person with a religious demon be identified?

A few of them are extremely obvious in society. There are the "Jesus Freaks" that have stickers all over their cars and Jesus written all over their persons. They are especially weird in order to turn the unsaved not toward Christ, but away from Him. In other words, the unbeliever reasons, "if I have to act like this freak, I want no part of Jesus Christ!" The other obvious group are those who end up on mental health medication who are also "religious." Demons of fear and anxiety often join up with the religious demon to cause a person to fear the destruction of the earth and the final judgment. Several of these persons will end up on medication also.

Nevertheless, the major premise in this book is that the ones who are the most dangerous are the ones that are the most difficult to discern. Many of this kind may have big grins on their faces and tell you that Jesus loves you and even invite you to their church. Generally though, a person with a religious demon who goes to church is usually out of balance in some way. For example, they cannot receive correction, they are rigid in their interpretation of scripture, often taking scripture out of context to put either themselves or someone else into bondage, their emotions are unstable---others are either reaching for the stars filled with ecstasy at the glory of God or momentarily they find themselves in the deepest valley of despair and depression. Some of these people will leave you long sermons on their telephone answering machines, can not say a sentence without saying "amen, praise the Lord, I'm blessed" etc. Some will appear to love being passive and victimized, as they believe that they are "suffering for the Lord."

Though by no means an exhaustive list, here are some reasons to "raise a spiritual eyebrow."

1. ALWAYS the most noticeable in a worship service---ie dancing, shouting, wailing, falling slain in the spirit, doing the "holy dance"--- yet there is known, repetitive sin in their lives. Their Christian walk does not manifest the 9 fruits of the Spirit. Jesus said "you shall know them by their fruit." Although they may be intelligent and successful, the fruits of holiness: love, joy, peace, long suffering, goodness, gentleness, faith, self control, and meekness are not apparent.

2. They are extremely NARROWMINDED, CRITICAL, JUDGEMENTAL,AND LEGALISTIC. They are skillful at keeping in bondage those "less spiritual" than themselves.

1.Some cannot be distinguished from people in the world because they openly gamble, swear, smoke reefer and the like, yet they wear big crosses around their necks, claiming that they love the Lord and that they are saved. Their thoughts and conversations will align sin, the world and the flesh together in one neat package. More often than not, these folk don't go to church.

4. They love worship and church more than they are concerned about saving souls and casting out demons.

5. They do not want to hear about Satan, demons, deliverance etc.

6.The most outstanding character trait in a person who may have a religious demon is PRIDE.

7. They consistently say "God told me this or God told me that."
It should also be noted that even people who are good tithers may have a religious demon. In short, the best religious demon is a "wolf in sheep's clothing." Sheep praise the Lord, they tithe, they support the pastor, and they pray. To recognize a wolf, one needs the Lord to reveal him or her to you, as well as bless you with the wisdom to know how to handle the situation, once the wolf has been identified. Most of the profiles presented in this book are faces of wolves or spiritual predators who are very skillfully disguised.

Here is just one of the examples in my experience that caught my attention early on---the first of several manifestations of the religious demon that I witnessed in the AME Zion Church. One day, a visiting minister preached a sermon with the title "DRY BONES", taken from the familiar passage from the book of Ezekiel. After the service, a woman well known to me whom I will call Sister Ann came to the altar with several others who were gathered. Sister Ann was a frequent churchgoer, having grown up a Baptist in the deep south. Her deceased father and several brothers were preachers. The message had been fiery in the traditional style of African American Baptist preachers, including a lot of hooping. Hooping is similar to rap music, however it sounds more like the way BB King sings the blues---more a song lyric than a rhythmic beat of words in a rap song. Anyway, Sister Ann was holding a small baby in her arms. All of a sudden, Sister Ann uttered a loud, piercing scream, threw the baby up in the air, and fell out on the church floor in a strange frenzy, rolling around like a wild animal, completely out of control. It took five strong people to try to restrain her, to no avail. Somehow, someone caught the baby before he hit the church floor also.

This is what some black folk call "shouting." At the time, I was completely ignorant of the workings of a religious demon. It was just that my spirit knew that the manifestation that I had just witnessed could not be from the Lord. Would the Lord put a helpless infant in jeopardy of losing its life just so that one of his own would praise Him in such a wild way? I don't think so! When this woman "came to herself", I began to question her after service to try to understand what had happened. I was careful with my questions. As I opened the discussion with, "Sister Ann, what were you thinking about just before you "went into the spirit?" she replied, "I was thinkin bout my Daddy. My Daddy used to always preach a message called "Dry Bones." I knew her father, a black southern preacher, dead and gone.

I believe that such a manifestation is a clear example of how a religious demon will use a carnal, emotional worship experience for his own pleasure. Do I believe that this woman is saved? I really don't know but based upon her cold, unfriendly personality toward other Christians, I doubt it. One thing I do know from a first-hand, up front view. Sister Ann was not "faking it." She was completely unconscious, oblivious to the fact that a religious demon was inside of her, mocking the Christian experience. However, there are others who will "fake it" and that is also the work of a religious demon. Fakers are more prevalent in charismatic churches because of "sign seekers."For example, religious pride will cause one believer to become more demonstrative in a worship service than others---

running up and down the aisles, waving their hands, rolling on the floor--- because a competitor had also just been very "expressive" to say the least. Others will "fake it" to try to either impress the Pastor, or to attempt to prove that a particular ministry is anointed. Recently, I have heard a Charismatic sister say that because there were visitors in her church, she "fell out slain in the spirit" when her pastor touched her. She didn't want her pastor to be embarrassed if no one else "fell out." I wonder how many others do the same thing!!!

Jesus made a very plain yet profound statement concerning counterfeits, so basic and elementary that believers often neglect to consider His rather simple admonition, "you shall know them by their fruit." The case of 92 year old Bertha from Nebraska is an outstanding example. A woman who claimed to have been a born again, a charismatic believer for 72 years, Bertha continually suffers with obsessive compulsive disorder (OCD) for the same length of time. In her incessant need for cleanliness, the outward manifestation of OCD involved various rituals of hand washings, and the wearing of rubber gloves during visits to her own toilet. Bertha would also scrub any surface area that she observed any visitor touch in her home. The washing rituals became increasingly intense for Bertha in any public area. Having been hospitalized for over a year in her mid twenties, she also received shock treatments to her brain, which were of no avail. Unable to raise her children and to fulfill her duties as a wife for many years, Bertha still remained a devout, religious Christian.

In the assessment stage of pre-deliverance counseling, I discovered a connection between the onset of the OCD and Bertha's account of her baptism in the Holy Ghost with the manifestation of speaking in tongues. Even though I did not automatically assume that her spiritual experience was a counterfeit, I routinely proceeded to try the spirits to see if they be of God. As I sought for fruit, I kept in mind that anyone who has been saved, who has experienced the baptism of the Holy Ghost, and who has been a woman of prayer for 70 years most definitely have access to the mind of Christ. Yet it was rather strange that Bertha's mental disorder first became apparent practically simultaneous to her receiving of the Holy Ghost. In my mind, this was not only an obvious contradiction to the Lord's life and power but even more, a subtle affront or insult. It naturally follows that a "fruit" of Bertha's salvation would be her enhanced ability to overcome a perpetual affliction, at least after 70 years!

By standard procedure, my first step within the assessment stage of pre-deliverance counseling is to seek to know whether or not the client has a clear knowledge of the basic elements of salvation which includes repentance and an understanding of the Lord's resurrection. In Bertha' case, my eyebrow was slightly raised because even though Bertha accepted the doctrine of being "born in sin", she really did not seem to understand it. As counseling progressed, it became evident that Bertha had never experienced herself as a lost sinner needing Jesus as her substitute for the crime of falling short of the glory of God. In fact, she viewed sin more as an act of "doing" than as a state of being. She reasoned that she had never experienced the glorious kind salvation that others have attested to because she never really sinned as others did--- no fornication, adultery, swearing, drunkenness, lying, stealing or any such behaviors.

Moreover, since the only sin that Bertha could identify with in 92 years of life was eating a piece of candy that was stolen by a friend when she was 8 years old and coming home late from school one day,   I was somewhat concerned that Bertha never really experienced the godly sorrow that brings forth a rebirth in the spirit. Therefore, when I carefully asked Bertha to consider whether or not the fact that she did not raise her own children might be considered a sin, I was not expecting an outraged confrontation. In fact, her resistance was so strong that counseling could literally go no further. Bertha even prompted one of her sons to call me the day after the session to apprise me of what a wonderful mother Bertha has been, in spite of the fact that is grandparents raised him.

The problem in continuing in pre-deliverance counseling with Bertha was that her 70 years in Christiandom was seriously shaken after only 3 sessions with me and reading one chapter of "War on the Saints." Even so, Bertha was committed to continue in pre-deliverance counseling with me if and only if, I had submitted to her terms. Her primary concern was that I expressed doubt of a renowned, well known evangelist about the word of faith phenomena of "falling slain in the spirit." At meeting when Bertha was a young woman, she claimed that she fell out so powerfully in the spirit when this evangelist laid hands on her, that she had to be carried off the platform. Bertha explained that she was "out cold" and it took several minutes for strength to return to her body. The issue at hand is that Bertha has based practically her entire religious experience upon the divine origin of this supernatural occurrence at the evangelist's meeting. As such, she really could not be in agreement and join forces in counseling with anyone who does not believe in being slain in the spirit, in general, or in the renowned evangelist, in particular. In fact, not only did she become defensive but she put up an aggressive and strong counter attack by fiercely declaring "suppose YOU were confronted by the fact that no one with the background in New Age and witchcraft that YOU have experienced could EVER be saved nor could YOU be anointed with power from the Holy Ghost to cast out devils?!!"

So, finally, here it was. The spirit of Jezebel spoke through the pride system of this outraged 92 year old upstanding and highly moral senior citizen, a demon covertly bent on "killing off the minister sent to set its captive free." Rather than shout back "get thee behind me Satan," I answered Bertha calmly, without defense or malice and simply replied:

> "I have been so confronted over the years and so I have already put ALL of my supernatural experiences to the test, including the day that I got saved and the day that I spoke in tongues. I assessed it ALL by the word of God. Where my salvation experience is concerned, I experienced myself as a lost sinner who needed a Substitute to take the punishment for my sins. In a moment, in the twinkling of an eye, I knew without a doubt that Jesus Christ of Nazareth was that man who is God, resurrected from the dead. I confessed Him as Lord over my life. Where the speaking in tongues is concerned, since I received this manifestation when I too was a young woman at a Kenneth Hagin convention in 1983, I have periodically questioned it. I have recently vowed not to speak in tongues in public until the Lord grants me the gift of interpretation. I also no longer pray in tongues either. Where all other supernatural experiences are concerned, some of them have proved to be counterfeit, including the phenomena of being slain in the spirit."

Bertha was certainly not prepared to hear that I recognized the spirit of Jezebel in her as she might have succumbed under the shock of such a revelation. Nor did I not get an opportunity to share with Bertha my impressions concerning her manifestation of OCD from a spiritual perspective. The primary spiritual benefit that one receives from repentance is the overwhelming sense of forgiveness and cleansing that comes from receiving Jesus Christ as a Substitute for one's personal sins. Only a sinner saved by grace can testify of what it feels like to "come out of the wilderness." I myself will never forget it. I cannot state too often that as a 33 years old, I felt like I had just been born and like I had never sinned. I was washed and I was cleansed. I understand why Bertha admitted in our first session that her salvation experience was "not so glorious". It simply happened that one day in church, she knew it was time to make a commitment and so she simply "got up from the pew, went forward to make a decision for Christ." It came to me after that first session that Bertha's perpetual need to wash and be washed may be related to the fact that since she never saw herself as a sinner, she never got cleansed in the spirit.

Could it be that the compulsion to wash physically is a sign that she has not been washed spiritually? I don't know. However, if this be true, then Bertha is still in her sins, and she never really got saved. Moreover, if she never got saved, then the spiritual language that she spoke did not emanate from the Holy Ghost. In like manner, Bertha's joy in worship and her devotion of 60 years to a good and moral life is merely a natural byproduct of clean living, obtainable through Buddhism, Hinduism, or any other religion. On the contrary, the joy of salvation in Christ is to know by faith that you have been lost and that through the sacrifice of Jesus and His resurrection that you have been found. This is worshiping the Father in spirit and in truth. Unfortunately, some prefer to keep their religious life in tact, even though they may be worshiping in the flesh and in error.

Along with the daily OCD rituals, Bertha reports that she takes Holy Communion every day and has great fellowship with the Lord every morning, a joy in Him that completing her assignment to read various chapters in "War on the Saints" was seriously beginning to hinder. According to Jessie Penn Lewis, people like Bertha are the most difficult to reach with deliverance for several reasons:

> ...Devotion, singing, preaching, worship,--- all rightful things--- MAY SO POSSESS THE MIND AS TO CLOSE IT TO ALL PERSONAL KNOWLEDGE OF THE NEED OF DELIVERANCE FROM THE ADVERSARY'S DECEPTION2....In the moral realm comes an attitude of infallibility, positive assertion and unteachableness, with loss of real power of choice." (War on the Saints, 9th edition, pp. 176- 177):

It should be noted here that in Bertha's case, she truly wanted me to convince her to continue with pre-deliverance counseling because she was clearly confused, stating that 'she did not know what to do.' However, I realized that I could not compete with the glorified image that she continued to maintain of the renowned evangelist, a key hindrance to any continued pre-deliverance productivity with me. Moreover, there are occasions when someone will seek my services for one reason, and then I discover later that either the Lord or the devil sent them for another purpose entirely.

I could be wrong, but in the case of Bertha, I believe that her contact with me w crucial and important where her own eternal salvation is concerned because the P' Spirit used the late Jessie Penn Lewis and myself to shake Bertha's foundatior served her "a wake-up" call. I personally believe that its far better to check one's spiritual life BEFORE the night of death comes--- the final season which no man or woman can check or can change. (II Corinthians 13: 5,6) So, in my mind, a loss of 70 years of a fruitless Christian experience is better checked in time, in the light of day. For in spite of the best of human morality, all have sinned and fallen short of the glory of God, where the wages of sin is death and an eternity in hell.

As the case of Bertha suggests, it is crucial to understand that there are those who are not saved who appear more saved than many who actually are born again. The case of Ola is yet another example. My experience with this case is presented in more detail in later chapters. Nevertheless, Ola is mentioned now because even more than Bertha, Ola appeared to be saved. Not only did Ola speak in tongues, but she also manifested counterfeit gifts of the Holy Ghost that fooled the elect for years. Born a catholic from Nigeria, Ola truly believed that she was "born again" as a charismatic when she joined a word of faith church. However, in the course of her deliverance, she was completely "taken over" in a trance. During the deliverance, the witchcraft demon railed at me that he owned Ola because she had been given to him by her grandmother. Once exposed, a trilogy of demons became bold and confrontational, refusing to turn Ola loose. Ola's grandmother still remains a practitioner of Yoruba, a form of religious witchcraft practiced in Nigeria. Witchcraft is the practice of cursing and controlling with a counterfeit spiritual authority and power.

Therefore, it is mandatory to seek to uncover what caused the captive to become subject to witchcraft and its various forms. The captive's victory from deception and bondage is attainable if he or she is guided or counseled to be enabled to see the Lord clearly and serve and respect Him obediently. I am not suggesting that you will need to study darkness in any great detail. For example, you do not need to study every ritual, false doctrine or religious practice to realize that witchcraft and or the religious demon is involved. Utterly committed to upholding their own self image, captives in the grips of the demon Jezebel will fight to uphold an appearance of moral purity. Moral purity in this instance is not so much a desire to seek after true righteousness but more a desire to appear righteous to its public. The spirit of Jezebel is like her old testament predecessor in the flesh. Its desire is "to kill the prophets of God" and to crown false prophets that are obedient to Satan. In this regard, the religious demon has found a seat in the organized church, a pivotal position to fulfill Satan's goal of killing true prophets.

From the onset, I point out that a sensitivity and a compassion for those bound by this demon is essential to set the captives free. I myself am always prepared to help these captives to pick up the pieces of their shattered lives when the Holy Spirit confronts them to face their own wickedness. Remember also that the spirit of Jezebel will send demons of accusation, rejection, condemnation and fear as a means of counter attack, so it is imperative that one is wise as a serpent but as harmless as a dove. The key is to remain humble, repentant and forgiving.

I have learned to keep in mind that the face of Jezebel's objective is not only out to destroy the captive but Jezebel's main goal is to kill the minister. Therefore, one of my primary goals in pre-deliverance counseling is to determine whether or not the captive has been merely seduced by Jezebel or if the captive is completely overcome by this demon in his or her soul. I also realize that if the captive cannot come to repentance, I may have to walk away, and perhaps never look back, putting the captive behind me completely. A stage in counseling that I call "weeding" will be the testing ground for whether or not the captive will be cooperative by standing for his own deliverance. I refuse to stand alone against the spirit of Jezebel.

Endnotes

1. Dr. Rebecca Brown, pg. 188, "Prepare for War", by Whitaker House , 1997, first copy write 1987.
Be warned, that you need to be a mature Christian to read Dr. Brown's books. I have come across many believers who have put themselves into bondage by not having the maturity and the discernment to read her books. Some in the field of deliverance may disagree, but I perceive Dr. Rebecca Brown to be a spiritual trailblazer in the field of spiritual warfare and deliverance in our generation. Like myself, she puts herself on the frontline by revealing her own failures. I myself have reaped the benefits and fruit of Dr. Brown's willingness to be transparent in revealing the details of her struggle to set the captives free.

2.Harold L. Busséll, Unholy Devotion: Why Cults Lure Christians." Zondervan Publishing House, Grand Rapids Michigan, 1983 pg.111

3.J-P.Lewis, War on the Saints, the Ninth Edition, Thomas E. Lowe, Ltd, pg.176-177

4.Ibid, pg. 178

5.I have quoted from "Revolution: Worn Out on Church" in Chapter 2 where I have agreed with him. Generally speaking, I believe that according to his definition, I would be considered a "revolutionary." Barna's language is kind of "high brow" as it is written for the well educated professing Christians, upper middle class successful folk who are "Worn Out On Church." Where I disagree with Barna strongly, is on pg. 103. He compares the church revolutions of the 1800's and the 1900's, and for this day he writes this:

"The new Revolution differs in that its primary impetus is not salvation among the unrepentant but the personal renewal and re-commitment of believers." , I believe that such a statement is in direct contradiction to the word of the Lord Jesus Christ. No revolution or revolutionary is ever permitted to change the Lord's priority for the salvation of souls. The Great Commission is at the top of the list of priorities for EVERY generation. What I am finding is that just because church folk may be growing tired of traditional church, does not mean that they are saved. In fact, my biggest focus within the revolution is not based upon re-commitment of believers but an examination of whether or not those who claim to be in the faith are actually IN it. This is because for decades now, people have been responding to church invitations and have not understood repentance or the resurrection. Also, my primary goal in the Revolution is to preach in the spirit of John The Baptist, not only emphasizing repentance but the coming of the Lord in our time.

I agree with Barnar that "rather than relying on a relative handful of inspired preachers to promote a national revival, the emerging Revolution is truly a grassroots explosion of commitment to God that will refine the Church and result in a natural and widespread immersion in outreach. This is the Church being restored so the Holy Spirit can work effectively through the body of Christ."
The Lord does have His remnant. People like you, the reader, are called to play a

significant role in the Revolution, people who may not be preachers in the traditional sense. However, I believe that our part in the Revolution is still to "get folk saved," particularly those who have been churchgoers. This chapter is a warning to the revolutionary to insure that pew warmers are actually saved, and that the Lord will not return, look at them and say "I never knew you." All you were was just "worn out on church."

Chapter 5 Doctrinal Mixtures

The Apostle Paul of Tarsus predicted that in the last days, teaching spirits would rise and deceive many with a plethora of false doctrines. I believe that these teaching spirits are actually religious demons who literally specialize in bringing forth false doctrine. By stringing together several non-related scriptures from the word of God, they have entrapped countless for centuries. According to "War on the Saints," scripture is generally used as the basis of these teachings--- skillfully woven together line by line like a spider's web, so that the un-suspecting are caught in the snare.

"Single texts are wrenched from their context, and their place in the perspective of truth; sentences are taken from their correlative sentences, or texts are aptly picked out from over a wide field, and so netted together as to appear to give a full revelation of the mind of God; but the intervening passages, giving historical setting, actions and circumstances connected with the speaking of the words, and other elements which give light on each separate text, are skillfully dropped out." (War on the Saints, pg.20 9th edition)

How true, relevant and timely are these words in their application to what has happened in recent times. Since the love of money is the root of ALL evil, it is not surprising that the leading false doctrine of the religious demon in the present moment is the prosperity gospel---an out of context teaching that obligates God to bless the giver in all ways, with an exaggerated emphasis on financial prosperity, with an added emphasis that a believer can actually buy a spiritual blessing from God with their financial giving. The message is even down to a formula: whatever you give will have a one hundred fold return: 100 dollars for a one dollar offering, one thousand dollars for ten dollars, 10,000 dollars for 100 dollars, and so on. Those who preach this doctrine use scriptures to support this teaching that in no meaningful way are even connected to financial prosperity.

I believe that it is truly an abomination to twist the Lord Jesus Christ's own words as the foundation for this materialistic teaching. One outstanding example is John 10:10: "I came that they may have life and have it more abundantly." These words of the Lord's have been used to spawn countless charismatic churches that even draw their names from this scripture, calling their churches "Abundant Life"...congregations where financial prosperity is emphasized from the standpoint that wealth can be expected to flow from the pulpit to the pew. For as the members bless the pastor financially, this false and out of context teaching proclaims that God will bless the members financially in response to their "blessing of the anointed man or woman of God." Those who preach this "abundant life" fallacy have paid absolutely no attention to the fact that in the Greek language, there are six different words for "life:"

Bitkiós means "natural or present existence; bios means "livelihood;"psuche means "breath or the life of the soul;" biosis means "the manner of life or one's lifestyle;" pneuma means "the spirit life;", either human or divine" and zöe means "divine, eternal life." The Greek word that is translated "life" in the words of Jesus concerning abundant life is the word zöe, or abundant "eternal," divine life in Him--- an interpretation that is consistent with the Lord's overall message of eternal life. If Jesus was saying that "I came that you might have an abundant life financially, then the word used for "life" would have been "bios."

So what about the prosperity preacher who declares today: "I am rich, because the Lord Jesus Christ has made me wealthy from your tithes and offers and therefore, I have need of nothing?" (Revelation 3:17)In other words, what about the leaders that scatter His flock with false or mixed doctrine? The fact that demons are looking for doorways of vulnerability should not be surprising. The major doorway Satan benefits from is that "the word folk are not rightly dividing the word" and preach an "out of context" gospel. For example, Satan unsuccessfully employed this very same tactic with the Lord Jesus Christ. Satan assumed that Jesus was vulnerable because He was hungry and thirsty after a 40 day fast in the wilderness. Then he confronted the Lord Himself with "the word of God out of context." Even though this strategy proved unsuccessful with the Lord, it should not be surprising that the Destroyer would continue to apply the same tactic against vulnerable sheep.

Where charismatic leadership is concerned, the witchcraft demon is attracted to a person with a soul that is predisposed to the 3"P's" of position, prestige and power. This was why I myself was so susceptible in the 70's to the New Age Movement before I was saved. The former, unsaved Pam was stuck in the 3 "P's. Those who wish to dominate, to acquire fame and prominence can become a safe haven for the witchcraft demon. In such cases, the personality of a charismatic leader will be a secure hiding place in which demons of a similar nature will be able to maneuver without discovery. This is because no one will ever suspect that the pastor's ambitious striving for control and domination will be demonic because he or she has continued to demonstrate over time a steady pattern that propels them to seek power. Simply put, every one just assumes that the pastor is merely being true to the nature that is required to fulfill his calling or anointing. Today, there are countless pastors, known and unknown, where the witchcraft spirit has mingled with his or her personality.

For this reason, James warns those seeking to be masters that theirs will be the greater condemnation. Jesus mocks you, Oh Laodicea, by declaring to you that you are "wretched, miserable, poor, blind and naked." He further counsels you to buy gold from Him that has been refined by fire so that you will be rich in what is spiritual. Poverty can be an effective refining tool for the proud. I believe that those who do not preach the whole counsel of God are in great jeopardy. Why? Because those who handle the word of God are Satan's primary targets to bring damage and destruction upon the sheep by that very word that they so confidently preach. It is a very clever tactic indeed---so much so, that we now have the term "spiritual abuse" in our Christian vocabulary.

Spiritual abuse is more closely addressed within upcoming chapters. When considering spiritual abuse, generally we focus our attention on obvious cults and false religions. However, spiritual abuse is equally rampant within the organized church. In fact, I believe that the emphasis on the prosperity doctrine is perceived by the Lord to be equally damaging, as the love of money is the root of all evil.

To combat this evil, the Lord revealed to me in 2003 that He was allowing the spirit of poverty---a demon--- to bankrupt those of His people who anchored their faith into a false teaching that was sent to them by seducing spirits and doctrines of devils. The reason

He is allowing His people to become bankrupt is to prove to them that they will not become rich by investing in a word of faith ministry as "seed planted into good ground." The prosperity doctrine as preached first by well known mega and television evangelists, is now being taught by practically every word of faith church, regardless of size, race of the congregation---in fact, this false doctrine is now being preached and taught all over the world.

If you the reader listen to Christian radio, watch Christian television or read Christian books, undoubtedly you have heard the expression, "planting seed into good ground." The "sow seed" expression is taken out of context from the words of the Lord Jesus Christ in Matthew Ch: 13, called "the Parable of the Sower." The Charismatic Movement has taken the term "good ground" and the use of the word "seed" out of their spiritual context in order to fit a natural interpretation of financial and material prosperity.

To the word of faith preacher, "good ground" is a symbol that represents his or her ministry or church and "seed" stands for money. Therefore, the logical understanding is that if the sheep plant their seed by way of a tithe, offering or donation into the "good ground" of a flourishing ministry, the giver will reap a natural harvest of material wealth from the Lord. Lately, this doctrine has become even more damnable because the mega preachers are now declaring that for giving money, not only will the giver's return be material, but it will also be "spiritual." In other words, if you "sow" money, you will reap a healing, a deliverance,   or perhaps a marriage will be restored.   Damnable!!! Blasphemous!!!! Woe be the fate of those who teach it.

Ironically, the parable of the Sower, is a very easy parable to understand primarily because Jesus took His disciples aside and explained it Himself. Jesus clearly states in Matthew Chapter 13 that "good ground" is the heart or soul of a person and "the seed" is the word of God. This parable has nothing at all to do with material giving. In fact, Jesus uses the parable to describe the required condition of the heart or soul to receive the word of God and become born again. In order to be born again or saved, the soul of the sinner must be good ground. As Jesus explained, the sinner's soul is good ground when he is able to "hear the word of God AND understand it." Once the sinner understands and responds to the gospel of Jesus Christ, he will be fruitful in his or her spiritual growth and progress in the Lord.

Another related out of context blunder is in regards to tithing, with the insistence of the present day churches, (particularly the word of faith and charismatic ones) that tithing is mandatory. If tithing was a new testament mandate, then my question is "why is it mentioned only once in the new testament, and particularly to the Hebrew converts?" (Hebrews 7:5-9)   I suspect the answer is that it is because tithing is an old testament practice that the Hebrew Christians were very familiar with. In fact, the scripture that is often used is really about Melchizedek, with tithing as an incidental or secondary thought. Mentioned a few times by Jesus in the gospels, we must remember that while on earth, Jesus Himself ministered under the old covenant, yet He never gave a direct command to His disciples concerning this subject. In fact, Jesus was more impressed with the widow woman who gave all that she had,-- the little "mite"---, then he was with the hypocritical tithers who precisely divided even a tiny mint leaf into 10   equal pieces so as to be "religiously perfect." (Mark 12: 41-44, Matthew 23:23)

I personally believe that tithing was an old testament practice meant solely for the 12 tribes of Israel. New testament believers are not under the law but by grace we are expected to be cheerful givers, prepared to even give above and beyond the tithe---in fact, like the widow woman, ready to give our all to God based upon any individual standard that He Himself sets for us. A part of our new creation in Christ Jesus, love overrides everything, and so if our hearts are not in accordance with our actions, then our spiritual walk is hypocritical. After all, if we can't give cheerfully but we have given because we have been coerced, the irony is that since our hearts were not right with God when we gave, how could we possibly expect the Lord to bless our giving with a financial return?

Considering coercion, I was shocked when I recently learned that some mega ministries not only conduct a credit check and require its members to submit pay stubs to actually assess the tithe by the gross income, but that 10 percent of a church member's income is often directly deposited into the church's account. Just as a heat bill may be automatically removed from a person's checking account and directly deposited in a fuel company's bank on a monthly basis, the church is demanding its ten percent off the top. I believe that the religious bondage inherent within this issue is definitely a form of demonic oppression where scare tactics are employed to fleece the sheep. For example, a few years ago, I received the following email from a member of mega church in Washington DC. These are the exact words of that member:

> "My pastors are turning me off because I remember that Juanita Bynum came to our church and held the longest offering in history. She used a scare tactic on giving in relating her message to a couple in the New Testament who died because they lied to the Holy Ghost. (Sapphira and Ananias) People were giving their furs, shoes, watches, diamonds, emptying their wallets, closing out their checking accounts; you can go on with the rest. I distinctly recall an ex member who after coming to his senses a couple of days later asking for his $1000.00 offering back and the pastor became angry with that particular ex-member! You know a few months ago, the co-pastor had the audacity to tell the congregation how gullible we were in letting someone come in our church and intimidate us like that. I thought 'you and Bishop are supposed to be the protectors of this flock that you fleece ALL THE TIME!' Something is wrong!"

I agree with this frustrated mega member. Something is definitely wrong. Television is the vehicle that the religious demon has successfully used to spread this damnable doctrine. I have also noticed over recent years that when each mega preacher "takes up the offering" on the a popular Christian broadcasting network, every last one of them have used out of context scriptures, even texts that have little to nothing to do with finances, in order to seduce people into giving to receive blessings from God. Perhaps these TV preachers feel indebted to the producers for exposing each of their ministries to the insurmountable benefits that accompany regularly televised broadcast appearances. In is my belief that one of the most disreputable messages of this kind was preached by Juanita Bynum, a corrupt sermon that was entitled "Divine Release."

At first, it appeared to be a powerful, serious teaching about righteousness, holiness and walking in faith, as the prophetess began to expound on her text from I Peter Ch 2, with a line by line discourse. Then almost instantaneously, a bona fide word degenerated into a confusing, manipulative melodrama of out of context, wrongful division of the word of God, into something I can only call "spiritual babble." In fact, I personally do not understand how she arrived at making her profane statements from Peter's epistle. Turning her own self coined phrase upon herself, what at first appeared righteous seemed to evolve into a "hustle for the kingdom," with herself and the broadcasting network as the hustlers and gullible black women as the marks. The following excerpts from "Divine Release" was recorded almost word for word, transcribed statements from a taping of that program:

> "To be authentic in the spirit, the only proof that you have that you have been called of God, that you are the righteousness of God, that you have a bona fide ministry, is that you demonstrate that you have the unction to release seed. (money.) The higher you go in God, the more you will 'release." If you are righteous, then built into you is the unction to 'release."

As the Prophetess was speaking forth these words, a man in the television audience threw his "seed" to the floor in the aisle. The Prophetess then remarked, "This man has proved and confirmed this word. For what is divinely given is the only way that you can divinely receive." Simply put, the prophetess indicated that this man's actions of throwing his money to the floor served as a prime example of the actual unction of divine release. Therefore, according to her premise, the Lord will send this man a "divine release." Sounds to me like how men throw their money to the ground when they are gambling, particularly shooting crap.

Then the Prophetess did what I personally consider to be deplorable,--- an actual shakedown, not of the rich, but of the poor and struggling. To the rich,--- those who are evidently not a part of Bynum's target group of supporters---, she retorted: "those who are multi-millionaires who can give $20,000 are not capable of a divine release because they are not desperate." So in an appeal to her target audience, single mothers of color, Juanita Bynum reached out with these words:

> "You've tried everything that you could. That hundred dollars or that $300 that you have to pay your bills is not enough. The seed you have in your hand cannot pay your bills, so you should release your seed to this TV network. Your seed is your favor with God. To seven thousand people in TV land, God is saying to you that He is requiring you to release that seed of $300 or $1000 by midnight. The Lord has revealed to me that once you do, then divine release will go into action within a few hours."

Then came the veiled threat to the fearful and the superstitious nature of some black folk, fearful of receiving a curse from God if they don't obey the prophetess and "release their seed, particularly for the needs of the Mother Land!

> "God has a call on my life to send me with to Africa but some of you refuse to release your seed. How dare you watch us go, and not feel the unction in you to release your seed?"

Yet, one of the best messages that I have ever heard preached by anyone was preached by Juanita Bynum on 8/14/02 and aired on the morning of 3/18/03. There was no hype, and there was no performance, just the pure unadulterated word. This was a sermon that exposed the frivolity and compromise that exists in the present day church with special emphasis upon the secularizing of worship through its acceptance of worldly music. The Prophetess warned that thousands have come to the Lord but not through the brazen altar of repentance for sin, nor by the cleansing power of the blood of Jesus Christ that empowers us to walk in righteousness. She even uplifted the storefront churches who may only have 10 righteous members yet who are more useful to God then a large congregation with 10,000 members who are unclean and unchanged.

As Paul wrote, we wrestle not against flesh and blood but against principalities and powers. (Ephesians 6:12) Therefore, the issue of out of context preaching and teaching is not about specific television evangelists but about the unseen force that empowers them. I believe that the religious demon and the witchcraft spirit are behind the scenes, working on the lust of men and women for fame and fortune, and using them to impart false doctrine through the airways. Are they anointed preachers of righteousness who have cleverly found favor with powerful Christian television networks through various money raising antics so as to have opportunities to reach multitudes with the pure gospel or are they the best false prophets that Satan himself has ever designed and placed in the Body of Christ? If Sister Lewis were alive today, I believe that she would say that they are messengers of God who have not tried the spirits and who have been seduced by the enemy to mix truths with lies. Yet this is one area where I disagree with my 19th century mentor. I remember the words of the Lord where He declared "you cannot serve both God and mammon." (Matthew 6:24)

These very words from the mouth of Jesus chill my very bones. For I myself recently came through an escape from the fires of hell, where the spirit of Jezebel tried to lure me with money. My own experience humbled me to consider that perhaps the ministries of Juanita Bynum, Kenneth Copeland, Creflo Dollar, Benny Hinn and countless other mega ministries that preach the prosperity gospel truly started out with Jesus. Yet a sincere desire to spread His word may have been seductively corrupted by either a ministerial need, a desire for recognition and prominence, or a lust for mammon. But for the grace of God, I myself could have fallen in a big way.

Ironically, my telephone introduction with Violet from Hollywood began with a conversation about the prosperity gospel. After visiting my website, Violet called me to express how she had been planning to attend a conferences sponsored by a prosperity preacher but after reading some of my articles, she had decided against it. We had a rather lengthy discussion which ultimately led to Violet joining my web ministry about a month or so later.

Almost immediately, Violet became the biggest, most consistent financial supporter that my ministry had experienced to date, other than for a few isolated donations of others. I don't know how wealthy she was even though she claimed to be the daughter of a well known movie star. However, much more than her money, I myself had never experienced anyone to dote upon the word that I personally preached as much as did Violet. She literally wanted to have in her possession every word that I ever preached or taught—be it a book, a training manual, an audio message on the website, a CD or a tape. In fact, she was up early in the morning and even late at night listening to my teachings, taking notes and sending me several emails a day.

In all of my days as a minister, I had never experienced anyone who appeared as hungry for the word of God as was Violet. On more than one occasion, I had to restrain her from flying from Hollywood to New York in a heart beat. I am a very private person, and I have learned not to be pushed into premature fellowship with those that I have never personally met. Even so, I remained mildly cautious, primarily because Violet admitted that she had been a church hopper most of her life. At the time of our contact, Violet had made a decision not to become a pew warmer in any organized church.

On one hand, I was pleased with decision. However, I suspected that perhaps there was a spirit of strife, division and even rebellion in her that may have caused her to refuse to serve under anyone. However, most of my caution was based upon the fact that she had been involved with just about every well known deliverance ministry in the country. Admitting to having digested into her spirit a great deal of false and mixed doctrine, particularly as the word of God relates to casting out of devils, I realized that re-training her might be challenging. Furthermore, Violet also mildly expressed concern over the fact that even though she went through deliverance from a judgmental, legalistic demon, she was only somewhat assured that she was completely free. Therefore, in spite of her zealous support of my ministry, I kept myself guarded, proceeding with discretion.

In order to seduce me to believe that Violet was being sent to my ministry by the Lord, a religious demon cleverly used a Christian colleague to send me a personal prophecy about 8 days prior to receiving Violet's first offering:

> I bless you my sister and speak ZOE life and total wholeness to your very being. Because of the call upon your life, you have and will touch the lives of thousands, and now you'll move even higher into the glory realm to bring wholeness and healing to others. That old carnal mind (flesh) is dead and I can see that about you, and God is truly raising you to a level of where there will be no more pain. The old pain has been merely a stepping stone to your future, and Pam I hear the Lord say, Rest in Me. Though you have thought you were resting, the time has now come for a sure resting place, and I am that place my daughter. For I have taken you on a journey, a journey of wills, and pain, hurts and tears, but you now daughter enter into a glory realm that you've not known in the past. The old has surely passed away, and the new is now rapidly approaching, and you will drink of the new wineskin, for old wine cannot be poured into the new. So, be assured, that you will see a new light, a new day, and a new wine, and in the newness of all of this you will bring more healing, more wholeness, and more transparency. And even finances will begin to flow more abundantly over the next few weeks, your bank account will change, the way you handle money will change, for I will use people to pour into your coffers and yes you'll be surprised, though you've heard this before. So rest now, and look forward to drinking of the new wine."

By nature and experience, I am consistently cautious of unsolicited prophetic words of this kind, particularly those that contain predictions. However, when eight days after this prophecy, Violet sent in her first offering that blew my mind with the number of zeros behind it, the religious demon tried to use this particular "word of knowledge" to convince me that Violet was the first of many who would "pour into my coffer."

This is how the religious demon works to deceive gullible Christians with what is commonly known as "confirmation." In this case, the religious demon's strategy was to tempt me to comply with Violet's hidden agenda by relying on the validity of a supernatural prediction that actually came to pass since someone had actually poured thousands into my coffer within the prescribed time line of "a few weeks" requiring some banking changes, just as the prophecy had predicted.

The way that I tried the prophecy to see if it be of God was simply "to wait." It took about four months for me to perceive whether or not this word of knowledge, placed in the mouth of a professing Christian prophetess emanated from God himself of if it was an act of divination sent by the spirit of Jezebel. After four months, the Lord revealed a message to my own spirit with insights gained from my experiences with Violet and with others---guidance diametrically opposed to depending upon people for donations.

The truth is that the Lord has no intention of using people to pour into my coffer. Actually, He has already poured into my personal bank account, finances gained by inheritance and other legitimate business transactions. In truth, I believe that the Lord has made it clear that the only way that I can ensure that I will not dilute or compromise His message based upon the lucrative offerings of others, I am to use my own personal money to finance the work that He has called me to do. Moreover, the incident herein described was the true confirmation that my spirit needed. In spite of what the enemy meant for evil, the Lord used a temptation sent by a religious demon to cause me to understand that it is impossible to maintain an un-compromised word if one has to depend upon the tithes and donations of people, whether the givers be rich or poor.

Generally, what I have learned is that unclean motives will be exposed early on within a relationship if one "has an ear to hear." From the onset of the "lets get to know you" stage, Violet admitted that her 35 old daughter was an avowed lesbian. Once she tested the waters to see if I was homophobic, Violet was pleasantly surprised to learn that in my flesh is a special affinity toward homosexual men. In fact, she learned that before I was born again, I was known to prefer gay men as my best friends instead of women, in an era when homosexual discrimination was prevalent in this country.

Looking back on the situation, I believe that Violet's primary motivation was originally unconscious. Furthermore, her "hidden" agenda from both herself and from me was progressively twofold. The first step was for her daughter Johnnie Mae to be accepted into a credible ministry where she could not only use her secular marketing skills to promote and build a ministry, but also become re-integrated into religious life. Then, once involved in that ministry, I suspect that Violet anticipated that Johnnie Mae would eventually be persuaded to submit herself to it for deliverance from a demon of perversion. So it was imperative that Violet find someone who specialized in casting out demons. As an aside, I repeat that I don't believe that Violet was completely conscious of her motives early on in our contact but that these imaginations may have evolved over time.

The initial eyebrow raising experience occurred when Violet asked me to professionally counsel Johnnie Mae. Once I learned that Johnnie Mae had been molested by a relative as a child, I too suspected demonic infestation. I was not adverse to counseling Johnnie Mae, until Violet offered to pay for the counseling without her daughter's knowledge.

She claimed that "Johnnie Mae was too proud to let her mother pay for my services." Therefore, Violet wanted this financial arrangement to be an anonymous gift. Quickly I denied such a request, based upon its lack of ethical integrity and un-professionalism.

As time progressed, I watched how Violet made several more unsuccessful attempts to maneuver Johnnie Mae and I together, in hopes that I would cast the spirit of lust and perversion from her daughter. Johnnie Mae was living as the "husband" in a lesbian partnership, planning to adopt a child. I appeased myself by reasoning, "Pam, this is just a mother's love" and I chalked up these manipulations as just the natural behavior of a doting parent. However, later on I would discover that her daughter's deliverance was Violet's primary motive for ingratiating herself to me.

Although Violet had asked me several times not to hesitate to apprise her of anything demonic that I may have discerned in her own behavior, I did not immediately confront her with what I perceived to be her manipulative, controlling ways. Even though she indicated that she was receptive to all and any of my insights, I have to honestly admit that I unsteadily walked a chalked line. Simply put, I really did not want to risk offending Violet because of her consistent and, in my mind, extravagant financial giving. Not used to these kinds of offerings, I simply did not want to "rock the boat."

It is important to note here that I never once asked her to tithe nor did I coerced a penny from her. In fact, I never even knew what to expect from her financially , but I frankly did not want those offerings to stop coming. Let's face it. Truth is truth. Not that I was ever in danger of being co-opted by the almighty dollar in this instance. Nevertheless, I literally racked my brain as I earnestly searched for ways to "speak the truth in love" yet simultaneously avoiding any unnecessary confrontations that Violet might take offense to. Therefore, I did a lot of spiritual dodging. Since this is really not my usual style, I was beginning to feel an uneasy sense of bondage.

In truth , the power struggle between the demon Jezebel and myself began within days of putting Violet to work within my ministry. Eventually, the religious side of Jezebel stood toe to toe with me and I could no longer side step or dodge Violet's increasingly obvious manipulations. A woman of deep convictions and a desire to know God, I could be wrong, but I don't believe that Violet was ever free of her hidden unconscious agenda, which I finally was compelled to face myself. As previously stated, I believe that what Violet really wanted from me was the securing of her daughter's deliverance from lesbianism by the Holy Spirit.

Even though Violet truly believes that I am genuinely anointed, her commitment to my ministry palled in comparison to her ultimate goal of obtaining her daughter's deliverance. Ever maneuvering me toward her desired end with each contact, Violet periodically continued to try to steer Johnnie May my way as well. With the spirit of Jezebel guiding Violet's progressive steps toward maximizing her pre-conscious agenda, the religious demon also tried to used her to to either buy me or steer me toward compromising my stand on homosexuality so that my ministry would continue to receive her substantial offerings.

So when Violet suggested that I allow Johnnie Mae to use her Hollywood connections to obtain guest spots for me on Christian radio and television, I found myself between a rock and a hard place. A public relations expert with marketing skills, under different circumstances, I would have welcomed Johnnie Mae's help. So trying to walk in wisdom, I didn't immediately say "no", but I knew that if forced to, I would. So I spiritually dodged this bullet with the truth. I was not yet ready to go on radio or television but that I would get back to her in the near future. I hoped that in time, Violet would forget about it and I would not have to deny her request outright.

Very much an "Eager Beaver," I reasoned in my mind that as Violet impulsively considered one idea from another, she would soon forget about me appointing Johnnie Mae as my public relations director. To consistently keep it real, in the back of my mind were those generous offerings. Yet in all practicality, I also realized that if I could not effectively deal with Violet's issues, she would be of no value to me in the Lord's work. So once again, I was in a catch 22 situation, damned if I do, but in worst shape down the line, if I don't. It is imperative that I not allow anyone to misrepresent my ministry in the public eye or to control me by their generous offerings. For an avowed lesbian to be my public relations director was clearly an impossibility in my mind.

Yet with every passing day, I was truly concerned about Violet's impulsiveness to jump in and act without thinking or counting the cost of potential ramifications or consequences. A true test of my patience, I found myself continuing to explain basic, simple instructions because of Violet's desire to do things "her way" coupled with her impaired comprehension skills. The reality is that in spite of the fact that she was not very intellectually advanced or well-informed, she had the personality of a "know it all", intensified by a willful stubbornness clothed in a "Movie Star" type of charm and grace that was difficult to say "no" to. Furthermore, on more than one occasion she would trivialize my instructions and too often than not, I found myself ever so gently but much too persistently being called on the carpet by her for one thing or another. By the time that the actual confrontation erupted, I was beginning to feel like I was being maneuvered toward Violet's desired goals, with her spiritual hands pushing me forward ever so gently toward her daughter Johnnie Mae.

Finally, the proverbial last straw was deposited on my spiritual back when she proposed to arrange for me a convention in Hollywood, first suggesting that I stay in her home, and then offering that I stay in Johnnie Mae's home. Of course I did not want to offend her but in my mind, I always prefer a hotel. Yet once she went so far as to say "Johnnie Mae's partner Louise so hopes to cook one of her sumptuous meals for you," the crucial moment had taken place. Not only did she offer me Johnnie Mae's hospitality,--- the indoor-outdoor swimming pool, tennis court, bowling alley and all the other hi-style accouterments, Violet also indicated that the lesbian couple was going to plan a reception for me on their palatial estate. According to Violet, the couple planned to invite all of their influential friends, both gay and straight to this reception so that they might encourage their associates to "pour their money into my ministerial coffer."

Most assuredly, I could have side-stepped this issue as well, and simply turned down the trip with an acceptable excuse of some kind but I truly needed to know if I would be able to work with Violet or if our association was headed for an abrupt end. In this regard, I was compelled to finally confront her with the word of God about "keeping company with brethren" who are living a sexually immoral lifestyle. Consequently, I declined her daughter's invitation on the basis of I Corinthians 5:11. Hidden behind the actions of this doting, domineering mother, the demon Jezebel's confrontation compelled me to stand for righteousness and not yield to temptation based upon Violet's mammon.

Nevertheless, even though she may have had her own motivations, I would not be at all surprised if she was completely unconscious most of our association of the religious demon's hidden agenda. What was concealed from both of us when we first met was made subsequently made known to me by the Holy Ghost. Violet was being unknowingly used by the spirit of Jezebel to tempt me to yield to the lust of money,--- the true root of all evil---, sent to me as my greatest supporter to cause me to compromise for mammon, confirmed by a prophecy given before she sent my ministry one cent, no less!!!! These are the wiles of the devil.

The religious demon will certainly try to seduce a true child of God whose soul is conducive to the spirit of domination and control, beautifully arrayed in sheep's clothing without any evidence of the wolf's fangs. In an article that I found on the Internet entitled "Unmasking the Evil Embodied Within the Spirit of Jezebel'", Sister Nadine's description of personalities tainted by this demon is both accurate and informative. She writes that captives to the spirit of Jezebel's manipulations and maneuvers are well known by their intimate circle of family and friends to manifest domination and control within relationships. In this regard, I suspected that other members of Violet's family were very familiar with her darker side. Once I assigned her to mentor some of my sheepfold, it became evident to me that most people don't really get to see Violet's true nature because of her soft spoken façade and her repetition of religious sounding platitudes like "God loves you. You are the special apple of His eye." Even at the conclusion of every conversation, Violet gently and sweetly purrs--- "Love you." or "I love you very much."

Sister Nadine suggests that friends who remain outside of the inner circle will not only cover up for Jezebel types but they may even fiercely defend them against all criticism or correction. Although I was socially uncomfortable with her profuse flatteries of my spiritual gifts and her ingratiating ways, I simply minimized my lack of ease and comfort in our communications as merely a by-product of her cultural norm. In fact, I have grown to truly appreciate long distance spiritual relationships because it is a lot easier to not know people after the flesh, but after the spirit. Weary of the carnal contacts that I consistently received from Violet every day concerning non-spiritual matters and other mundane concerns and activities, I realized how challenging it would be for a person like me to have someone like Violet as a neighborhood friend. I could literally be overwhelmed as my only worldly interest is long distance swimming, a feat that I usually carry out alone.

Incongruent as it may seem, it was her zealous belief in the ministry of casting out devils ---a rarity among professing Christians---that I found rather appealing. Therefore, Violet's commitment to deliverance opened the door to my acceptance of her rather obvious efforts to try to prove to me that even though she was raised in a racist family, she herself "loved black folk." Not only trustworthy, Violet convinced me that she was worthy of being taken into my confidence and capable of being assigned to mentor some of my weaker captives. I literally walked into Jezebel's trap by making these assignments. According to Sister Nadine, most people with this sort of demonic influence are "looking to birth disciples to eat from their own tables," particularly attracted to the weak and the vulnerable. This began to happen almost immediately.

Simply put, disregarding the prophecy that I had received four months before, I was led to try the spirits to see if Violet was really led to me by God to support my ministry. My strategy involved presenting Violet with some of my professional insights about her relationship with Johnnie Mae. In short, I told Violet that she was meddling in her gay daughter's life. I also advised her that I was beginning to feel like she was unconsciously manipulating me and that I am a person who cannot be steered beyond my own will.

In this regard, I pointed out that women who feel powerless tend to develop passive-aggressive styles geared toward "trying to get their own way by maneuvering others into doing what they want them to do." Without a doubt, I expected that Violet would experience extreme but well controlled anger and offense, that she would respond graciously, but that in no way would she ever again desire to be involved in my ministry. I had grown to really care for Violet, and I truly hoped that my assessment was incorrect. I admired her love of the Lord and I prayed beforehand, that if Violet was sent by the Lord, that she would rise above her own flesh reaction to my observations, and allow her commitment to the ministerial work override any personal resentments.

As Sister Nadine points out in her article, the spirit of Jezebel refuses to be corrected by anyone and this demon will cause its captives not yield to any spiritual authority. Unfortunately, Sister Nadine was right and so was I. Violet withdrew not only her financial support but also Christian fellowship with my ministry. I was truly saddened and disappointed. However, the day that I stood on the word of God, confronted the issue of homosexuality head-on and subsequently overcame the temptation to compromise the word of God for filthy lucre, I cannot remember ever having felt more powerful in my entire life!!! I could have run over a troop, scanned a wall and healed every lame person in sight!!!!!

Besides the prosperity gospel, I believe that the gay and lesbian lifestyle as an acceptable Christian practice is probably one of the loftiest doctrinal mixtures perpetuated by the religious demon since the white man used scripture to justify slavery in America. The key factor here is that when a believer in Jesus Christ defies a clear word in the scriptures through disobedience, the religious demon will answer his or her prayers concerning what is obvious in the bible with a lofty, spiritualized response. The following words of Luke, an avowed "Christian" homosexual clearly demonstrates my point. Luke's refusal to accept the clear word of God on sodomy has subjected him to delusional thinking:

> " It just amazes me to see some of the Christian ministries like yours who claim to be Christ led yet they don't know a thing about Him or what exactly Jesus taught. How in the world would you think that God's wrath would come upon Gays and Lesbians who love Christ and serve Him everyday of their lives? You need to come into the new fold, Sistah! To even bring up Old Testament judgment is under estimating the will of Jesus. Why on earth do you think Jesus came to the earth? So that "whosoever" believes might be saved. You people kill me with your Pharisee ways of thinking. Oh and by the way, re-read the Sodom and Gomorrah story and you will see that all the people of the town were outside the door. Yes, it does say men, buy if you read the original Hebrew that would include woMEN too. It was Queen...oops, I mean King James who twisted things to deal with his own "demons."

> "If you knew my story and that of others, you would know how saved I am. I don't believe in cheating. I believe in having a monogamous

relationship, in my case, a relationship with one man. We have had in our church well known preachers who have been skeptical of our church, but once they actually came to see for themselves we gay and lesbian Christians, they all say the same thing---that the Spirit of God is truly with our church. One of them even apologized for preaching against who and what we are. We have many, many couples in our church, where everyone is welcomed, straights as well as gays. Our church is blessed double fold because of the faithfulness and characters of the people in our congregation. I too, continue to be blessed in my life.

"We do not get angry with folk such as yourself anymore. We just pray for you. We realize that we don't want to be used as a weapon against straights by the enemy so we simply pray for you. I believe God's word which declares that no weapon formed against us shall prosper. Why do you want to be a weapon in the enemy's camp against us? Do you think that if we weren't born the way that we are that we would choose to be gay? Would we choose to be bashed, to be preached against to be discriminated against as we are? Even the 10 Commandments, chosen laws of God given to Moses say nothing about homosexuality. Why pick and choose what scripture to use against us? Do those among you eat pork or shellfish? Do the men not touch their wives or girlfriends when they are on their menstrual period? I have been with women sexually twice. Both times, I vomited. This was prior to my having had a sexual encounter with a man. Today, my dear, after me and my husband have sex, we play gospel music and praise the Lord for blessing us with each other."

The deception clearly manifested in Luke's own words is reflected by his gross lack of scriptural understanding, indicative of how the religious demon operates in a confused mind that has denied a clear word. Of one thing, Luke is correct. A homosexual can be saved like anyone else. Nevertheless, once a homosexual becomes saved or "born again", in the spirit he is no longer considered a homosexual by God. Yet, if he continues to walk in the flesh, then he will remain a homosexual and will never rise above his carnality to a true worship in the spirit. The key is that since the Lord expects all those who believe on Him to not walk in the flesh but in the spirit, for Luke to insist that the Lord chose him to be a homosexual, borders on blasphemy.

Clearly, in the spirit there is no gender, either male or female or any other mixed gender of gay or lesbian, for we are all one in Christ. (Galatians 3:28) If a gay or lesbian chooses not to allow his or her flesh to be crucified, then he or she will continue to embrace a corrupted gender. However, Luke and others like him should heed the warning of Paul to the Corinthians, a warning that applies to us all:

"Know ye not that the unrighteous shall not inherit the kingdom of God? Be not deceived. Neither fornicators, nor idolaters, nor adulterers, nor EFFEMINATE, nor abusers of themselves with mankind, nor thieves, nor covetous, nor drunkards, nor revilers, nor extortioners, shall inherit the kingdom of God. And such WERE some of you: but ye are washed, but ye are sanctified, but ye are justified in the name of the Lord Jesus, and by the

Spirit of our God. (I Corinthians 6: 9- 11)

The operative word here is "were." In the spirit, an idolater like I used to be is no longer a witch in the spirit--- nor a substance abuser an addict--- nor a bank robber a thief--- nor a whore a fornicator--- and in keeping with this same line of thinking, nor an effeminate, a homosexual. In fact, even the term, "homosexual Christian" is a misnomer, a corrupt phrase of two words that should never be linked together, not even with a hyphen. When people like Luke pray under the assumption that his or her lifestyle is acceptable to the Lord, then the Father will allow a religious demon to answer that prayer with an sublime response that will lead to even more spiritual confusion. In such cases, if rebirth actually did transpire, continued disobedience to the word of God could lead to the Holy Spirit turning such folk over to a reprobate mind. Once reprobate, repentance becomes impossible. (Hebrews 6: 1-6)

With captives like Luke, the religious demon has formed a partnership with the spirit of lust and gluttony --- the unclean spirits that oversee a larger class of demonic activity: rape, child molestation, sodomy, incest, masochism, sadism, bondage and other forms of sexual perversion. Since a captive's first memories of gender or sexual confusion undoubtedly occurred in childhood, it is a logical assumption for those so affected to believe that they were "born that way." Therefore, proponents of the belief in a genetic predisposition to homosexuality are unaware of the fact that the demons or groups of demons of perversion can be transferred in childhood by a process of predator to victim contact. With the sex act itself being the doorway or entrance for demons who specialize in homosexuality, the captive becomes "one flesh" with the predator. Such contact explains how a victim becomes a predator, transferring the demon of perversion to other victims, and the vicious, invisible cycle is perpetuated from perpetrator to victim in widespread proportions. Thus, the reason behind Paul's admonition to "flee fornication!" (I Corinthians 6:15-20)

When the religious demon and demons of sexual deviance are conjoined, I have found homosexuals actively participating within some phase of worship within the organized church---as choir members, choir directors, musicians and very often, as ministers, all of whom appear to be extremely anointed in their particular craft. In several situations, I have observed men dressed in women's clothing and make-up, robed, as they boldly processed into various choir stands with the unspoken approval of the ministry and the laity. Where the preachers are concerned, they generally fall in the "down low" category---closet homosexuals--- married with children---perpetuating a damnable fraud and a clear and present danger to transmitting a sexual disease to their spouse. In fact, I recall one particular minister, well known and accepted throughout the AME Zion denomination for my entire tenure there--- a sought after evangelist around the country--- even though he was obviously gay. In this regard, I suspect that the tacit acceptance of gay men on "the down low" has been silently recognized and intrinsically established within the organized church for not only the two decades of my own experience, but quite possibly, for several decades and even for centuries.

One of the most prominent arguments for openly allowing homosexuals a prominent place in the life of the organized church is that many gays are gifted not only in music but in preaching as well. Gifts of song, music and oration are considered evidence of anointing, and anointing suggest the oil of the Holy Ghost. Yet the nail in the coffin of such an excuse is that Satan himself has always been anointed, both before and after his rebellion. Referred to by God Himself through the prophet Ezekiel, Lucifer is "the anointed cherub that covereth,"known among the angelic hosts for his musical prowess , as even his frame consists of built in pipes and tabrets. (Ezekiel 28:13,14) Therefore, if Satan operates from a corrupted anointing, then is it not obvious that the gifts and talents of his disciples also flow from that same corrupted anointing? Didn't Paul warn the Corinthians concerning this same issue?

> "For such are false apostles, deceitful workers, transforming themselves into the apostles of Christ. And no marvel; for Satan himself is transformed into an angel of light. Therefore, it is no great thing if his ministers able be transformed as the ministers of righteousness; whose end shall be according to their works." (I Corinthians 11: 13-15)

Moreover, the bondage that the religious demon has imposed upon the issue of women in ministry is typically "Antichrist" in nature, yet people with sound minds and a modicum of commonsense believe that Jesus would eliminate from ministry an entire gender of people who literally fill up the churches today. As a woman who is not only a pastor but who is also called into the entire fivefold ministry, I have never really debated the "should women be ordained" issue. I don't profess to be a bible scholar or a student of Hebrew and Greek. Rather, I approach the issue not by my own understanding of what the Apostle Paul has written concerning women of his day, but by knowing the Lord. And because I know the Lord, particularly through the gospels, I believe that the best understanding of "the woman question" should be viewed from the Lord's perspective. After all, Jesus is the Lord of the Army. He is our spiritual "UNCLE SAM" and He knows what He is looking for in His recruits.

Once Jesus called me and I answered, The Lord referred to me as "a front line warrior" and so since the battle we fight is not carnal,---- it is not flesh, then it really does not matter "the nature of the flesh." That which is flesh, is flesh. That which is spirit is spirit. Since the battle is "of the spirit", then we must enter into battle, not knowing each other "after the flesh." I myself do not preach "as a woman." I minister as a spirit who happens to be clothed in a female body. This is embodied in the Lord's words regarding worshiping Him in "spirit." A part of worshiping Him in spirit is also to "preach" in spirit, to "teach" in spirit, to "pray" in spirit, and so on.

In order to eliminate more than half of the Lord's army, the religious demon uses the meanness of church die harts who "major on minors," taking advantage of spiritually blind churchgoers' concentration on flesh. What we don't seem to understand, is that the Lord has had His reasons for "restraining" people until the time is right. For example, when the Lord first sent out the Apostles in Matthew 10, he told them to only preach to the Jews and not to the Gentiles. Why? Because of timing. The timing was not yet right. Also, because of "readiness." The apostles were culturally insensitive to the needs of gentiles and Saul of Tarsus had not yet been converted. In fact, Peter didn't even think that salvation was for the Gentiles until 10 years after Pentecost when the Holy Spirit had to give Peter a vision to "shake him up." And what did Peter say? Well, Peter had the audacity to say "NO, LORD." (Acts 10) THOSE WITHIN THE ORGANIZED CHURCH ON THE WRONG SIDE OF THIS ISSUE HAVE SIMILAR AUDACITY.

In other words, those who profess to be God's people are saying "no Lord!" Is this not the way of the Antichrist in His denial of all that will build the Lord's kingdom? I believe the reason why the Lord has allowed women to be restrained in ministry throughout church history is because of the hardness of His people's hearts on this issue and the fact that women were in bondage in the world for so may centuries. Because of prejudice and ignorance, women have been restrained from gender equality and equal rights on all levels. Those who declare ,"NO LORD" relative to women as pastors are without understanding of the Lord's heart, His ways and His timing.

Blinded by the out of context interpretations of a few scriptures, women who feel a call on their lives have been put into bondage by legalism. Whole denominations have split over this issue. The religious demon has compelled the ignorant to restrain women in ministry for 2000 years. However, the restraints are off. Wake up Church. Eve was forgiven at the cross. We are in the 11th hour. The Lord is calling out to those who have been idle for 2000 years which includes not only women of all ages, but those among the men who have been left out of ministry: the young visionaries and the old dreamers. (Acts 2:17, 18) WHY??? The middle aged man is responsible for the state of the church today and I believe that the Lord is about to replace him. Perhaps Jesus has saved His best wine for last.

Besides the prosperity doctrine, the gay-lesbian issue and women in ministry, the religious demon has inspired the doctrines of "name it and claim it", slain in the spirit, drunk in the spirit, that everybody has a "prayer language," that everyone must have a covering to minister, that Jesus was reborn in hell, that man is or will be a god, that Satan's teeth have been pulled and that the devil is merely " gummin folk", that the Father can be ordered around, that it is a believer's lack of faith that causes him not to be healed. Then there is the false doctrine that suggests that the church is going to establish dominion over the earth as taught by Latter Rain, the Manifest Sons of God and related theologies, including Kingdom Now Theology, Progressive Revelation, Replacement Theology, pre-tribulation rapture, and countless others, too numerous to mention them all here.

The Religious Demon and Endtimes

A responsible examination of scripture will be careful not to overlook the spiritual significance of the connection between the world's acceptance of sexual perversion and two catastrophic volcanic eruptions: the flood in the time of Noah and in Abraham and Lot's generation, the destruction of Sodom and Gomorrah. In Noah's day, the cosmic powers were sexuality intimate with the daughters of men and monstrosities were birthed. (Genesis 6:1-8) In Lot's day, his wife was stoned because she looked back at the destruction of a notorious city of ill repute. (Genesis 19:24) Sodom was so infamously recognized for anal sex, that the perversion itself was later named "sodomy" in dishonor of this condemned city.

Worth mentioning also is the debauchery associated with the worship of the golden calf . The Lord God was prepared to destroy the entire nation of Israel, relenting only at the intercessory plea of Moses. Apart from God's longsuffering and merciful nature, my cursory reflexion upon biblical history highlights an interesting correlation between increased fornication and other forms of sexual sins and a corresponding increase in earthquakes. Since Jesus predicted that an increase earthquakes is an endtime sign, by chance the eroticism of our day is directly connected to increased earthquake activity around the world.

With the recent national election, the country said no to gay marriage, and the church took a sigh of relief, ignorantly accepting the outcome of the election as an indicator of the church's positive impact upon society. However, as previously pointed out, the organized church has compromised with undercover homosexuality for decades and perhaps longer. I believe that the present day issue of homosexuality and religion is an issue of life and death and that any nation that embraces this perversion is most likely doomed for destruction by the hand of God through devastating natural disasters. Ironically, the recent floods of Katrina in New Orleans, Louisiana occurred on the very weekend that a national gay pride event was traditionally scheduled, a spiritual eyeopener that the spiritually blind in America overlooked or minimized.   I also believe that if we are to escape the wrath that is to come, then it is imperative that those who profess to belong to Jesus remain a righteous people. As the Lord declared through the prophet Isaiah:

> "Come, My people. Enter thou into thy chambers, and shut thy doors about thee: hide thyself as it were for a little moment, until the indignation be overpast. For behold, the Lord cometh out of His place to punish the inhabitants of the earth for their iniquity,: the earth also shall disclose her blood, and shall no more cover her slain." (Isaiah 26:20, 21)

Once we consider the foreboding words of the Lord Jesus about the increase in earthquakes immediately prior to His return, His own admonition recorded in Matthew the 24th Chapter could be extremely relevant to our times. Within His prophetic warning, the Lord referred to a period in time as "the beginning of sorrows." These sorrows serve as signs that although the end is very near, we who believe on Him should not be troubled because "THE END IS NOT YET!" For those of you who are unfamiliar with the sorrows, here they are:

1.THERE SHALL BE WARS AND RUMORS OF WARS.

2.Many will come in the Lord's name saying that Jesus is the Christ, but they shall deceive many.

3.NATION WILL RISE AGAINST NATION, KINGDOM AGAINST KINGDOM.

4.There will be famines, earthquakes and pestilences in various places.
5.They will deliver Christians up to tribulation and kill many of us. We will be hated by all nations for Christ's sake.

6.Many (Christians?) will be offended and will betray one another and hate one another.

7.Many false prophets shall rise up and deceive many.

8.Because lawlessness shall abound, the love of many shall wax cold.

9.The gospel of the kingdom will be preached in all the world as a witness to all the nations.

10.THEN SHALL THE END COME.

There is a mixed teaching previously mentioned along with others called "the Dominion Doctrine" that has been spread abroad by the Charismatics of the non-denominational faith movement. This teaching suggests that the Lord Jesus will NOT return for His Bride the Church until she becomes glorious, without spot or wrinkle or any such thing. I have heard charismatic evangelists metaphorically describe the church of today as a toothless old hag, whose bridal gown is torn, dirty and tattered. It is true that a large portion of the church today is permeated with sin. However, the subtle insinuation that it will be a long time before Jesus returns for His Spotless or Sinless Bride is dangerously misleading.

Most assuredly, the Lord already has His glorious church without spot or wrinkle. Every time a saint of God passes on to "glory", he and she put on their spiritual bodies which are glorious. Because of the blood of Jesus, the spiritual body of the believer is not tainted by the spots and wrinkles of sin once it departs from the sinful nature of its flesh. Out of each generation, the Father has gained a harvest of true believers who have "put on glory." Charismatics have repeated so often that "Jesus said He's coming for a church without spot or wrinkle or any such thing", that those who have heard it have assumed that this saying is out of the mouth of the Lord.

However, no where in the Bible is it recorded that Jesus ever spoke any such words. This is yet another scripture taken out of its original context from the writings of Paul the Apostle to the Ephesians. Paul's major focus in this scripture is not the return of the Lord, but upon Christian marriage. He is merely making a comparison of the Lord's love for His Bride, the Church, and how a Christian husband ought to love his own wife in a similar fashion. Paul wrote that Jesus intends to present His church to Himself "a glorious church, not having spot or wrinkle, or any such thing, that it should be holy and without blemish." (Ephesians 5:27) There is absolutely no reference at all that would suggest that the organized church must be without spot or wrinkle BEFORE Jesus returns. Every Christian who dies is without "spot or wrinkle." Those who are alive when He comes back will be instantly changed from mortality to immortality and therefore, they too will be without "spot or wrinkle." To be without spot or wrinkle has nothing at all to do with a clean up of the literal organized church. To be without spot or wrinkle is to be redeemed completely, not only in spirit, but also of soul and body.

Now it IS recorded that the Father said to the Son "sit at My right hand until I make your enemy your footstool." Here again, the charismatics assume that these words mean that Jesus will not return until the Lord uses the church, (particularly themselves) to defeat Satan, not recognizing the spiritual truth that Jesus has already defeated the devil. Paying attention to the list of sorrows that Jesus Himself predicted would occur just prior to His return, particularly #2, #5, #6, #7, and #8. Do these particular sorrows approximate an all powerful church that has victoriously made the enemy the Lord's footstool? No, they most definitely do not.

The church that makes the enemy the Lord's footstool is led by the Lord Himself, when He returns with true believers who have been made glorified, first through their death and and then completely by resurrection. Those who are alive at His coming shall be instantly changed from mortality to immortality and they too become "glorious" as previously stated "without spot or wrinkle or any such thing!" It is clear to me that this event that the church calls "the rapture" does not happen until the end of the tribulation when the Anti-Christ and the False Prophet are defeated, the wheat and the tares are separated, the battle of Armegeddon is won by the Lord and His glorious army, and Satan is bound for 1000 years. Then, ALL of the Lord Jesus Christ's enemies SHALL BE HIS FOOTSTOOL! It is the only scenario that makes sense to me, according to the scriptures and the nature of God.

The job of the church in all ages continues to be to preach the gospel of the kingdom. And this we shall do until the end. Why? Because the Lord foretold that we would. I believe that there are already 7 different types of churches on earth right now. Jesus addressed the 7 churches of the early church 2000 years ago as recorded in the beginning of the book of Revelation, in the first three chapters. Two of those church "types" are definitely overcomers: The church at Smyrna and the church at Philadelphia. It seems that the church at Smyrna will be martyred and the church at Philadelphia will remain alive throughout the tribulation and shall be victorious. Thank God for the church symbols of Smyrna and Philadelphia, the martyrs and the survivors among God's people in the time of the earth's devastation.

However, as we see in the list of sorrows, false doctrine and false prophets shall abound in five "church types" of the final age preceding the Lord's return. For example, I believe that the church at Thyatira is the present day Roman Catholic Church. Undoubtedly, Catholics have moved beyond scripture in its deification of Mary. Moreover, many of the denominational churches today are like the church at Sardis--- traditional, dry and lifeless churches where the Holy Spirit is so grieved and quenched, that He is barely in their midst. The Lord advised the faithful few in these places to strengthen what little remains that is under the sentence of death and that the members make sure that they themselves do not become tainted by the weak spirituality of their churches.

Furthermore, the church at Pergamos consists of those who uphold false doctrine about the Lord, denying His divinity yet calling themselves "Christian." Several churches fall in this category. These are the churches, whether denominational or charismatic, where Satan has established himself within its organizational structure and has obtained "a seat." For example, Sun Yun Moon has already infiltrated the African American Baptist Churches by tempting them with money. Yielding to this temptation, the Baptists have allowed Satan to have a seat. Some of the Presbyterians have been supporting the gay and lesbian lifestyles among the laity as well as the ministry, where avowed lesbians are pastoring. Satan has obtained a seat. The Laodicean church is very visible and obvious today. These are the "prosperity seekers." Some,---not all--include the mega churches birthed by Christian television. The Laodicean church today has become so proud and so boastful, yet they are like clouds without water. Self-centered and blind, Satan has used very subtle methods to draw multitudes into this deceptive trap.

Satan has established himself a seat.

Another doctrinal mixture with an end time focus is what I believe to be the fallacy of the pre-tribulation rapture. The hidden agenda of the religious demon is subtle and clever in this instance. If believers are convinced that they can simply escape God's final wrath upon earth, then why prepare to stand? I myself am expecting to escape, either by death or by a "Red Sea" type miracle. Therefore, I heed my Savior's advice as I prepare for His

Second Coming. I do not fret as I watch and pray.

Moreover, in a book entitled "Endtime Delusions," the author makes some rather discerning observations that expose the strategy of the religious demon to keep believers ignorant of endtimes through a misinterpretation of Daniel 9:27. This scriptural misunderstanding is confronted on the basis that there is no biblical evidence of a 7 year period of tribulation. In fact, Steve Wolhberg declares that the current debate over pre-mid-post tribulation rapture is a clever demonic smoke screen. In "Endtime Delusions", Wohlberg re-awakens believers to the fact that the early forefathers of the church unanimously concurred that the Anti-Christ is the Roman Catholic Vatican, a religious system that was conceived after the fall of the Roman Empire.

Wohlberg also presents an historical update that reminds us that the Vatican ruled the entire known world for the period outlined in Daniel's prophecy of 1260 days, according to an interpretation that is based upon God's calendar of "a day for a year." In addition, Wolhberg points out that the church forefathers all agreed that the countdown to the coming of the Antichrist began shortly after the fall of the Roman Empire, with the 1260 years coming to an end in the year 1798. In that year, Napoleon destroyed the rule of the papacy by placing the then Pope Paul VI into exile. As predicted by John in the book of Revelation, once dead, the papacy was miraculously healed and today remains a formidable political, social and religious power of our times, in spite of the sex scandals permeating throughout its clergy. 2 (Revelation 13: 1-18)

So at the conclusion of this chapter, I anticipate the reader's question: "How do we know if we have accepted a counterfeit or a mixed doctrine?" I know myself the indescribable feeling of clarity that follows, once my own eyes were opened to the truth about several false doctrine that I myself had formerly believed. So in keeping with my style of expression, I conclude this chapter by answering this question with a quote from "War on the Saints," since once again, the late, great Sister Lewis has provided the answer beyond my own ability to explain:

> "When believers first hear of the possibility of counterfeits of God, and Divine things, they almost invariably ask 'How are we to know which is which?' It is enough, first of all, for them to know that such counterfeits are possible; and then, as they mature or seek light from God, they learn to know for themselves, as no human being can explain to them. But they cry 'We do not know, and how can we know?' They should remain neutral to all supernatural workings until they DO know. There is among many a wrong desire to know, as if knowledge alone would save them. They think that they must be either for, or against certain things, which they cannot decide are either from God, or from the devil; and want to know infallibly which is which, that they may declare their position: but believers can take the attitude of 'for' or 'against' without knowing whether the things they are in doubt about are Divine or Satanic; and maintain the wisdom and safety of the neutral position to the things themselves, until, by a means which cannot be fully described they know what they have wanted to understand."
> (War on the Saints, 9th edition, pg. 59,60)

Endnotes

1. Sister Nadine, "Unmasking the Evil Embodied Within the spirit of Jezebel." http://www.sweety.com/Jezebel.pdf#search='Narcissistic%20personality%20and%20Jezebel'

2.Wohlberg also exposes the religious demon's tactics to keep people blind not only about who the Antichrist is but also about the rapture, Israel and the end of the world. I strongly recommend that you purchase his book, "Endtime Delusions," published by Destiny Image in 2004. I also recommend his website at www.endtimeinsights.com

3.Note: On April 28, 2006, I received a word in the spirit that Roe vs. Wade will soon be overturned by the Supreme Court and that abortions in this country will once again be illegal. However, when this momentous event occurs, Christians are going to foolishly consider it a victory for the church and that because of their prayers, America has escaped the wrath that God intends to impute to this country. The foolish virgins will rejoice in a false hope. The way to try this word to see if it be of God is to watch, pray and wait. As recommended by Sister Lewis, I myself maintain "a neutral position."

Chapter 6 Mental Disorder and Jezebel

Located in a pdf file on the Internet is an article that I first referenced in Chapter 5 that defines the spirit of Jezebel as the mental health disorder known as narcissism, authored by a Catholic nun, Sister Nadine. It seems irreconcilable in this instance that the religious demon would work against itself by revealing truth through someone who is herself deceived by the Jezebel spirit within the Catholic church's adoration and deification of Mary, the mother of Jesus. Proceeding with caution in referencing this article, I have found very often that a religious demon will release a particular truth through a prophet or messenger because Satan is seeking to draw his prey into a deeper trap. Yet in this case, so as not to throw the baby out with the bathwater, I find that Sister Nadine's description of the spirit of Jezebel as comparable to narcissistic personality disorder   is both accurate and informative:

"The 'Jezebel spirit' is named after King Ahab's wife in ancient Israel, Jezebel---the first woman in the bible, with much written about her, that clearly displayed the symptoms of a ' malignant Narcissist.' This spirit is born out of witchcraft and rebellion and is one of the most common spirits in operation today. It is a powerful enemy of the 'body of Christ'---the church, just as it's namesake was. It operates freely on even sincere believers whose hearts are for God individually and has also attained positions of power within the churches. In the secular world, these people are often thought to suffer from 'narcissistic personality disorder', 'Paranoia' and are often labeled as 'Psychopaths' or just 'plain evil.' Yet, the most accurate and complete description of the characteristics of these people is to be found with a with and against 'evil'---not psychiatry, which has just recently started trying to come to terms with the term 'evil'. Religion is where 'evil' has most often been described and discussed, and its books mention it often as the end-result of un-repented sins." 1

Sister Nadine describes the mission and purpose of this personality type iss fivefold:

1. to masquerade as a protector

In order to gain access to it's captive, the spirit of Jezebel will enter through negative emotional doorways that have already been opened by other demons, including fear, rejection, jealousy and anger. As a protector, the spirit of Jezebel promises its captive ultimate elevation through recognition and domination of the lives of those around him or her---befriended targets that will eventually be spiritually back stabbed. Though not adverse to sexual seduction, spiritual seduction is Jezebel's religious goal. The Jezebel demon tries to convince those in Christ---particularly leadership--- that the captive is spiritually mature, trustworthy, loyal and reliable---persons who by virtue of their works are prematurely granted privileges and opportunities to minister and to hold positions of authority. In most cases, those with this demon can be found at the right hand of those in spiritual authority.

2. To kill the prophets.

As was the case in the life of Ahab's wife, a religious demon will seek those who by nature have a jealous, envious spirit, hostile to all spiritual authority. Like a shark or a snake, these captives can be most cleverly vicious and dangerous, particularly to those who are called to the fivefold ministry. For example, these captives will circle the lives of others within a congregation, looking for teachable, fleeceable, controllable disciples of his or her own. For these captives like to birth spiritual babes unto itself, disciples that will eat false doctrine from their own tables. Toward this end, some of these captives will seek out others who are in rebellion, yet who are weak, wounded, or those who are in conflict with their pastoral leadership.

3. To emasculate all men.

Through projection, these captives are generally bent on destroying evil in others, completely blind to the evil within their own souls. When life threatens their blameless self image of perfection, the Jezebel spirit uses these captives to be actively engaged in hating and destroying those who resist them, usually in the name of righteousness. Generally people of deep convictions, these captives may have a zeal for God and a desire to serve Him, which leads them to be convinced that they are serving the one true God. Even so, their true hidden agenda is self-worship.

Although biblical Jezebel is a woman, the demon that bares her name is a spirit, and therefore is neither male nor female. Therefore, the Jezebel nature can be found in both sexes. These captives tend to be strength snatchers, extremely jealous when others receive recognition and acceptance. Whether male or female, these captives may appear to be mild mannered and somewhat passive, serving at the feet of some prominent male figure, whom the spirit of Jezebel will use these captives to destroy.

4. To curse others.

A master of criticism, murmuring and complaining, captives will believe that their stand is righteous. With callous disregard for the well-being and independence of others, these captives have been convinced by this seductive demon that others who disagree with the captive deserve to be cursed. The Jezebel spirit is compatible with demons of fear and discouragement against anyone who confronts it. It will put a spiritual contract out against anyone who goes to war with it, not taking defeat 'lying down.'

5. To appear to desire to destroy evil.

Yet another facet of the hidden motives behind the Jezebelian form of religiosity is to seek self exaltation as well as to blind the eyes of the last generation to prevent the necessary preparation for the return of the Lord in His Second coming. Rick Joyner adds additional light to the motives of this demon, particularly as it relates to Sister Nadine's viewpoint concerning "killing the prophets":

> "Jezebel demands recognition for herself while serving as the enemy of
> the true prophetic ministry. Jezebel was the greatest enemy of one of the
> Old Covenant's most powerful prophets, Elijah ,whose ministry especially
> represents preparing of the way for the Lord. The Jezebel spirit is one of

the most potent forms of the religious spirit which seeks to keep the church and the world from being prepared for the return of the Lord. This spirit especially attacks the prophetic ministry because that ministry has an important place in preparing the way of the Lord. That is why John the Baptist was persecuted by a personification of Jezebel in the wife of Herod. The prophetic ministry is the primary vehicle through which the Lord gives timely, strategic direction to His people. Jezebel knows that removing the true prophets will make the people vulnerable to her false prophets, which always leads to idolatry and spiritual adultery." 2 (Epic Battles of the Last Days, pg.137)

The Narcissistic Personality and Spiritual Strangeness

When bordering on mental illness, a phrase that I have coined called "spiritual strangeness" can manifest in deep depression, the hearing of voices, visual appearances that are invisible to others and   manifestations of narcissistic personality disorders of different varieties. (See The Making of a Prophet, pp. 165-178) Where the demon of Jezebel is concerned, at the core of the mental illness is a pride system that reinforces false or counterfeit religious beliefs and   practices. Psychic phenomena like telekinesis and astral travel emanate from the witchcraft side of the face of Jezebel. As such, when supernatural manifestations are present, the spirit of Jezebel is generally the lead demon. The Jezebel demon is also at the root of self absorption, where legalism, perfectionism and self righteousness will progressively debilitate the soul. I suspected that previously mentioned 92 year old Bertha was also personality disordered, particularly as it relates to her perfectionism and the confusion and despondency she experienced when even mildly challenged or suspected of being in error. Although Bertha manifested symptoms of perfectionism, a more classic influence of the face of Jezebel is more clearly evident in a professing Christian whose name I have changed to Pearl.

Claiming to be a doctor of holistic medicine, Pearl contacted me by email with a rather desperate and impertinent cry for a deliverance from an alleged physical infirmity that she believed to be demonic. She reported that she was without any physical strength, continuing to cough, vomit and remained without appetite. By virtue of her New Age profession alone, I was immediately aware that the spirit of witchcraft was definitely unmistakable. Moreover, the fact that Pearl professed faith in Jesus Christ while simultaneously misquoting the Lord frequently, I suspected that I was dealing with not only Jezebel, but perhaps the spirit of the Anti-Christ as well. For example, Pearl views herself as "Christ-like", not at all considering that her 30 year practice of homeopathic healing is an occult practice, nor would she consider that her own beliefs could in any way be demonic.

Working with a captive bound to the Jezebel spirit is no easy task. The complexity of the situation is that when helpless and in the middle of a crisis, the captive is usually cooperative and approachable. Due to the urgency of Pearl's situation and the importunity of her emails and her phone calls, I overruled the steps and stages of my usual procedure. I confronted the demons by telephone in order to bring Pearl some immediate relief. By reversing the process, I cast out the demon of torment first so that Pearl would be free to work on her other issues and problems. For example, her adult son had threatened to commit suicide if Pearl did not stop interfering in his life. As is the case with this personality type and the Jezebel spirit, Pearl's life is one of chaos, instability, confusion and broken relationships.

Once I exercised the authority of the Name of Jesus over the demon of torment, the spirit of Jezebel and the spirit of the Anti-Christ were clearly exposed, discernible in Pearl's transparent self love and obvious sense of superiority. Pearl obtained immediate relief. Interpreting her well being as a sign of a complete deliverance, Pearl backed off from any further counseling, disregarding and opposing all of my suggestions and comments that she was not at all "delivered." With much debate and contention, Pearl conceded that "the Lord DID use me to set her free," but she vehemently refused to address those underlying characteristics that permeate her very proud personality. Considering the length of time that she has been narcissistic, it is only logical that she would tenaciously defend her own self concept. Therefore, in Pearl's mind, she is "as SHE says she is"---loving, giving, honorable, forthright, righteous, selfless, the perfect mother, superior---to name but a few.

It is apparent to me that Pearl is one of the unsaved professing to be saved. Notwithstanding, in Pearl's mind, she is "Christ-like" even though she defied several of His words and His ways as evidenced in her emails. Once relieved of torment, the contradictions between Pearl's actual character and her idealized image of herself became so obvious that it was amazing that she could not perceive it with her own self proclaimed intelligence. On the contrary, Pearl is consistent in her ability to ignore the unconcealed. In fact, Pearl would only accept the reality of demons in her life as being sent to her through the jealous witchcraft practices of others, never once considering that she could be in any way responsible for her own torment. This inherent blind spot coupled with her adamant resistance to authority is the most serious obstacle to a complete deliverance. Furthermore, within her emails are numerous statements that would cause a knowledgeable Christian to seriously question her salvation. Unwilling to be broken in spirit, the religious demon's motive is self evident. Pearl's solution is to do away with all demonic doorways of a personal nature by declaring herself "above it all."Pride has hindered Pearl from taking a realistic assessment of those un-submitted areas of her soul. As Paul wrote, "God resists the proud but give grace to the humble." (James 4:7)

The religious spirit in personalities of this kind targets both pride and fear from the root of their character flaws, where the pride is so vulnerable that the captive develops a spirit of fear to try and protect it. According to Rick Joyner, "the religious spirit seeks to have us serve the Lord in order to gain His approval, rather than from a position of having received our approval through the cross of Jesus. Therefore, the religious spirit bases relationship to God on personal discipline rather than the propitiatory sacrifice of Christ."3("Epic Battles of the Last Days", pg. 125)

The strengthening of pride is the logical outcome for Pearl, the climax and consolidation of the process initiated within her search for self glory. Pearl needs to be given time. As Joyner points out, like Pearl, the original Jezebel was prone to false religion. Due to this predisposition, the Lord gave the Jezebel spirit in the church at Thyatira time to repent because the roots of her pride system went too deep for a speedy deliverance:

"However, even though the Lord gave Jezebel time to repent, He rebuked the church of Thyatira for 'tolerating her." (v.20) We can be patient with people who have religious spirits, but we must not   tolerate their ministry in our midst while we are waiting! If this spirit is not confronted quickly it will do more damage to the church, our ministries, our   families, and our lives, than possibly any other assault that we may suffer." (Joyner, pg. 125) 4

Multiple Personality

The case of Ann manifests a much more dangerous side of the spirit of Jezebel than does Pearl as Ann has been diagnosed by the mental health system   as suffering from Depersonalization Disorder and Multiple Personality Disorder, which today is called DID-Dissociative Identity Disorder. The psychiatric mental health system refers to a group of disorders   as "Dissociative"." Considered to be psychiatric disorders, these disorders are identified by a disruption in consciousness, memory, identity and perception. The term Dissociative means   an experience of loss of identity as a person. Although these two disorders are lumped into the same category, they differ a bit in its manifestation within an individual. Depersonalization and DID are similar in that the disorder takes over a person's faculties involuntarily for a period of time. There is no designated time period as to how long this "take over" could last.

Captives diagnosed as DID seemingly have no control over this involuntary action. As stated in the definition of Dissociative Disorder: memory, identity and perception if "not working correctly...causing significant distress within the individual." Therefore I believe that this is the main similarity between the two disorders. Depersonalization is "when a person 'looks at themselves from the outside,' and observes their own physical actions or mental processes as if they were an observer instead of themselves." In addition, Depersonalization is also described as: a dreamlike state, recurrent feelings of being detached from one's body and mental processes, unreality and other characterizations. (See the DSM-IV)

It would seem that DID is more intense than depersonalization. The individual would not only be taken over, but will emerge with distinctive identities or personalities called "alters", each with its own relatively enduring style of perceiving, relating to, and thinking about the environment and self. These personalities will emerge at will, taking over the individual's personality. Also, the "alters" will 'take control' of a person at different times, with important information about the other identities seemingly out of conscious awareness from alter to alter. It seems that the major factor that differentiates Depersonalization and DID is the issue of conscious awareness. A person suffering from Depersonalization is aware of their actions, even if it seems as though it is dreamlike.

Conversely, a person suffering from DID is not conscious of the emerging personalities that paralyzes him or her. Depersonalization Disorder tends to have what is termed as "Reality Testing." Reality Testing is an individual's ability to discern, perceive, appreciate or 'test' the qualities of their surroundings. On the other hand, captives with DID also manifest an inability to recall important information that is too extensive to be explained by ordinary forgetfulness. Unlike Depersonalization, the beginning roots of DID are associated with severe psychological stress in childhood, most often ritualistic sexual or physical abuse.

Therefore, with Depersonalization and DID as backdrops, the case of Ann comes into focus. I received a telephone call from this 46 year old African American woman, a history teacher from Buffalo, New York. Ann claimed that though not computer literate, a person in Florida did a search on the Internet and came up with my name and number. Since her voice was urgent, loud and desperate, as in the case of Pearl, I made an exception to my normal procedure and agreed to a face to face interview and assessment with Ann. I personally picked Ann up at the Greyhound Bus Station in Albany New York and drove her to a motel. Counseling sessions took place in her motel room for three hours prior to the deliverance session. Since I considered Ann a case of crisis intervention--- a deliverance emergency--- it should be noted that I did not expect that Ann would be completely delivered.   Rather, my concern was to address the demon of gluttony that allegedly threatened to cause her to gain 800 pounds. When Ann advised me that she had already gained 50 pounds in two months, I arranged   this visit to ease her torment and then to subsequently enroll her in deliverance counseling for a prolonged period.

Here is Ann's self assessment of her problem in her own words:

"I have been a Christian for over 17 years, I have the Holy Ghost. I love the Lord. I am experiencing demonic oppression and obsession for the last two years. I am pulled left. I don't want to scratch my head but my hands are doing it and my hands cannot be removed. I would be driving in one direction and they would alter the direction. They also speak through me and tell lies. When I don't want to sit down, they force me to sit. They say 'we will show her who is boss.' They seem to have control over my body. They have a mocking song they have sung for the last 5 years. It is about Jesus. Years ago when I would pray, sometimes they would affect my speech and I would stutter. When I don't want to cry, tears flow. They are also having sex with me causing me to have orgasms. When I am not tired, they attack me with a spirit of sleepiness. It has caused me to have an auto accident. They do this sometimes in the classroom while I am at my desk.

When I give the words of God and speak the blood of Jesus, it is to no avail. They told me that they were influencing spirits. I had never heard of influencing spirits. They are demons. This is still continuing. When I read, they put music to the words I read and slow down the pace. Several months ago, they said they were going to make me gain 800 pounds. In two months, I gained 50 pounds. This is an example of what they force me to do. My hands are frozen and when I try to pry the food out of my hand, it won't release. One half a box o f cookies, hamburgers, cupcakes, pizza, slices of bread, beef patties, cereal, fruit, pancakes, a half container of potato salad and sandwiches all in a day. While I am walking down the street, they will force me to eat out of the garbage cans and say "Let's save money on food" and where is your God now?!
This is hell! I am the dead among the living. I can't take it anymore. Their torment is constant."

It was apparent that Ann had learned to live with demonic oppression for five years or more, depending upon which of her accounts of its origin is correct. I believe that the only reason she was as persistent in seeking help was because she was afraid of gaining more weight. She even admitted that years ago she had been obese (250 pounds) and that she had lost significant weight. She never mentioned HOW she lost the weight but she apparently lost more than 100 pounds. During the interview, she indicated that she had been taking care of a sick relative, lost concern for her own wellbeing and therefore lost weight. Ann also admitted that she does have a fear of being obese. It was clear from one of her comments that the fact that I myself was overweight at the time of her visit, caused her to challenge my credibility. In a passive-aggressive manner, she made an indirect comment such as "I was normally a chunky kid, normally obese--- kind of like you are."

When she called about 5 days before her visit, she could not control her eating. Yet, by the time she arrived, she claimed she had not eaten in 3 days and that it was quite a relief. She acted like it would be wonderful if she never ate again, which is irrational. Unless she was acting when she originally called, the woman who faced me was not the same fearful, practically hysterical woman who begged for an immediate appointment over the telephone. Even this first encounter could have been a performance. Nevertheless, if the information Ann provided is valid, I believe the Lord allowed her torment to serve as a blessing. For Ann heard for the first time of the possibility that she might not be saved. Such a revelation is itself "the blessing." Where this intervention did not succeed was in convincing Ann to spend the time to truly equip herself for complete freedom and deliverance. However, as frugal as I believe her to be, it was a catch 22 situation. She never really intended to go into even a brief counseling for the simple reason, she did not want to spend the money. In her mind, the workman is not really not worthy of his meat.

A tall, pretty yet rather plain woman, I was shocked to observe that not only was she not obese, but she did not look more than about 160pounds. At her height, of about 5'11", it was hard to imagine that Ann had only weighed 110 lbs two months ago, since she claimed that she had gained 50 pounds in two months. In fact, if this were true, then Ann must have appeared very emaciated, gaunt and frail, as she was a big boned woman. Actually at 160 lbs, Ann looked thin. She had a rag tied around her head in a kind of turban on a 90 degree day. When questioned about wearing the bandanna in the midst of so much heat and humidity, Ann claimed that "she had not gotten her hair done." I was shocked to learn that with all of the advances in hair care for black women, Ann still had her hair pressed and curled with hot combs and curling irons, an obsolete method. This would mean that Ann's hairdressers were senior citizens, as hot iron pressing has been out of date for at least 25 years in the African American community. Her facial expression remained without affect, dull and blunt. She expressed pride in the fact that she is a "cool, calm and collected person."

There were several discrepancies in various details of Ann's story of torment. For example, when she filled out the assessment forms, she indicated that she had no mental health history or involvement. However, when questioned later, Ann admitted that she had been to a psychiatrist six months ago, where she was diagnosed as suffering from depersonalization, and was prescribed Zoloff. Since she admits to having a lying demon, it is difficult to distinguish truth from lies in the information that she provided. Ann also claimed to have only slept with two men in her life, indicating that the orgasms that she continued to receive from the demons are distasteful and she wanted them to stop. I personally have my doubts about this statement also. She is a single woman, not in any relationship, used to having orgasms with her former lover, and yet she claims she is not enjoying these spontaneous orgasms.

Ann's childhood also seemed relatively normal, free of trauma and abuse. She claimed that as a child she was "the smart one" of 5 sisters and 2 brothers, both parents living. She adored her father, a daddy's girl, yet she remembers one time when he touched her inappropriately with his leg on her leg as they laid across the bed watching TV when she was a teenager. Her father never molested her, and this seemed like it was a harmless incident but she claimed that "it didn't feel right." Her mother loved her but "didn't like her." Ann expressed a belief that she reminded her mother of her mother's sister Sandra. Ann expressed a belief that her mother was jealous of her Aunt Sandra because she was like Ann---ambitious, smart and pretty." Where her religious background is concerned, Ann spent 25 active years in the Baptist church as a nominal Christian, serving as an usher. Her great aunt was involved in witchcraft. This great aunt favored Ann. Ann's mother was given various emblems and statutes by the great aunt. These were in the house when she lived with her mother. She checked the box indicating that there was some Masonic lodge involvement in the family. She also reported minimal experience with astrology, palm reading, the catholic mass and yoga.

The most outstanding highlights in Ann's self reported assessment are these: the fact that as a nominal Christian, Ann lived with a Muslim man for 11 years. But most important, Ann believes that she became born again by chanting "alleluia" with a Pentecostal woman who claims to have been praying for Ann's salvation for 17 years. This is even more interesting since for a good portion of those years, Ann was an active member of a Baptist church. Perhaps because for 11 years Ann was obviously living in sin, this was an indication to the Pentecostal friend that though a churchgoer, Ann was not saved. Ann also had two abortions. Once I learned that she came to Jesus while tarrying with Pentecostals in a home prayer group, I immediately suspected that she had opened herself to a religious demon at that time.

I also suspected from the first telephone session with Ann that the religious demon was at the root of the torment, along with an incubus sexual demon and a gluttonous demon. When I inquired by telephone as to how she became born again, Ann responded by telling me of her tarrying experience. With revelation and enthusiasm, I hollered out, "that's it. I've got it." In the same voice as the captive, the demon answered me and said "you don't have shit, bitch!" Then Ann apologized. "Excuse me. That was one of them." It was this demonic manifestation that caused me to change my procedure and to arrange for Ann to travel to my area immediately. In hindsight, I believe that the demon may have baited me because he knew that he was not coming out due to the fact that the captive would not accept my insight that "she is not saved." The religious demon knew that "his territory" was safe, protected by the captive herself.

The first hour was spent in an initial interview. The last two hours consisted of additional assessment. Though not overtly disrespectful, Ann was very challenging after the completion of the second hour. She questioned me intensely on my background and continued to ask me to demonstrate to her satisfaction that I was called to deliverance. For example, she wanted to know my success rate as well as how many others I had delivered. In fact, she asked me if I was a charlatan, out to get her money. I remained composed but firm. I reminded her that she was not being charged a fee for deliverance, only for my time in pre-deliverance counseling. I also advised her that if she did not trust me, the deliverance would not be successful, and therefore, I would take her back to the bus station, without charging her for the two hours that I had already been engaged. Ann decided to continue. In hindsight, I realize that I should have declined the case. The religious demon's motive was clear. Ann was deliberately sent to me to weaken my faith in the area of deliverance ministry.

Even so, this challenging confrontation served to show a side to Ann's personality---a hostile side--- covered by her outwardly passive, aloof, and polite demeanor. An educated, Master degreed woman, Ann obviously valued her intellect and her intelligence. To find herself with a demonic force in control of her mind was indeed a blow to her ego. However, in spite of the obvious torment she was in, I somehow sensed that Ann would prefer to be that one special case that the Lord could not or would not deliver. Since she had never heard of a religious demon, she chose to apply her own names to them. In fact, on the assessment form, Ann wrote: the spirit of forgetfulness, the mocking demon, demons of filth that dig up the nose, rub my feet and then smell it, the demon that talks through me, the demon of sleepiness, a demon that causes me to cry, demons that have sex with me and the demon of gluttony. She could not give a name to the demon that takes control of her body.

Counseling focused on trying to cause Ann to provide indicators as to how she gave up so much ground to the enemy. Other than for obeying every "holier than thou" voice that she heard, the root of the problem was not uncovered in just a few hours. Once relief is obtained upon deliverance, Ann agreed to enroll in counseling. However, she admitted that she is extremely frugal as evidenced by how she interacted with the motel clerk. I had previously advised her that the rate was $69 a night, but that it was $79 on summer weekends. When she was charged only $54, she began to suggest to the clerk that it was too much. I interrupted her by stating that she was being undercharged by $25. She took the key and went to her room without further comment.

At the completion of the deliverance session, Ann made a clear statement suggesting that she was going to handle her situation on her own. The problem with Ann is pride. I found that even though she was in torment and that she realized that she needed to seek help, she was not willing to admit that she does not have all of the answers. However, Ann's most outstanding resistance to deliverance was that she refused to even consider the possibility that she might not be saved. In hindsight, in spite of her torment, I should never have conducted a deliverance for two main reasons: I did not believe that she was saved and Ann challenged my credibility inappropriately. I believe that a deliverance counselor should consider the credibility issue prior to deliverance for if two cannot agree, demons will not be bound. My mistake with Ann was that I should have taken her lack of respect for my authority as a barrier to deliverance.

Furthermore, as I drove Ann in my car from her motel room to my office, driving on the highway at about 65 miles an hour, she reached across the car from the passengers side and grabbed the steering wheel. Struggling to maintain control of the vehicle, I shouted at the demons and commanded them to stop in the name of Jesus Christ of Nazareth. Jumping back over to the passengers side and removing her hands from the steering wheel, Ann was very nonchalant about the matter and stated, "they say that during the deliverance session, they are going to have some more fun with you." Then she continued riding for another 10 minutes, as though nothing had happened. This was witnessed by a passenger in the backseat, a deliverance team member from my church. The following consists of notes taken from Ann's case file concerning the deliverance session. "Ct" is an abbreviation for captive, and stands for Ann's name:

Prior to the session, the ct. signed the Deliverance Disclaimer Form, witnessed and paid in cash with $150 for 3 hours of counseling. Those present at the session were Doris B., Susan F. and myself. The session transpired for about two hours, with extensive prayer, additional inquiries, commands and expulsions. Manifestations occurred throughout, primarily coughing up mucous. There were some shrieks, head shakings, and movements from her stomach up her esophagus and out of her mouth.

The most hostile demon of all was the religious demon. It was mocking and insulting. When confronted, a religious demon caused the ct to walk toward me as though she was going to strike me. When blocking the confrontation, the team indicated that the ct.'s body strength was limited, and if necessary, she could be "taken down" without much effort on their part.

When she appeared to be completely delivered, the ct. took a tissue, threw it across the room and then said "they did that. I didn't do that." This was an indication that we had wrestled with this thing for two hours to no avail. The next morning on her way to being driven to the bus station, the ct. asked various probing questions, like could this be happening to her because the Lord wanted to use her in deliverance ministry.
At the conclusion of the session, I had a personal sense that although there was a great deal of manifestation, the ct. was not delivered because she did not believe that she had a religious demon. In other words, she felt that she KNEW who these demons were, and we didn't, particularly me. I also felt that she may have unknowingly been sent to me by the devil to try to shake my confidence in the power of the Name of Jesus to deliver. This assertion was motivated by the fact that she seemed to glory in the fact that "she was still in bondage" by throwing a piece of paper across the room and saying, "they did that, not me." Once we actually saw demons manifest and believed that they were out, I sensed a certain kind of "self satisfaction" in the ct. to affirm that our efforts to set her free had failed.

The ct. was advised that I changed my normal procedure to reach out to her in her desperation, but she was in no way impressed by my concern and compassion for her. Since she was not familiar with the Internet, I provided her with assignments for about two or three months on a floppy disc. By the nature of her post deliverance session questions, I got the impression that she would either not use the material or use it on her own. I pointed out to her that since this was copy written material, I was preparing to publish it. Therefore, if she was not going to follow procedure, she should return the disc to me.

She indicated that she planned to continue with the telephone counseling when she returned home. However, as she was getting out of the car, she returned the disc. She asked me if she could simply call from time to time with questions. Later that evening, I called her and left a message on her answering machine that if she wanted questions answered, she should register in the SEW Training Program.

Within 24 hours of her departure, I left another message on her cell phone answering machine as an inquiry to her well being. She did not respond. So I waited a full week to try again and she answered her home phone. Her voice was aloof and cool. She told me that her condition had not changed not one bit, yet she contradicted herself by admitting that she was no longer having problems with gluttony. She attributed this change not to our intervention but to the "influences simply changing their strategy." Where she had insisted prior to the deliverance that I should confront a demon of gluttony, on this last phone call she said the following: , "I never had a demon of gluttony. I have a demon that simply uses my body for different things: eating, sex, going here when I want to go there. That's all. I don't have a demon of gluttony."

Then she asked "what about these little deliverance storefront churches that are around? Are they any good?" I quietly said to her "are you suggesting that because we did not set you free that we are not any good?" She calmly replied "no, but I have to keep trying." My response to her was that I could not make an assessment of those whom I do not know. I advised her that I would pray for her and that if the Lord gave me any special insight to her problem, that I would call her and let her know. Then the conversation ended.

In spite of the fact that I believe that Ann was sent to me by the enemy to bring doubt and discouragement to me for not being able to cast out demons from her, the true blessing of our brief encounter was that I was able to let Ann know that without repentance and a belief on the Lord's bodily resurrection, no one can be saved, even though chanting at a tarrying altar produced a manifestation of speaking in a tongues. She was apprised of the fact that her tongue speaking was a counterfeit.

Endnotes

1.Sister Nadine, "Unmasking the Evil Embodied Within the spirit of Jezebel." http://www.sweety.com/Jezebel.pdf#search='Narcissistic%20personality%20and%20Jezebel'
There is much insight in Sister Nadine's article, yet the irony is that she remains blind to the Spirit of Jezebel as the demonic force behind the deification of Mary, the Mother of Jesus Christ.

2.Rick Joyner, Epic Battles of the Last Days, Whitaker House, 1995, pg. 137

3.Ibid, pg. 125

4.Ibid, pg. 125

CHAPTER 7 CHARISMATIC WITCHCRAFT

The case of Maxine is a classic example of how the Jezebel spirit can find a haven within the charismatic, word of faith churches. One of the advantages to email counseling is that a constant recording of each session can be saved in writing. This client sought my services because she was being tormented by demons who constantly accused and condemned her. She heard these demons as "voices in her head." She also stated that she could literally feel them moving about inside of her. She further reported suicide ideation, having made a definite plan that was thwarted. Maxine had recently experienced a great deal of grief, depression and loss over a boyfriend who had committed suicide within the year. Since she also functioned as a part time mortician, she had recently prepared the corpse of a very young man who had committed suicide, an incident that Maxine claimed precipitated her own suicidal plan.

A very intelligent 37 year old Caucasian female, born and raised in rural South Africa, mother an alcoholic, father a devout racist, a hater of black people. Maxine claims that her father had murdered a black woman more than two decades ago, without consequence. A former prostitute, Maxine is unmarried, mother of one child, having had 4 abortions. Several of Maxine's friends had committed suicide. She admitted to using drugs and alcohol but is not an addict. She was un-churched until her salvation experience about two years ago.

At the time of contact, Maxine was an active member of a large Charismatic, word of faith church. From her answers to questions concerning salvation, Maxine seemed to understand repentance. However, she was unclear about the meaning of resurrection. She described "resurrection" as "re-birth", "revival" and "renewal." It is crucial to note that there is no area of the occult that Maxine has not been involved in, including hypnosis. She reported having sent and received curses, astral projection and travel. Tatooed on her back was the Python snake. She sent me a picture of her back by email. It was hideous, to say the least. Even though she has never received mental health treatment in her country, Maxine has heard voices telling her about the future, voices that also condemn and accuse her.

During the assessment process of pre-deliverance counseling, Maxine described her salvation experience in the following email:

> The night I was "saved", I had tried to commit suicide-and I remember God speaking to me. He said "well, you don't know how to make yourself happy there—I can see-and you don't want your life—I can see. Give it to me. I will take it and show you more happiness than you've imagined. Come with me and trust me." From that point in my life forward-I've been a "different person"—and I left family/job/possessions etc. to go to the country, where I lived a life of total God dependence and met Jesus through a group of good Christian folk. I was not "born again" until I met Jesus."

Maxine further reported that once she "got saved", she lived in a place called the "Miracle House" for a year. She indicates that this is a Christian church that has been described as a cult. She further states that once she joined her present word of faith church, she renounced the Miracle House's control over her life and moved away from their teachings. She wrote "I hope, but I suspect they are still an influence)---they teach that the world is not real and that there is no devil."

It was clear to me that Maxine was not saved. To my pleasant surprise, it was not difficult to convince her of my suspicions. Within a week, Maxine listened on the website to a sermon that I preached called "I'd Rather Have Jesus", and reported that the loathsome nature of her sins was revealed to her and that for an hour or more, she cried deep, wrenching tears of repentance. At this point, I suspected that the client was now saved, since I had also explained to her the true meaning of resurrection and she also confessed that Jesus was raised from the dead.

Shortly thereafter, Maxine reported having the following experience:

> "Yesterday, I went into the mountains with my dog. I got out of the car and it started raining and we went walking together. I fell to my knees several times, I addressed the demons-I felt like the Holy Spirit was upon me. God and Jesus with me—and I commanded the demons to know that I was with Jesus of Nazareth—they had no choice but to leave, that God Himself would not allow them to live in my flesh any longer. My tattoos were covered with red ink which I had done earlier, pleading the blood covering of the cross. I called out that I do not have the mark of the dragon on me anymore, that only the mark of Jesus had authority, only His blood.

> It was still raining and I had an experience like a blood transfusion with the blood of the cross and the Holy Spirit. I felt/saw the blood go through my flesh, slowly traveling down, through every artery, through every muscle and I then felt like I had dead black corpses in me. I removed them by reaching inside. I felt freer than I had ever felt in my life. I experienced a glimpse of who I was, in Jesus, and I was very happy. And yet, there was a spirit still inside. Even so, I knew that the process had begun, but as not yet finished. That the main demon would have to be fought down the track. He controls the others. His skin is scaly. He is a serpent and there are spines down his back. He is black. He doesn't want to leave. You are right. He has made a claim on me."

Although Maxine believed that this experience was from the Lord, I had sufficient doubts, particularly because demons "do not die." All spirit is eternal. Secondly, I was uncomfortable about the reference to a "blood transfusion." The concept of the blood of Christ is symbolic and spiritual and not physical or literal. At this point, I began to suspect a religious demon at work. I now believe that the motive behind this "spiritual experience" was to suggest to both Maxine and to myself as counselor that the witchcraft spirit was the lead demon. Eventually it was uncovered that the witchcraft demon was covering for the religious demon in a subtle "counter espionage" type of strategy.

In the beginning of our counseling "email" interactions, Maxine was very self effacing and gracious, with constant words of thanks and gratitude for my work, very often accompanied with complimentary remarks of praise as to my skills and spiritual discernment. She was also very compliant to all of my instructions. However, I was concerned about her constant fasting, but then again, I didn't think that the fasting would hurt the deliverance and I considered that it might even help it. As Jesus declared, there are some demons that will not leave except by fasting and prayer. Experience has also revealed that much of that fasting should be conducted by the captive himself, since very often he or she will vomit during deliverance. Therefore, I was initially very impressed by her desire to stand and actively participate in her own deliverance.

A month later, Maxine wrote the following:

> I was reading the bible when I remembered the name of the demon that has either used me or was given to me in the past. The name is "NIMOWAY". I never told anyone else this name because I was instructed not to. The passage in the bible seemed to be addressing the transgressions of this spirit—and it was telling this spirit that it would be exiled. This demon has a deep, voice, very guttural, like an animal. His presence is so black and powerful, so obstinate and evil."

Immediately, I searched the web to research the name "Nimoway" and to my surprise, I found out that Lady "Nimoway" was the name of the woman who started the cult known as "WICCA." It is a witchcraft group whose "bible" is called "the Book of Shadows." WICCA considers itself a "nature" demon, and WICCA ceremonies are often carried out in the woods.

(www.angelfire.com/realm2/amethystbt/ladyofthelake.html)

Once again, the witchcraft demon prepared yet another cover-up for the leadership of the religious demon, as the remainder of pre-deliverance and post deliverance counseling subsequently unfolded. I would not be surprised if Satan rewards humans that serve him by naming lesser demons after them. In this regard, I was reminded of Maxine's experience in the woods and once again, I did not believe that her spiritual experience was from the Lord.

In response to what I discovered about Nimoway, Maxine writes:

> "I feel that I know her in my soul, she is a familiar spirit. Is it strange that I should feel affectionate toward her? I love her, I know her, when I looked at her , I knew her! I knew her! I did not tell you that I had an experience with 'another Maxine' a few years ago in the mountains. She was watching a video "Mists of Avalon" and she sent out a "call in the air" for another familiar to join her. I turned up and we watched it together and talked about what it was like when we were there, and we laughed like pagan witches together and rolled round on the floor in laughing ecstasy. It was if I was transported to another time and space. Now this Maxine is a very, very powerful Egyptian alchemist. She used to let me play with her 1,000 year old essences from Egypt among other places. I always felt/confessed that I fell in love with her. If I'd been "into" women, I would have married Maxine right there and then."

Keep in mind that when Maxine expressed her encounter with her Egyptian "alter ego" or spirit counterpart, she was an active member of a word of faith mega church in Australia. Maxine also did street ministry around the brothels of her country. Up to this point in pre-deliverance counseling, our email contacts were friendly, serious and most definitely professional. There were times that I shared a personal testimony, primarily for the sake of encouragement and support. Maxine continued to help herself by attending various charismatic worship services and prayer meetings. Initially, I thought that constant church attendance would prove to be beneficial to Maxine being able to withstand her deliverance. However, I began to get several emails such as the following:

"I have had an amazing weekend, at a prayer/repentance meeting Friday night which was led by a South African preacher who GLOWED with the GLORY of our Lord, and again on Saturday morning. Very powerful. Very humbling yet uplifting. Joy, dancing, repentance---the whole works. On Saturday I went to the South African fellowship meeting. I just love to dance for the Lord and it seems that is the way of the South African which I fall into and feel great fellowship with."

As a result of this email and others like it, I was beginning to discern that in this case, the religious demon might be even more powerful than the witchcraft demon. At this stage within the preparation process, Maxine had remained open to my counsel and advice. Then one day she mentioned that she had gone out on street ministry with one of the church members. She stated that she told one of the sisters that she herself had been a prostitute and the sister gave her a hug. I did not criticize Maxine. I merely made a suggestion that the Lord no longer viewed her as a prostitution and that unless led of the Spirit, there was really no need to confess this matter to anyone. To my amazement, Maxine became outraged at my statement, claiming that she was as spiritual as me and therefore her discernment was equal to mine. After several months of constant work, it was finally clear to me what I was dealing with. I had come face to face once again with the spirit of Python, the Jezebel spirit mentioned by Jesus to the church at Thyatira:

"Notwithstanding, I have a few things against thee, because thou sufferest that woman Jezebel, which calleth herself a prophetess, to teach and to seduce my servants to commit fornication and to eat things sacrificed to idols. And I gave her space to repent of her fornication; and she repented not. Behold, I will cast her into a bed, and them that commit adultery with her into great tribulation, except they repent of their deeds. And I will kill her children with death, and all the churches shall know that I am he which searcheth the reins and hearts; and I will give unto every one of you according to your works." (Revelation 2:20-23)

After carefully and rationally pointing out to Maxine how the demons were using her pride to destroy her confidence in me to stand in the gap for her, the telephone deliverance was finally scheduled. There were several demons that were expelled: including the spirit of death and suicide. The religious demon was confronted with no manifestation. From the sound of Maxine's testimony 1 and due to the fact that she could no longer hear the tormenting voices , it would appear on the surface that Maxine's deliverance was a glowing success. (See the testimonials in the Appendix.) On the contrary. Her testimony is merely more "religion" from the Jezebel spirit. Maxine had signed a deliverance disclaimer form which included a statement that she would continue in post deliverance counseling for at least 5 sessions. Furthermore, on more than one occasion, she was advised about the vigilance and care that must be taken to prevent a more intense captivity. So after about three weeks had elapsed without any contact from Maxine since the deliverance, I emailed her. In her own words, she responded as follows:

Dear Pam:

Since the deliverance, many, many things have happened. I guess it is only really now through trying to explain to you, that I realize how much. I've been wondering how I could write it all down and do justice--- and yet not come under fire from you, for there are many things that could certainly be interpreted many ways when one is not the individual concerned, some revelations are so personal from God, they only have meaning for me.

I do not mean that I fear you or anything. It is just that I've lost the need to explain myself, to let the world know what I am thinking. I seek to understand, not voice my mind. It has also become apparent that my role has shifted from "seeker" to "minister". I have been ministering to people not about stuff I know, but about stuff I wasn't so sure of. I have been ministering to myself through people, if you know what I mean. The Word has taken root, scripture can be recalled and quoted more readily, and I find that I am gentle and patient (not just pretending), but that my mind feels peace, at rest, and I've all the time in the world to listen to people and to understand.

It does not matter about demons now, in the sense that they are not the threat they once were."

After I reviewed this email, I realized that the religious demon had taken charge. Yet another month passed, and Maxine was sent a casual follow-up note inquiring as to her well being. It was clear that the witchcraft side of Jezebel was giving deference to the religious side. It was also evident that since the deliverance session, the religious demon definitely became stronger. Simply put, Maxine fell into sin less than a month after her telephone deliverance, became pregnant and had her 5th abortion without any sense of sorrow, remorse or repentance. In fact, the religious demon used her to remind and subtly accuse me of the same sin, a sin that the Lord forgave me for more than 20 years ago. Furthermore, she refused to participate in my deliverance correspondence training course, claiming that instead, she planned to enroll in a Christian bible school in her country.

It was not until my final communication with Maxine that I revealed to her the presence of the religious demon. The power of the religious demon is rooted in the pride of its victim. God resists the proud, but gives grace to the humble. I have found that the pride of word of faith, Pentecostal types is their biggest stumbling block to deliverance. Once Maxine decided that she did not need post deliverance counseling, I realized that the religious demon was in charge.

Perhaps I did not pray for Maxine enough. The Lord knows. After 3 months of intensive email counseling, I eventually acquiesced and allowed her to define our relationship. I realized that this was the only way that I would have any communication with her at all. Because I wanted to serve her, I tried to become what she wanted me to be. This former client now insisted on being my equal relative to my role as minister and counselor. She claimed that she was going to bible college, putting down any mere bible correspondence course that I had to offer her. I tried to avoid the spirit of jealousy within her, but it was not possible because of the prominence of the Jezebel spirit. The religious demon in an ambitious person has the tendency to become jealous of those that appear to be more "spiritual" than itself.

When she mentioned the fact that I myself had committed the sin of abortion, I used this as an opportunity to share with her the seriousness of this sin, particularly since the Lord had revealed to me that this sin had brought with it a curse upon my life in the area of my relationships with men and with husbands. The purpose of my sharing with Maxine from my own sinful past in the first place was to minister to her as a testimony to the power of the blood of Jesus when He set me free from condemnation. However, after her last communication, I confronted Maxine with the straight and the narrow of it --- that fornication is a sin that she must flee and that abortion is the sin of murder that will bring with it a curse. The fact that Maxine had no remorse and felt no desire to repent of her 5th abortion is another sign of the spirit of Jezebel.

In retrospect, Maxine is not unique within my experience as both a counselor and a pastor--- captives who have appeared congenial and compliant during times of demonic torment, whose true natures are subsequently unmasked once the torment has been removed. For example, I have discovered that the demon of Jezebel can only wear the disguise of mild mannered passivity for a short while because it truly hates humility and repentance. Like Maxine, easily apparent in any Jezebel captive is complete self exaltation and self righteousness, ---evidence of flesh that has never come to the cross to be crucified.

The dilemma is that although preached in charismatic assemblies, the cross is truly an offense to those who have given place to Jezebel. Actually unable to repent, these captives are among those that like the rich young ruler, it is almost impossible for them to be saved. Defiance of and a lack of submission to legitimate spiritual authority will usually manifest itself clearly, and as in the case of Maxine, give itself away. The light of truth and discernment provided by the Holy Ghost will shine very brightly in His exposure of the total darkness of this very evil demon, even when it appears to operating in bible toting, faith professing, tongue talking folk who love to sing and dance in the congregation and wave their hands toward the sky.

Restated throughout this book, the irony is that once truth has penetrated and pride has been overshadowed by humility and meekness, the religious demon could be the easiest to leave. A good example of a spirit of error is manifested in the woman at the well. Could it be that the woman at the well had a religious demon that immediately left her when faced with the truth? Looking into the eyes of Jesus as the Truth, I believe that the spirit of error immediately fled and released her, without even a command from the Lord. Like Maxine, the Jezebel side of this un-named woman's nature included regular worship while continuing to fornicate. As Jesus discerned by the power of the Holy Ghost, the unknown woman at the well   was living   with yet another man who was not her husband. Jesus did not condemn her and I did not condemn Maxine. What is impossible with counselors and ministers like myself is possible with God.   I keep Maxine in my prayers. I am grateful to her for providing me with a spiritual education. Because of this experience, I do not waste precious time when I recognize the challenge of Jezebel to my spiritual authority. As her case was officially closed , I repeated to Maxine the words that Jesus spoke to the woman at the well in the first sentence of the last email that I sent to her.

" YOU DO NOT KNOW WHAT YOU ARE WORSHIPPING. YOU ARE NOT READY FOR MY COURSE OR BIBLE COLLEGE, AT LEAST NOT AT THIS TIME. YOU WILL SIMPLY JUST BECOME MORE "RELIGIOUS." Try to step outside of yourself and look at the very disdainful way that you wrote about your recent boyfriend and his family. I could not hear in your words any desire in you for those people to come to know the Lord, get delivered from drugs and witchcraft, and become born again. Even while in sin, you remained "religious." This too is classic behavior for someone who has a religious demon.

Pride is what keeps the religious demon around. Pride goeth before a fall. I say this to you as a servant of the Lord that I have done whatever I could to reach you. You wanted a friend and I became your friend, when what you really needed was a teacher and a pastor. You have resisted me in this area from the beginning, and what you have written in this email is the result, as well as the other events that you previously described. The wages of sin is death.

Beloved, I realize that you are on a different path now, and it is clear that I am not the one who the Lord will be using to mentor you.   I humble myself to that fact. However, I could not just let you move on, without sharing with you the truth as I see it. If I am wrong, I pray that the Lord will have mercy on me. Anyway, I pray that you will hold on to this email. If we never communicate again, this email will eventually mean more to you than what happened during the telephone deliverance. In regards to your deliverance, I will quote to you what Jesus said in Matthew Chapter 12:

When the unclean spirit is gone out of a man, he walketh through dry places, seeking rest, and findeth none. The he saith "I will return into my house from whence I came out; and when he is come, he findeth it empty, swept, and garnished. Then goeth he, and taketh with himself seven other spirits more wicked than himself, and they enter in and dwell there: and the last state of that man is worse than the first. Even so shall it be also unto this wicked generation.

Maxine, your house was almost empty but not quite. I believe that this was the reason for the struggles that I had with you prior to the telephone deliverance session. It was because of the religious demon. When you appeared to relent and to submit to the fact that the Lord was backing me up, I went forward and conducted the deliverance. The problem is that your religious pride coupled with your ambition to minister hindered your deliverance. You see, I believe that once the other demons were bound, the religious demon became more powerful as well as more evident.

If you resist this demon by humbling yourself to the truth, it will leave you and you will not need me or any one else to participate in your deliverance. I will pray that you put on the girdle of truth and allow truth to set you free. I will also pray that if any other demons have entered your "house", the Holy Spirit will take charge and cast them from you.

I perceive now that my services are no longer needed and your case is officially closed."

Actually, I believe that I waited too long to close Maxine's case and that I should have done so long before the actual deliverance session due to strong and continual manifestations of client resistance and rebellion that was an obvious sign of impending failure. My problem was that I had done so much work that I didn't want to consider it a waste. Unfortunately, as committed to deliverance as she was, in fact, following my instructions and completing her assignments to the letter, Maxine unknowingly fought against her deliverance by covering and siding with the lies and deceptions of the religious demon. As I am a fighter by nature, the enemy knows that it is a weakness of my flesh not to ever retreat in a battle. I have since learned that rather than go forward, sometimes it is wise to stand still and wait for a more conducive opportunity to advance. The words of Jessie Penn-Lewis once again clarify and express my problem with Maxine in a nutshell:

"The will may be set, and declared to be for deliverance, yet when the truth is given, evil spirits manifest their presence in the circumference of the person, or where ever they may be located, by arousing feelings of rebellion against the very truth, or messenger of truth, which the person in his will has chosen to receive." In such instances, to avoid doing more harm than good, it is best to stand still rather than to advance, carrying out the battle quietly in prayer for guidance. (War on the Saints, pg. 218)1

Since Maxine, there have been several other cases that demonstrate how the Jezebel spirit operates with word of faith believers to cause them to rebel against the truth, as in the case of Rose. Rose contacted me at her pastor's recommendation. A few months prior to my contact with Rose, her pastor left a prayer request on my answering machine. The pastor's prayer request was rather intriguing, so I saved it, not realizing that we would soon be in contact by virtue of the fact that Rose became my client. These are the transcribed words of Pastor Judy, practically verbatim:

"Hi Pastor Pam, this is Pastor Judy from the state of Washington. I came along your website on the Internet. Our church is a baby church, growing, about 2 ½ years old. We've been given many prophetic words and the supernatural power of God is manifest in our ministry. You see, we have a dream, a calling from God, but the spirit of Jezebel is trying to destroy us before we can fulfill our destiny in God. We have been under some heavy attack, intense warfare from the spirit of Jezebel, the spirit of control. We've even had witches to come into our church who have spoken curses against me and my husband, who is our Senior Pastor. He has definitely not been himself. You can hear in my voice that the warfare has truly been intense, as I am hoarse. Its hard to talk to other people who do not understand spiritual warfare and so we thank you that you can help us take this thing to prayer as we know that we are over-comers. We are grateful that there is someone else out there like you, who believes in heavy intercession and believes that they can tear the kingdom of hell down."

Generally, I delete all answering messages after I have heard them and responded. In this instance, I did not return the call because Pastor Judy had simply asked me "to take the matter to prayer." Since the prayer request was about the spirit of Jezebel and spiritual warfare, I was led to save it. Then a few months later, I received yet another phone call from Pastor Judy, indicating that she was in support of my ministry and that she planned to send several of her members to me for deliverance, with Rose as the first referral. When Rose sent me an email to begin the deliverance counseling process, she identified her problem as "having a spirit of Jezebel." When I asked her to explain why she believed that she was possessed by this spirit, she replied, "my pastor and the members of my church have strong gifts of discernment and the Holy Spirit has revealed to everyone that I have a spirit of Jezebel, and I believe them."

For all intents and purposes, Rose seemed a perfectly normal, demon free young college student, with absolutely no personality or behavioral indications of the demon Jezebel. In fact, for three months of pre-deliverance counseling, I only observed a few signs potentially suggestive of a legalistic perfectionism akin to a religious demon, but no signs at all of Jezebelian inclinations. Yet Rose's thinking patterns and interpretation of scripture seemed mildly legalistic. For example, I assigned her an article to read and to prepare a commentary in writing. The fact that Rose emphasized the "slip of the tongue" errors made by the author, I noted mentally that Rose clearly missed some of the main elements of this assigned reading entitled "Satan Seeks To Devour You!" This sermon turned article is one of David Wilkerson's many teaching sermons. In Rose's own words, I received the following email:

> I am really enjoying "Satan Seeks to Devour you." It is so true that many Christians don't realize when they are under a spiritual attack. But what gave me such a revelation was when he said "Satan's aim is always to tempt God's people to rebel against his word." It is such a simple statement but so profound. One small thing. The writer misquotes the bible twice. Once he says Satan led Jesus into the wilderness(It was the Holy Ghost) and he also says that when Peter spoke to Ananias and Sapphira the couple fell dead (Peter did not talk to them together). But it was really good and well written article. As far as the 4 foot holds of Satan. One that I know I have is unforgiveness. When I was in Argentina on a missions trip, some one was praying for me and they said there is a wall there and you need to forgive. Now I know how important it is to forgive and I am not even sure of everyone that I need to forgive. I have made lists of everyone I can remember that has hurt me (from the girl who stole my snack money in first grade to the boss at my last job that yelled at me) I have said out of my mouth I forgive but I guess it's a heart issue still."

I assessed this written communication as the first sign of perfectionism that could be characteristic of religiosity, a potential sign of a demonic doorway. I found her comment regarding Peter and the slain couple to be petty. David Wilkerson's intent was clearly evident regarding the deaths of Ananias and Sapphira and his article in no way suggested that Peter spoke to them together, nor did it matter if he did. They dropped dead, whether 5 minutes apart or 5 hours apart, it is of no real consequence. Actually, this comment was based upon Rose's own inference.

Since I could find no substantial evidence of the Jezebel spirit in Rose or any other demon for that matter, I obtained a Deliverance Permission Form (DPF) from Rose so that I could speak directly with Pastor Judy for the sake of clarification as to why the Pastor believed that Rose was under the sway of Jezebel. Notwithstanding, almost immediately, I sensed the spirit of Jezebel within Pastor Judy. In fact, it was clear to me that she was the latent pastor of their church and not her husband. In short, most of her comments about Rose were as wrong as they were shameful and degrading.

For example, Pastor Judy expressed that she "discerned in the spirit" that Rose had a lesbian spirit "because she wears men's pants to bible study." If she had simply asked Rose to explain, she would have learned that Rose had a very practical, understandable reason for wearing them. On bible study nights, most church folk dress casually and comfortably, saving their dress clothing for Sundays. Simply put, Rose revealed to me that she wears men's pants on occasion because she is tall, her legs are long, and therefore, men's pants provide a better fit than do women's.

Moreover, an email from Rose confirmed my original suspicions---that both the church and the husband and wife co-pastor team were caught up in fleshly worship. Furthermore, Pastor Judy's accusation that like Jezebel, Rose was an attention seeker, may have been connected to the fact that Pastor Judy did not appreciate the attention that Rose was apparently obtaining from her husband, Pastor Sam. It should be noted that right after the comment about the lesbian spirit, Pastor Judy also claimed that Rose frequently came to bible study with her cleavage exposed. The following response from Rose shed some light on this matter:

"When we were in the building we had before now, we had folding chairs. It was not an uncommon event if we wanted more room to dance and move around during worship to fold up the chairs and lean them against the wall. In our new building ,there is more room and usually I will come out of the rows and stand on the far right side and have room to sway, twirl, dance or wave flags. One night Pastor Sam was in "my spot." I didn't want to crowd him out. The chairs we have now are padded "church chairs" that connect . Since there was no one in the row behind me, I disconnected two of the chairs and pushed them back with my foot so I would have a little more room.

For some reason Pastor Sam found this very funny. He laughed for about 5 minutes. At our next service, when he was talking about worship, he used my moving back the chairs as an example (I don't remember the exact words) but he was saying that you shouldn't let anything get in the way of worship and how as he saw me kicking the chairs and he could imagine me thinking "out of my way chairs you aren't going to get in the way of my worship." For my part it wasn't that deep. I guess that is where Pastor Judy gets the idea that I want people to watch me because they see things like that."

Virtually an outsider with these two women, as a counselor I was in an unworkable dilemma, stuck in the middle between Rose and Pastor Judy. Since Pastor Judy was not my client, my sole responsibility was to set Rose free. Yet Rose's relationship with this church and its pastors was full of contradictions. In spite of the fact that Rose admitted that doctrinal error was being preached as a result of the co-pastors' association and affiliation with various unprincipled "mega ministries", her affection and commitment to this pastorate was inflexible and unshaken. For example, throughout the 3 month extended period of pre-deliverance counseling, Rose became fully conscious of the issues and discrepancies of this ministry, yet she continually manifested a tendency to minimize and even ignore the obvious. She also made it very plain to me that she would not tolerate any unfavorable assessment of Pastor Judy. With my hands so bound, there existed no favorable or common dwelling ground for truth and error to co-exist.

Once I perceived that a demonic soul tie existed between Rose and Pastor Judy,--- ironically, a soul tie formed by the Jezebel spirit of control that Pastor Judy claimed to be spiritually wrestling with to save their "baby church,"--- I realized that no amount of deliverance counseling would prevail if I had to restrain from presenting Rose with the truth. In retrospect, the one who should have sought counseling was Pastor Rose herself. Unfortunately, this case did not turn out well. Rose was invested in remaining in that church for reasons that I did not have the time to uncover. In spite of the fact that Pastor Judy "fronted" with me about all the members she was going to send to me for counseling, I learned from Rose that their church consisted of 7 members, including both pastors and their daughter. So its clear that in spite of her disapproval of Rose, Pastor Judy was prepared to lie to keep one of the sheep from leaving their actual sheepfold of four.

I believe that there is a fundamental principle here that cannot be escaped. I was sought to free Rose from a demon that she did not have, by a pastor who clearly is demon oppressed by that very demon. Deliverance from believing lies must be overturned by believing truth. Therefore, whether demon oppressed or not, it is evident to me that Rose really does need to be set free. It is unfortunate that her own passivity is holding her captive to this ministry. In this case, both the sheep and the pastor were invested in maintaining the status quo of their corrupted relationship. Actually, on a pre-conscious level, I suspect that Pastor Judy truly wanted Rose to leave their church, in spite of their few in number.

Considering her original telephone message when Pastor Judy sincerely sought intercessory prayer against a Jezebel spirit she believed to be attacking her ministry, shortly followed by her referral of Rose as one of her members that she adamantly believed to be oppressed by a Jezebel demon, it is not too far fetched to assume that Pastor Rose believed that Rose was sent to her little church to destroy it. When I spoke with Pastor Judy about the case, she made it very clear to me that she moved in the gifts of discernment and that her ministry was highly favored of God, chosen for a high calling in His kingdom. Through a strong confidence that God has spoken to her and revealed that Rose had a Jezebel demon, I sensed that Pastor Judy was unteachable and unyielding, with a positiveness leaning toward infallibility.

I also assessed that in spite of the fact that although Pastor Judy tried to ingratiate herself to me with subtle offers of promoting my ministry,---a manipulation suggestive of connections and power that were subsequently confirmed were not actually available to her,---- she would not listen to me. What she desired from me was the word of faith need for confirmation of her own "gift of discernment." In truth, I believe that word of faith ministers as deceived as Pastor Judy are themselves praying to the devil more often than not, because their emphasis on praise and worship is so sensual. Since Senior Pastor Sam believes that kicking chairs around is "real worship," an open invitation to the religious demon is inadvertently granted. In "War on the Saints" , this condition is aptly described:

> "The counterfeit presence of God is given by deceiving spirits, (religious demons) working upon the physical frame, or within the bodily frame but upon the senses. We have seen the beginning of this and how the first ground is gained. Control is advanced by these sense-manifestations being repeated, ever so gently, so that the man goes on yielding to them, thinking this is truly 'communion with God'---for believers too often look upon communion with God as a thing of sense, rather than of spirit. So he starts praying to evil spirits under the belief that he is praying to God. The self-control is not yet lost, but as the believer responds to or give himself up to these 'conscious' manifestations, he does not realize that his will power is being slowly undermined. At last, through these subtle, delicious experiences, a conviction is established that God Himself is in possession of the body, quickening it with felt thrills of life, or filling it with warmth and heat, or even with 'agonies' which seem like fellowship with the sufferings of Christ and His travail for souls, or the experience of death with Christ in the consciousness of nails been driven into the bodily frame, etc. From this point the lying spirits can work as they will, and there is no limit as to what they may do to one who is deceived to this extent. (War on the Saints, Abridged, pg. 113)" 2

In the end, Rose believed that Pastor Judy was above reproach--- in fact, that both of her pastors are in direct, special, personal communion with God. Therefore, to question any divine direction given particularly by Pastor Judy was the height of sin. I discuss matters of this kind more deeply in the chapter on demonic soul ties. Yet it is appropriate to acknowledge at this point that my biggest mistake was communicating with Pastor Judy one on one. Rose should have been present on a conference call. Even though I informed Pastor Judy that I would be sharing our commentary with Rose, this information did not stop Pastor Judy from outright lying. I could definitely have disproved her, yet I knew that both women would find a way to reason away even concrete evidence of Pastor Judy's lies. Be warned that those who refuse to face the truth will remain under the oppression of the religious demon and the Jezebel spirit.

Another damnable mixture of witchcraft and religion is the practice of freemasonry. Strongly rooted within the culture of African Americans both within and outside of the church, it has been my experience that the work of the religious demon, the demon Jezebel and the spirit of the Anti-Christ merge in a blasphemous trinity to kill, steal and destroy. In a venomous attack against the families and loved ones, particularly the significant others connected to the professing Christian lodge member, the demon's wrath frequently falls. Since this trinity hates everything and everyone who claims to belong to Christ, it has no mercy on Christians who belong to freemasonry, yet continue to give worship to Jesus. Even though denominational churches welcome the Masonic Lodge to hold their various gatherings and celebrations within church walls, the witchcraft demon and the spirit of the anti-Christ detest being forced to enter into sanctified halls where Jesus is continually worshiped and praised.

Therefore, with great enmity, vengeance is enacted upon the family and loved ones of Christian lodge members. For example, Fred was the president of the trustee board while simultaneously holding the highest position in his masonic lodge when his family experience several tragedies. His son, a prominent lawyer, was jailed and disbarred from practicing law for vehicular manslaughter. He himself was in a tragic car accident that left him permanently impaired. The Rev. Martin Mackey, a masonic lodge member for years is no exception. His wife, afflicted with a disfiguring facial disease that left her with a foot and leg that looks like an elephant, both his children afflicted with schizophrenia, sadly, I could cite many strange and tragic examples of a similar kind.

Dr. Rebecca Brown offers a plausible explanation:

> "The sins of our ancestors DO have a grave effect on our own lives and the doorway of inheritance must be closed by prayer, confession, and the cleansing power of the blood of Jesus Christ. Specific abilities and demons are passed down from generation to generation. A commonly accepted example of this the the ability to 'water-witch'. Especially damaging is any involvement in the occult, any idol worship which is really demon worship. (I Corinthians 10:14-21), any demonic infestation, any oaths taken by parents or ancestors which are binding upon descendants (as are most occult, pagan, Mormon, Masonic oaths, etc." (He Came to Set the Captive Free, pg. 143) 3

The following personal testimony of one of my former clients who held the highest ranking position in the Eastern Stars in her particular state is presented in her own words. Sophie is a clear example of how sex, religion and witchcraft are intertwined within freemasonry:

> "When I was a young girl, I was visited by a demonic spirit. I remember to this day, what his form looked like and how I faced him as a child. When I told my parents, they took it as a dream. However, I knew better. From the moment that I encountered that demon, my life was never the same. As a child, I suffered numerous attacks by men. I was never ever safe again. I suffered continuously. I was molested as a child by a cousin who is now a pastor in my home town. As a teen-ager I still encountered the same things, including numerous attempted rape attacks. As a young woman, I began to rebel against those attacks and when Satan sent another demonic force into my life, I fell into the belief that I was born gay. I was a practicing lesbian for approximately 5 years, including moving to another state and separating myself from my family to live that lifestyle.

While there, I became born again, receiving Jesus Christ into my life. I also received a call to ministry. It was the most joyous time, to feel the love of God. I was so eager to live, eat, breathe the word of God. I also was the first female to be ordained into my family---which is a family of ministers. My father and uncles are all pastors. Three years after being ordained, I began to discern darkness around me and I even began to discern that same darkness around others also. My fear of what was going on in my life had left me stagnant. I was not growing in the Lord and I maintained an overwhelming feeling of being lethargic.

My nights were terrible. I could barely sleep. I would wake up in the night exhausted, go to the refrigerator and eat. I was no longer reading the bible or praying. I was living a lie and I knew that all the battles I faced as a child and an adult were minimal compared to what I was going through spiritually. At this point in my life, I contacted Pam for counseling. I felt like soon I would be exposed for the nominal Christian that I was. I knew that I was faking it, and that my anointing seemed as though it was gone. Pam was very patient with me even though I was wavering. I knew that I should resign from the Eastern Stars cult, but I just couldn't seem to send in my letter of resignation and I was continuing to discuss the matter and receive counsel from women who were steeped in the Eastern Stars. Furthermore, I booked a flight to New York, but then because of job responsibilities, I had to cancel.

Pam and I entered into a relatively extensive email counseling communication. She assessed my problem and advised me that the root cause of my present bondage was centered in the witchcraft demon in collaboration with a religious demon because of my involvement in the Masonic lodge. She also assessed that I was being oppressed by an incubus demon, a demon that specializes in sexual lust with either men and/or women. She advised me that the reason why I was so exhausted was because the incubus demon was causing my own spirit to travel to the men that I hated to try to destroy them.

Then one day, a rather strange thing happened. I began to cry and could not stop. It frightened me, so I called Pam late one evening. She counseled and prayed for me for about an hour. She advised me that the Holy Spirit was causing me to repent and that this was a "good thing" and nothing to be afraid of. As I have learned from Pam, repentance is the first key to deliverance. Shortly thereafter, another supernatural thing occurred. All of a sudden, I knew in my head who the demons were that were tormenting my life. I received three names: Metosite, Xastur and Jamia. This was extremely unsettling because we both looked these names up on the web, only to find out that these are actually the names of demons. In the short of it, Metosite was the witchcraft demon,Xastur the religious spirit and Jamia was the incubus spirit, the sexual predator and hater of men.

By now, I was really frightened. I even found a picture of Jamia. She looked like a cross between a cat and a bear, very voluptuous looking, with a long tail. Pam continued to urge me to send in my resignation to the Eastern

Stars and I continued to procrastinate. This strengthened Jamia which seduced me into sexual sin. It seemed that a force had control of my will, and I could not submit my resignation. However, Pam was there for me, one of the saints the Lord used to help to restore me." 4

Sophie eventually did submit her resignation to the lodge and her complete deliverance is among the testimonials in the Appendix. The torment inflicted upon professing Christians who practice freemasonry is similarly akin to the torment experienced by African converts to Christianity. Simply put, the tribal gods or demons become outraged. Both a case study and the testimony of an African who I have called "Jacque" are also in the Appendix. My experience has been that the tribal demons will vex and harass anyone in whom they dwell who "take them to church." The warfare is truly deep when the captive is also inflicted with a religious demon whose mission is to go to church out of its own lust for counterfeit worship. There have been times when out of necessity, I have had to require African captives not to do anything "religious" until I can cast out the witchcraft demon.

Moreover, the key factor to remember about the enemy's attack on Christians who believe in the power gifts of faith, healing and miracles is that the religious demon will often employ apparently contradictory strategies against the gifts of the Holy Ghost. For example, on one hand, the very same demon will vehemently cause its professing Christian targets to completely deny the power gifts while simultaneously employing an apparently contradictory strategy with Charismatics. Since faith cannot really be explained or "proved," when a healer attempts to authenticate a healing or a miracle, the door is opened to the religious demon's counterattack with the various rational or natural explanations of doctors and scientists.

This reality was strongly impressed upon me, as I recently watched a TV show of a recurrent medical series called "House." In this particular episode, while a young minister "who talked with God" was hospitalized for an unknown medical condition, he laid his hands on a cancer patient whom he apparently healed. As the cancer patient's hope and faith was increased, the doctors sought to disprove an apparently divine intervention. Yet to the doctor's dismay, Xrays clearly showed that the patient's tumors had significantly decreased in size. Yet determined to disprove divine healing, ---supposedly so as to protect the terminally ill patient from false hope,--- the doctor discovered that the young minister had herpes. Well known in the medical community that herpes can temporarily decrease the size of tumors, the doctors seemed vindicated with their own medical rationalization.

Yet, the episode ended with a subliminal suggestion that although faith and hope itself may prove spiritually beneficial to the coping skills of the terminally ill, divine healing itself is really non-existent---- yet another message to an unsuspecting world that falls in line with the underhanded attack of the spirit of the Antichrist against the gifts of the Holy Ghost, in particular, and the Lordship of Jesus Christ, in general. This TV episode is a pertinent example of how the religious demon employs his strategies and wiles so as to surreptitiously discredit divine healing. Consequently, I personally believe that the biggest mistake a bona fide faith healer can make is to try to prove, defend or justify God for anything, healing included. The religious demon will certainly capitalize upon our errors in wisdom and in judgment. In order to mock Jesus , the religious demon's goal is to do so by causing one of His disciples to look foolish, once the world thinks it has found its "rational explanation."

I demystify the faith healing issue with a strategy of my own. By never stooping to search for evidence to prove to a skeptic that a miraculous manifestation has transpired on anyone on whom I have either cast a demon from, prayed for or laid my hands upon, I stay out of the argument. I leave the proving to the Lord and to the captive as I go about my Savior's business, heeding His commands to lay my hands upon the sick and to cast out devils. Healing and recovery belongs to the Lord Himself. Since I believe in healing, I do not give the enemy place by trying to prove anything to a skeptic. I simply preach the gospel, in season and out of season. God's word will not return to Him void but it will accomplish what the Lord Himself intends. His intention is to heal the sick and to set the captives free, whether the world believes He can do it or not.

Yet another way that the religious demon maneuvers against the gifts of the Spirit is to distort a true gift. To illustrate with my own gift of healing, on my website is a picture of me, taken on the day that I preached my trial sermon, on October 25, 1981. Standing beside me on my left hand side is a huge head of a gargoyle,---approximately two feet long--- outlined in green, in a three quarter pose, the nose slightly turned in my direction. It also has a very large ear. With its green eyebrow crossing my entire left hand, today I understand why my healing gift has been distorted for almost 25 years. During the course of writing this book, a revelation came to me that as long as I held a false belief, that green eyebrow of a demon assigned to me was allowed to touch my hand.

Since I have known that I am called to heal, I went forth and laid hands on the terminally ill for the first 15 years of my ministry. People would live longer than their projected date of death. For example, if they were given a few days to live, some have lived as long as two years or more. However, I was never satisfied with that because I knew that their healing should have been complete and enduring and that when they eventually died, it should not have been from the very same disease that I had laid hands upon them to heal. Furthermore, I am ambidextrous, but when I lay hands on people, I use my left hand. I believe that the demon's eyebrow was over my hand in 1981 so as to distort my healing ministry once I got on the Lord's side after being suddenly snatched away from witchcraft. Yet even after I was saved, I myself created a doorway for this demon to touch my healing hand by not renouncing certain occult powers that remained.

I must admit that early on in my Christian walk, I ignorantly brought various occult practices into the Lord's house from my "New Age Days", due to my own spiritual blindness to the truth and the church's lack of supernatural power and discernment. The truth is that ever since I was a medium in 1974, I had the power to pull pain from anyone's body and this power continued into Christiandom until I recently renounced it. As the years passed, I noticed that healing seemed to be much more lasting if I simply prayed without touching or if I spoke healing into a person's life by a word of knowledge. But once I laid my hands on someone, even though healing came, for some reason unknown to me in those days , the healing did not last.

Even though I was not fully conscious of the problem, since I am led by the Holy Ghost, I simply stopped laying hands on people about 10 years ago without a conscious or rational cause. The last time I laid hands was upon a dying ferret just before Thanksgiving of 2005. As limp and near death Gismo was dropped into my hands, he was instantly healed and he leaped across the room as was his fashion. However, his life was short-lived, as his healing lasted for only 6 months and he just died a few weeks ago as I write this.

Already 7 years old, the natural lifespan of a ferret, his healing probably was not distorted and his owner is rather thankful for the increase of 6 months to Gismo's lifespan.

Once I began to cast out demons, I reasoned that this power to touch and remove pain was like a thermometer, a discernment for recognizing the presence of demons. Writing this book humbled me to know that it was not. Today I realize that it was an old, counterfeit gift that I acquired three years BEFORE I was saved. The truth has set me free to heal and cast out devils as never before. Therefore, this book is a testimony of how submission to the truth has prepared me to 'go forth' in the supernatural power of Jesus Christ and perform exploits that prove He is resurrected. I need not take the pain from anyone into my hands any longer. The Lord has taken our pain into His own body 2000 years ago!!!!

ENDNOTES

1. War on the Saints, pg. 218, 9th edition
2. Ibid, abridged edition, pg. 113
3. Rebecca Brown MD, "He Came To Set the Captives Free," Whitaker House, 1992, pg. 143
4. Sophie's Testimony: This captive was one of my clients who was successfully delivered from a witchcraft spirit as a result of her involvement in the African American branch of freemasonry for women, called "the Eastern Stars."

Freemasonry in the church is yet another face of the religious demon that has a seat in countless organized churches. Although the spirit of Jezebel, the organized church and the Masonic Lodge are not addressed in this chapter, I suggest that you read a rather understandable and concise teaching from an article on the internet. The website address is:

http://www.saintsalive.com/freemasonry/fmwitchcraft.htm

Excerpt: "The Masonic temple is a temple of Witchcraft! There can be little doubt about that. Veiled within its symbols are the deities and even the working tools of Witchcraft! As has been shown, the square and compasses are representations of the generative organs— the "sacred altar" of Witchcraft! The blazing star at the center of the lodge is the Witch's pentagram, symbol of the god of Satanism, Set! The Letter "G" stands for generativity, sexual potency."

Chapter 8 Mental Disorders and the Cosmic Powers

Countless cases of false mysticism have existed throughout biblical and religious history---an idolatry of camouflaged witchcraft and sorcery that has destroyed spiritual seekers for a lack of knowledge and have rendered some of them mentally incompetent and even reprobate, apparently doomed to damnation. (Hosea 6:4) The massive New Age Movement, a potpourri of doctrines which very often sound "Christian" are exalted under the guise of holistic health teachings or "cosmic growth", when in reality they are idolatrous Hindu practices that have rendered some professing Christians with mental health disorders. (Prepare For War, pg. 189)

Most certainly, I myself could have lost my mind. With objects appearing, disappearing and standing in mid air through telekinesis, with mediumistic demons stepping in and out of my body, overriding my own strong will, the cosmic power assigned to me clearly tried unsuccessfully to disorient me and render my mind useless. Such was also the case of the Babylonian mystic and king, Nebuchadnezzar. His idolatry mixed with self exaltation and pride caused this Babylonian king to be turned over to a mentally ill mind--- driven from men, feeding on grass like oxen, growing hair like eagles feathers,--in short, his mental understanding was taken from him for 7 years until he repented. (Daniel 4:31-37)

Likewise, one of the most baffling situations that I have faced in working with captives who are both mentally ill and religious is in trying to find the right moment to rightly divide the word to them, bring them to repentance and finally, to present the gospel in a manner that is causative to their understanding of the resurrection. To be capable of arousing their faith to believe in Jesus Christ of Nazareth and not some mythological being consistent with their own warped imagination have been truly a challenge. For example, a client who I refer to as "Sam" has suffered with Obsessive Compulsive Disorder (OCD) for more than two decades. Sam has come to various church altars on countless occasions, repeated the sinners prayer even more times, to no spiritual avail. I have also worked with mentally ill chemical abusers, captives to Borderline Personality Disorder and Paranoid Delusional Disorder with the same results.

Pre-deliverance counseling with a mentally ill captive has many built in challenges and difficulties that naturally hinder the process of being broken or crucified with Christ. Since a key to brokenness is the ability to repent and to accept full responsibility for one's circumstances, Jezebelian types are among the most difficult captives to bring to the cross. Various degrees of mental illness causes the captive to more or less externalize his problems, whether they be natural or demonic and so it is difficult for him to accept blame in general, and to repent, in particular.

Moreover, the mentally compromised captive has a tendency to experience his internal processes as though they are occurring "outside of himself." For example, the voices that he hears are not demons "inside" of him, but the voices of his next door neighbors, of those who pass by him on the street. Or his circumstances are such as they are because an enemy has put a curse on him. So projection becomes blame where the captive very naturally feels that his life for good or for evil is determined by "outside" forces. Those who do not accept responsibility for themselves are natural victims. Therefore, it is extremely difficult to motivate the mentally challenged to overcome passivity and to prepare them for battle.

Furthermore, in each pre-deliverance situation, targeting those times when the mind of a passive, victimized captive is coherent and logical enough to be saved has been preceded by at least a six month painstaking process of assisting the captive to cast down his imaginations and every thought that has rebelled against the truth about the gospel of Jesus Christ. (II Corinthians 10:4,5) Then there are those instances where the captive was not my professional client but a member of my church, whom I have come to know and serve for many years without observing any spiritual fruit that would suggest that they are "born again." As a pastor, I have worked closely with a MICA captive for 15 years and 8 years with a captive with an extensive mental health history, diagnosed as Borderline Personality Disorder (BPD).

There have been others that I have pastored for shorter lengths of time who had lengthy mental health histories. In spite of the differences in diagnoses, I have found that there is one factor they all have in common. They love religion---worship (particularly singing and music), bible study, prayer, even speaking in tongues, yet they are ever learning but never coming to a knowledge of the truth, professors of faith who have a form of godliness that deny the power thereof. (II Timothy 3:5) They also will not tolerate even the mildest correction, and will become menacing and even dangerous if their self concept is in any way challenged. As Paul admonished Timothy, in all but one case, I have had to turn away:

> "But know this, that in the last days perilous times will come: for men will be lovers of themselves, lovers of money, boasters, proud, blasphemers, disobedient to parents, unthankful, unholy, unloving, unforgiving, slanderers, without self-control, brutal, despisers of good, traitors, headstrong, haughty, lovers of pleasure rather than lovers of God, having a form of godliness but denying its power. And from such people turn away! For of this sort are those who creep into households and make captives of gullible women loaded down with sins, led away by various lusts, always learning and never come to the knowledge of the truth. Now as Jannes and Jambres resisted Moses, so do these also resist the truth: men of corrupt minds, reprobate concerning the faith; but they will progress no further, for their folly will be manifest to all, as theirs also was." (II Timothy 3: 1-9)

As 15 years of my 27 years in Christian services was as a pastor, it took me several years to learn how to "know them by their fruit." In "To Curse the Root", I believe that I have clearly defined fruit from a spiritual perspective:

> "Jesus said that we shall know them by their fruit. Therefore, as a deliverance counselor, you should search for the fruit and build upon it. When attempting to consider what fruit actually is, I can reveal to you what fruit is not. It is not church attendance, tithing, or praise and worship. It is not even going from door to door to witness, casting out devils, the power

gifts, street ministry or even winning souls. How could these things be 'fruit', when Jesus Himself declared that there will be those who have cast out devils, those who have said, 'Lord, Lord', and He will say that He did not know them." In other words, these people that Jesus is referring to were worshipers. Apparently they were not worshiping in spirit and in truth. They were probably worshiping in soul and in deception. It seems that soulish worship does not count with the Lord---AT All!!! (To Curse the Root, pg. 356) 1

Moreover, I define fruit as the power of the resurrection in a person's life---the demonstration in a believer's life that Jesus Christ is alive. Our faith in the resurrection is a demonstration of the power of the resurrection. Therefore, to bare fruit, is to consistently live by faith, in a manner that demonstrates that Jesus Christ is no longer in the tomb. When I consider various captives that I have had to turn away from for different reasons, the most outstanding commonality is that each person could not and/or would not demonstrate in their lives that Jesus Christ has overcome death.

George is one of those persons. His profile is presented in the Appendix of "To Curse the Root." 2 (pgs.360-367) In the next to the last line of the book, on page 367, I wrote in reference to George: "He is now saved.   What is impossible with men is possible with God." Unfortunately, circumstances that occurred after the completion of the book confirmed   that without a doubt, the religious demon successfully deceived me into making a false assumption. On New Years Day, George once again proved that he is without fruit. Having heard the gospel rather consistently for almost two decades, anyone who would come to church on a major holiday and without provocation, bring in a New Year by standing up in the congregation and testifying to a lie before the saints assembled could not possibly be saved.

George's testimony concerned how he had recently overcome a temptation to use drugs by the blood of the Lamb. It was a lengthy testimony, specifically detailed with how he walked into his sister's apartment to find a table full of all kinds of drugs and how the Spirit of God prepared a way of escape for him. George stood in front of the congregation, praising Jesus for his continued sobriety. Nevertheless, at the strike of the New Year, George was exposed to be a liar. Uncovered on the spot by an ice storm, George had been successful throughout the holidays to convince us all that he was consistently headed toward celebrating two years of sobriety. Since the roads were too hazardous to drive, particularly on New Years Eve, we all bedded down in the building. George had not brought his drugs with him to our service, expecting a ride home that evening, and so he missed his next dose of drugs. Consequently, George went into obvious withdrawal from heroin on New Years Day, hospitalized for detox by January 2!

I had been in ministry about 8 years when George joined one of the first churches that I pastored. A chronic drug abuser with a religious background in cults and Afro-centric non-Christian religions, George had grown to love Christian worship, particularly gospel music. Because of his strong, melodic baritone voice, George found favor in the African American churches, receiving several invitations   to sing   solos. With this qualification in mind, I began to perceive George as a ministerial asset when he was sober and so I did what I could to enhance his quality of life toward maximizing his recovery from addiction to drugs of all kinds. In fact,   I rented a room to him in the parsonage which he shared within the separate living quarters with two other similarly situated men in recovery.

For years I suspected that George had a religious demon, perhaps even the spirit of Jezebel. Drug abuse falls under the category of sorcery, with the original word for sorcery being connected to pharmacy or hallucinatory substances that produce euphoria. Sexual deviance is also compatible with the lustful facet of the Jezebelian demon. George has remained under the influence of both drugs and sexual perversion for about 50 years. Having committed murder in his youth, George also falls under a curse for the breaking of the the 10 commandments in "thou shalt not kill," serving 13 years for murder and an additional 5 years for stabbing a woman in an alleged act of self defense.

Detached from any genuine commitment to becoming completely drug free, attending church, tithing and other facets of religion became his antiseptic facade of righteousness. Since I've known him, George has kept his feet in two worlds: the underworld of drugs and sex and the church world of emotional and euphoric worship. Soft spoken and generous to a fault, he still remained a very dangerous man.

In terms of an extreme instance where my own life could have been in serious jeopardy, I believe that I was the next intended victim of this murderous demon within George that used his inebriated state to stab another woman. On a day that I will never forget, George had become extremely disturbed with me for correcting him about the mess he made in the communal kitchen of the parsonage. I found him in the kitchen frying pork chops, with grease and flour splattered everywhere. When I turned away and walked next door to the church office, a few minutes later I heard banging noises, with George screaming out obscenities.

So I went back door, quietly entered the flat , and to my amazement, George was alone, directing those obscenities in the direction of my office behind the thin wall. It was a chilling feeling to realize that he was railing at me for correcting him. Slipping out the back un-noticed, the next morning I caught George while sober and asked him to move. He moved out later that day. A few days later, a woman was stabbed and George was sent to prison for five years. Even so, he persisted to hold on to my pastorate by persuading the chaplain of the prison to invite me there to preach. I ended up preaching at that prison on a regular basis for the next eight years. When George was released from prison, he moved into the apartment that I found and furnished for him around the corner from our church, becoming an active member of Morning Glory in Saratoga.

Once a member, George became a literal thorn in my side for the next eight years. A sheer contradiction to everything my ministry stood for, his frequent relapses into drug abuse and his continued religiosity whether drunk or sober was a constant irritant to my patience. Proud to be known in the streets and alley ways of the city as "Preacher Man," George could be witnessed standing on the street corners, drunk as a skunk, praying and laying hands on the sick or preaching Jesus to the lost who were in far better shape than he was.

In cases of this kind, the hidden motive of the religious demon is to shame Christ. George served as a visual message to drug abusers in the city that they are better off with AA then following George to church and worshiping George's Jesus. Moreover, when addicts seeking recovery did come to our fellowship, George would ultimately draw them back into drug abuse or at least bum cigarettes from them. My soul was frequently tormented by George's consistent presence.

Several years ago, I received a revelation in the spirit that George and my ex-husband Richard were sent to me by a religious demon to destroy my ministry. It took years for this word concerning Richard to be confirmed as from the Lord. (More on this subject is presented in the chapter on demonic soul ties.) I reasoned that a word from the Lord would be infallible, complete truth on all counts. Therefore, in the trying of the spirits, I waited to see if this word would be confirmed concerning George, and it was---, eight years to the date of his release to my pastorate from prison. Notwithstanding, the religious demon put on a commendable performance of repentance to cause me to believe that George had finally gotten saved after 14 years of active church attendance:

> "As is his manner when sober, George brought a resident of the recovery program that he attended to church. I could see that this was a work of George's religious flesh. The man was in no way seeking after the Lord but simply was coming to church to be entertained. Anyway, back at the residence, George began to feel very disdainful and critical toward this man. Apparently, the man was a buffoon, one who likes to tell raucous jokes in his attention seeking effort among his peers. So the day before George got saved, he called me on the phone. 'Pastor, I just can't stand Victor. He is such a busybody, running his mouth like a fool. He is always up in people's business. I don't get in people's business. I mind my business. Pastor, I just felt like walking up to Victor today, and smashing glass all in his face. I just wanted to tear his face off." 2

Since I rebuked George very strongly for his evil and murderous thoughts,--- against a man he had brought to church to be saved, no less--- it appeared that my piercing words had penetrated George's soul like a knife. For the first time in his life, he could literally feel his own evil. When George could find no rest in his soul after my cutting rebuke, he telephoned me with tears and sobs imploring me to help him take his anguished, sinful nature to the cross. Consequently, I wrongfully assumed that he had repented with godly sorrow and that after being "churched" for more than a decade, George had finally become born again.

However, it did not happen. In retrospect, the key word is "godly"sorrow or grief toward God for our sinful nature being the reason for the Lord's separation from His father. This instance clarifies for me that being horrified over one's sinful nature alone does not not complete the kind of repentance that brings forth a rebirth of the human spirit. Godly sorrow is a heartfelt appreciation, a divine grief over what Jesus Christ endured for the sake of a sinner. Those with a Jezebel spirit cannot touch divine brokenness for Jesus' sake. The spirit of the Anti-Christ restrains them.

Like George, there have been others in my pastorate who appeared to possess a strong desire to come to Jesus, yet their seeking never seemed to come to fruition, which in my estimation is a contradiction of "whosoever will, let him come." 3 Hattie Mae was of this sort. Diagnosed as borderline personality disorder (BPD) by the mental health system, Hattie Mae was institutionalized for several years in her youth and young adulthood. Once released to independent living as an active participation in an on-going community mental health network of services, Hattie Mae soon became "religious" and began to attend a local Christian cult where she believed herself to be saved. During those years, she overcame cocaine usage and promiscuity, thereby assuming that she was saved. Once she joined the Jehovah Witnesses, Hattie Mae became extremely legalistic and paranoid relative to the book of Revelation and the end of the world.

Consistent with her mental health diagnosis, too innumerable to mention here are instances where Hattie Mae's very obvious bitterness and hatred toward God's people became evident. Her special brand of animosity against other professing Christians served as a clear indication of her unsaved condition, for we know that we have passed from death to life because we love the brethren. (I John3:14) For example, a conservative estimate of the number of times that Hattie Mae left Morning Glory Church over an 12 year membership because of interpersonal conflicts with myself or other church members would be about 24 times---an average of twice a year. Since she lived close to the church, she would return without apology, as if there had been no interruption of fellowship.

Though extremely crippled emotionally, at times Hattie Mae displayed a strong desire to give material things to various church members. Each such gesture was exposed to be a work of the flesh, motivated by a desire to "appear Christian. The likes and dislikes of her flesh and the self satisfaction engendered by pride in the fact that she had something to give that others needed was self gratifying. On a rare occasion, Hattie Mae would display an overstated vivacity and an awkward spontaneity,--- a short-lived enthusiasm overshadowed each time by discouragement, anger and even hatred.

In one very shameful situation, Hattie Mae developed a jealousy that bordered on pure hatred for a next door neighbor confined to crutches. A verbal confrontation ensued between them and Hattie Mae called me in a rage. I immediately got in my car and drove to her home, only to find her standing on the steps of her disabled neighbor's building . With her fists clenched, lips trembling, I looked into the face of the most hideous expression of evil that I have personally observed on any human being. Two onlookers had to literally restrain Hattie Mae from attacking a crippled person. With absolutely no concern for the consequences of her actions, her desire to attack this person was stronger than her fear of being arrested for assault. Over the years, I found Hattie Mae's mean and bitter spirit extremely distasteful, but as her pastor, I can look back with confidence that I walked in the spirit and did not fulfill the lust of my flesh by yielding to my aversion to her wearisome, narrow-minded, often loquacious personality.

I have not known why, but I have discerned in my spirit that I was not to attempt to cast out demons from Hattie Mae and from others similarly affected and so I held in check my inclination to confront Hattie Mae's demons until what appeared to be an emergency. Consistent with the behavior of the religiosity of mentally illness is for the captive to consider that the taking of medication is a weakness that is not consistent with being a charismatic believer. Hattie Mae was no exception, as she often unsuccessfully tried to detox herself , a situation that uncovered the evil in her heart on each failed attempt.

Therefore, since I knew that Hattie Mae had not taken her medication for a few weeks, I was not surprised to receive her phone call. On this particular occasion, Hattie May expressed sheer panic over her desire to strangle her pet rabbit. She was almost completely out of control. In spite of her mental illness and her self prescribed usage of her medications in the past, Hattie Mae had always been functional. In other words, she was able to "carry on" and avoid being hospitalized. She was neither delusional nor psychotic. Begging me to "do something" to help her, I spoke to her demons and commanded them to come out in Jesus Name."

Almost immediately, Hattie Mae was able to calm down and restrain herself from strangling her rabbit and for a week or so, her condition seemed much improved. About a week later, Hattie Mae was hospitalized for a chronic liver condition and she called me from her hospital bed close to midnight. When she called, I was in the middle of a crisis with another church member and I was rather wearied when I picked up the telephone. I learned the next day that Hattie Mae " did not like the tone of my voice." Since I did not have a chance to visit her in the hospital because she was only kept overnight, I anticipated trouble. Acutely aware that Hattie Mae's personality disorder coupled with her religiosity would combine to fortify her existing armor of self righteousness, I planned a home visit as soon as was conceivably possible, as I had to commute from my home in Albany to Norwich, a 110 mile trip one way.

It had been my pastoral experience with Hattie Mae that the slightest correction, perceived neglect or absence of special recognition would compel her to project blame and to strike out against me with various accusations. Since her self righteousness prevented her from accepting personal blame in any situation that arose, Hattie Mae consistently viewed herself to be the one that others have abused and victimized. Therefore, if I didn't take immediate action to do a home visit, I knew that I would suffer the consequences.

The night before my home visit to Hattie Mae's house , I had an alarming dream where I saw Hattie Mae attack me, try to kill me and I hit her over the head with a glass bottle. In the dream, I stood over her unconscious body, wondering if I had killed her. Upon my arrival at Hattie Mae's dwelling, she almost successfully hid the fact that her contempt for me had compounded overnight. Actually, she put up a concerted effort to be gracious and on some level, appeared glad to see me. Since Hattie Mae is one who takes great stock in dreams, as I was about to leave her apartment, I was led to share my early morning dream with her. To my amazement, she came forth with what was hidden in her heart. Once she heard my dream, Hattie Mae blurt out that she believed that I wanted to kill her.

Hattie Mae explained by reminding me of the fact that she had named Morning Glory in Norwich New York as her sole beneficiary in her will and that she now believed that I was planning to murder her to obtain the inheritance of $30,000 for the church. Once her suspicions were revealed, no amount of reasoning from anyone could change her mind. She wholeheartedly believed that I intended to kill her and knowing Hattie Mae, I anticipated that she was preparing a counterattack.

This is a time of great danger for a counselor or a pastor because the captive is subject to take physical action against you as a perceived enemy. The Lord has continued to bless me as I have walked through the valley of the shadow of death with quite a few people that I have either counseled professionally or pastored. In this particular case, Hattie Mae was hospitalized again within a few days, this time for paranoid delusions. The next time I spoke with Hattie Mae and her sanity had returned, she reported that she had observed a piece of paper stand up on the floor, turn into a little "paper man" and walk toward her.

In retrospect, I believe that after I confronted her demons to keep her from strangling her rabbit, Hattie Mae's mental health condition declined. Although she speaks in a tongue, it is evident to me that her condition worsened because in spite of her consistent church attendance, she did not get saved. Once her mental health improved with medication, she returned to the church, and the same religious patterns continued until I was no longer the pastor of Morning Glory and I lost contact with Hattie Mae. In cases of this kind, in practically every instance a mental health history combined with an involvement in idolatrous practices are the common variables. Furthermore, the manifestations have a supernatural bent of clairvoyance and clair-audience,---seeing things that others don't see and hearing things that others don't hear. One hundred years ago, I believe that Sister Lewis astutely described the condition of most mental health captives with backgrounds in the occult:

> " A very little consideration of the characteristics of those drawn into abnormal supernatural experiences, will bear out this diagnosis. The invariable effect upon such believers is the weakening of the mental force, the reasoning and judging power; a weakening in moral force and will and ofttimes a haunting sense of fear---fear of the future, fear of persons so that they cannot bear to hear them spoken of, or to speak to them; and a gradual general weakening of the physical frame. In time there comes an impatience---manifestly 'nervous' and not moral---and restlessness, and often an involuntary twitching action of the nerves." (War on the Saints, 9th edition, pg. 178)" 4

This particular viewpoint brings to my remembrance some rather uniques cases. Sam is a man in his 50's, raised into young adulthood as a Christian Scientist, both deceased parents remained steadfast followers to this Christian cult for their entire lifetimes. I believe that Sam and his only sibling---a sister—were cursed by the commitment of their parents to such a blasphemous religion. Rebelling against Christian Science in young adulthood, Sam dabbled in practically every New Age practice, including but not limited to astrology, transcendental meditation, crystals and pyramids.

It was difficult to ascertain in counseling whether the mental health problems preceded Sam's delving into the occult, as the time lines were close enough to have been concurrent. It could have been that the mental health problems led to seeking occult subjects, or vice versa. Even so, Sam's sister was reported to have had no occult involvement, yet like her brother, she too suffered from a milder version of obsessive compulsive disorder (OCD). A collector of anything in print,---newspapers, magazines and such,--- Sam's sister continues to create a fire hazard in her apartment because of the piles and stacks of paper that she literally cannot discard as rubbish.

Notwithstanding, Sam's manifestation of OCD is equally chronic yet much more severe than his sister's manifestation of this disorder. For more than two decades, every day of his life and several times a day, Sam sees dark shadows over everything---delusions and illusions that he believes to be human excrement. As such, he has developed various rituals to deal with this problem that include elaborate washings. Then on the other hand, he is afraid of the shower and so his infrequent bathing causes unsanitary conditions--- a foul, unclean odor is ever present. A professional patient, counseling for Sam was a way of life as well as going from church to church. In me, he could simultaneously indulge both his need to be a patient and his religiosity as a professing Christian.

After six months of intensive work, I confronted Sam's belief that his problems occurred as a result of a black man cursing him with an evil eye when Sam was about 30 years old. The two men had been best friends and colleagues on Sam's last and only job until "something happened" that Sam could not really explain. Shortly thereafter, Sam believed that the first signs of OCD were manifested and so he blamed the black man for putting a spell on him. During the course of counseling that lasted 6 months, I was able to trace Sam's problems back to factors that preceded this incident with the black man by more than 10 years. For example, Sam himself had been practicing the occult since he was in his late teens. According to Sister Penn-Lewis, lying spirits suggest causes and solutions to keep the captive bound:

> "They attack a person because they are in possession, but make him think and believe it to be an indirect attack, ie., through another person. The blame is placed on the man himself or someone else, or on anything but the true cause, so that the intruder may not be discovered and expelled. It is therefore important that all 'excuses' should be examined, i.e., the 'reasons' for such and such an unexplainable manifestation. The causes should always be gone into, for by believing a wrong interpretation of the manifestation, more ground is given to the lying spirits. The believer may be refusing ground on the one hand, and giving new ground on the other, unless he examines all the suggestions which come to his mind concerning his condition". (War on the Saints, 9th edition, pg. 176) 4

After exploring and exhausting every plausible cause for six months, I could see that counseling was ineffective primarily because Sam was not really a believer. He was merely "religious."So as an unregenerate soul, Sam remained adamant against any kind of spiritual change that required him to exert his own will power. Furthermore, it became evident to me that his mental health disorder was closely connected to the beliefs and practices of Christian Science. For example, Christian Scientists believe that both sin and death are illusions.

Following this train of thought, the Christian belief that Jesus died on the cross for sin is considered to be an illusion by Christian Scientists. I suspect that since Sam continues to "take the Christian Science demons to church", the religious demon is outraged. Feeling "betrayed," the demons are tormenting Sam because he rebelled against the fact that his parents had dedicated him to Christian Science from childhood. Therefore, his delusions and illusions are sent by the religious demon to mock and torment him for forcing them to attend traditional churches. This revelation brought a momentary relief so that Sam began to see a tangible reason for his troubles, but it was short lived.

The overriding stumbling block is that Sam could not apply any new revelation to his life because he internalized it as one who hears the word and either could not or would not do what it takes to mobilize its implications for himself. In fact, he upheld his own ideas as to the onset and the cause of his disorder, and no amount of evidence or reasoning could change his rather rigid point of view. Adamant and unyielding, Sam stubbornly refused to give up the notion that a black man had cursed him. Moreover, Sam was looking for the magic wand of Christianity to release him from his demons without making any personal effort to actively take part in spiritual warfare by standing "and having done all to stand, stand therefore!" (Ephesians 6:13,14)

I continued to adjust my procedures to accommodate his evasiveness and blatant laziness about completing required weekly assignments. However, once I insisted that he complete the work, Sam's response was "I don't have to do any weekly assignments with my psychiatrist." When he left a message on my answering machine stating that he had to reschedule because he was taking care of a neighbor's dog, I did not return his call. Two years have now passed, and I have not heard from Sam again.

Sam case is noteworthy because like others, he had been to many church altars countless times to be saved, recited the sinners prayer repeatedly, yet still could not stop himself from cursing God on a daily basis. The Jezebel spirit was in him so strong, that he could not read the bible out loud without coughing and even gagging. Although I remained convinced that he was being blocked from salvation and that his history with Christian Science as well as with the occult were the root causes of his dilemma, I also realized that I could not expect Sam to have any vital interest in my revelations as long as he continued to cling to his own particular beliefs and solutions.

I could have pursued Sam's case because he always looked forward to our sessions. A lonely person, I could feel his affection growing toward me and if I did nothing else, I became a caring human contact, concerned for and dedicated to his well being. Nevertheless, since my counseling is rather challenging, I realized that it was useless to continue with Sam as long as he persists to pursue his own way of resolving his situation. After all, he had made adjustments over a prolonged period: going from church to church, calling prayer lines at crucial moments for relief, counseling with his psychiatrist, taking his medication, and most important, engaging in his washing rituals. If I couldn't use the Name of Jesus Christ to magically deliver him with no effort of his own required, then in Sam's mind, I had no real solutions.

To work with captives like Sam takes time. The more entangled and the more barricaded a captive is, the more time is required. Such is also the case of Eric—a manifestation of paranoid delusional disorder. Sam's OCD was definitely a challenge but I must admit that Eric has been my most difficult case thus far. After six months of intensive work with Eric, I came to realize that no amount of pre-deliverance counseling would work. The demons have Eric so bound that they use his own passivity as a roadblock to hinder his preparation for deliverance. Every day, countless times a day, Eric hears voices that blaspheme, call him names, predict his death. When benign, "the voices" hold conversations with him and successfully direct and order his steps as though they were God.

Unlike Sam, Eric has a genuine desire to be in the kingdom, to see souls saved, and to go to heaven, yet like Sam, he too has bowed down at to too many different altars and repeated the sinners prayer countless times. Not really understanding repentance and resurrection, I thought that this was the cause. However, I myself have rightly divided the word to him and brought him to the cross on four occasions. I believe that Eric understands both repentance and resurrection and that he has faith to believe, and yet no fruit of salvation has yet been manifested to my satisfaction. Therefore, I began to seek the Lord very strongly on his behalf. I simply could not understand how Satan would be allowed to block Eric from basking in the light and truth of the glorious gospel of Jesus Christ. I needed to know how this would be possible. Consequently , I searched the scriptures to try to understand if there is any justifiable reason why captives such as Eric and others continue to seek Jesus yet do not seem to find Him.

The two most outstanding cases of mental illness in the bible is that of Nubuchadnezzar and the madman of Gedare. Even the mentally ill idolatrous Babylonian King ultimately bowed to and believed on the Father God. Since the The Lord's invitation is to those who are in the highways and the byways and He is absolutely no respector of persons, a correct division of the scriptures supports the belief that the Lord desires that ALL be saved. In truth, I could find no legitimate explanation, other than the scripture which refers to the prey of the mighty and the "lawfully" captive. Yet, even if there is an understandable cause, the Lord promised through Isaiah that "even the captives of the mighty shall be taken away and the prey of the terrible shall be delivered, for I will contend with him who contends with you and I will save your children." (Isaiah 49:25)

Without a doubt, the "mighty" and the "terrible" is referring to Satan in general, and I believe to the spirit of Jezebel in particular. The case of Elaine as presented in Dr. Rebecca Brown's first book is a salient example of how the witchcraft demon will put up a formidable fight to hold on to one it believes to belong to it by covenant rights. I don't know if Elaine had a mental health history, however for seventeen years, she served Satan as a High Priestess. Even in this case, Satan could not control Elaine's free will to believe on Jesus and to become born again. However, the fight to destroy Elaine's Christian experience was a formidable one indeed, a life and death struggle. In the compelling words of Dr. Brown there is a clue:

> "I was in the kitchen fixing dinner when Elaine came under the control of what I thought was a demon. I realized she was in the kitchen when I was stabbed in the back with the large knife I had been using to cut up the meat. I grabbed her hand saying: 'No demon. I bind you in the Name of Jesus. You will give me the knife.' I was surprised to hear a very feminine voice answer me. 'You can't order me around like some demon. I don't have to obey YOU and your stupid commands because I'm not a demon." (pg. 114, 115) 6

This "being" explained itself to be the spirit of a former friend of Elaine's from the witchcraft coven referred to as "Sally",--- a witch with an ability to project her spirit through the supernatural power of astral travel and attack people in the flesh. Considering that demons are liars, I myself doubt if this was actually a human spirit but that it was the work of what I refer to as a cosmic being. Finding myself far out on a spiritual limb here, I take you to the book of Jude and to the book Daniel. In Jude, the believers were warned not to bring a railing accusation against "dignities:"

> "Likewise, also these filthy dreamers defile the flesh, despising dominion, and speak evil of dignities. Yet Michael, the archangel, when contending with the devil he disputed about the body of Moses, durst not bring against him a railing accusation, but said 'the Lord rebuke thee.'"

(Jude: 8-9)

Jude leads me to ask, "Who are "the dignities?" It is clear that they are not earth bound demons that we have the authority to cast out in the Name of Jesus Christ of Nazareth. As Jude reveals, some of these dignities were chained in hell in Noah's time because they abused their power and were sexually intimate with women, who gave birth to mighty men of renown. ((Jude:6 and Genesis 6: 1-6) Are these "mighty men of renown" included among the dignities.? This is a question unanswered by that scripture. However, it is clear that all of these "dignities" are not chained. I suspect that to despise dominion is to treat them as though there were mere "demons." Instead, as did Michael in his dispute over Mose's body, I believe that if we find that there is no demonic manifestation when confronted, we should go to the Lord in prayer and ask Him to rebuke the dignities.

Just as the dignity disputed over the body of Moses, from what I have personally witnessed, the dignities tend to post themselves in the sky, directly above graveyards. Twenty five years ago, the heads only of two dignities were faintly imposed upon some photos that were taken of the sky directly above a graveyard by an amateur photographer: one apparently good dignity and another, an obviously evil one. If you go to my website at www.bewarechristian.com, you will be able to see scanned photographs. Both heads are so huge, that the word "giant" does not apply. From the size of the head, I suspect that the dignity could stand with his right foot in New York and his left foot in Florida.

The good or neutral looking one is in a blue sky at the top of the page and the evil one in red, is at the bottom. The "red picture" had to be rotated sideways so that its face could be seen. It's mouth is wide open, and the discerning will be able to see slight horns on each end of its oblong head. The wide-opened mouth is in the form of a circle, and I myself can see faint fangs inside it, protruding down from the upper gum. These photographs have faded over 25 years, but I myself can see these two heads almost as clearly today as when I first perceived them. PRINCIPALITIES AND POWERS ARE REAL, BELOVED! JESUS CHRIST IS THE LORD OF THE ARMY, WHERE EVERY KNEE, REGARDLESS OF HOW BIG IT IS, BOWS TO HIM!!!!

In this regard, I have often wondered why Jesus had a conversation with the demons called "Legion" who were in possession of the madman of Gedara, much less grant Legion's request to be cast into a herd of pigs. Were these beings among the dignities who had the right to make such a request? I don't know, but its something to think about. Along these lines, we see the rules of authority and protocol relative to dignities and angelic beings in the book of Daniel. Daniel had been in prayer and fasting for three full weeks in order to learn of the fate of the children of Israel when he received an angelic visitation from a being that resembled a man but had aface "as the appearance of lightning." A messenger from the throne of God, a supernatural being informed Daniel of the struggle he had endured in order to bring him a revelation of end times. In the 9th Chapter, Daniel had been visited by a being who identified himself as the angel Gabriel, the very angel who would have a major role in bringing messages to the virgin Mary and to Zechariah. However, in the 10th Chapter, we are not told if this angel is Gabriel. Much wisdom for deliverance is revealed in the angel's words:

> Then said he unto me, Fear not, Daniel: for from the first day that thou
> didst set thine heart to understand, and to chasten thyself before thy God,
> thy words were heard, and I am come for thy words. But the prince of the

kingdom of Persia withstood me one and twenty days: but lo, Michael, one of the chief princes, came to help me; and I remained there with the kings of Persia. Now I am come to make thee understand what shall befall thy people in the latter days; for yet the vision is for many days. (Daniel 10:12-14)

So who is the prince of the kingdom of Persia? I suspect that he is a "dignity" of a higher rank than was the one sent to Daniel but of a lower rank than Michael. I suspect that the only dignity that is of a higher rank than Michael is Satan himself. Otherwise, as recorded in Jude, Michael would not have had to yield to Satan and declare "the Lord rebuke thee." So then what should be our understanding of Paul's letter to the Colossians where he writes concerning the Lord's victory at the cross: "having spoiled principalities and powers, He made a shew of them openly, triumphing over them in it." (Colossians 2:15) I believe that all dignities must bow to Jesus but unlike demons, they do not have to bow to human beings when we use the Lord's name against them, and in this regard, we must come boldly to the throne of grace and ask the Lord Himself to rebuke the dignities on the captive's behalf. David also presents a clue as to how the Lord as Our Advocate functions with these dignities among "the congregation of the mighty." I myself am not yet ready to be as bold with the Lord as was David:

> God standeth in the congregation of the mighty; He judgeth among the gods. How long will ye judge unjustly, and accept the persons of the wicked? Defend the poor and fatherless; do justice to the afflicted and needy. Deliver the poor and need; rid them out of the hand of the wicked." (Psalm 82:1-4)

I interpret this scripture to impart that the congregation of the mighty not only includes the angels of the Lord, but also those dignities that serve Satan. Apparently, every knee must bow to the Lord, as He rules over ALL. However, although the dignities MUST obey Jesus, it seems that they can refuse our commands, because they are not earth bound demons. As a higher order or stature of authority than we are as humans, I suspect that the dignities do not have to obey our commands in the Lord's name. In His role as Advocate, the Lord defends our case and as Intercessor, I believe that Jesus delivers us from the dignities. I further contend that if we prepare our case according to the the the spiritual rules of law that David, Daniel and the saints of old were familiar with, we can successfully stand in the gap during spiritual warfare. In most situations, believers are the plaintiff and the dignities are the defendants.

INTERCESSORY PRAYER AND PREPARATION OF THE CASE

I have found that casting out of demons and preparing the captive to fight in mental health cases may not be the intervention strategy of choice. If it is the work of dignities to cause various seekers to be unable to be saved when they come to Jesus, as a deliverance counselor, I must be the one to prepare the case for intercessory prayer and ask the Lord to rebuke the dignities for the sake of the captive. In other words, I fall on the mercy of the court by coming boldly to the Throne of the Father, with Jesus as the Advocate. Prayer must be both effectual and fervent. (James 5:)

When something is "effectual", it produces the desired results. In truth, it works!! When a prayer is fervent, it is impassioned, ardent and fiery, filled with zeal and enthusiasm. If you've watched a trial in movie, the lawyer who wins is usually the one who is "fueled" in his presentation of an effectual plea to the jury. I believe that prayer in these situations and conditions is like entering an invisible court room to plea a case for vindication. I suspect that Satan is represented by his dignities, where they stand before God and petition the Father to be allowed to keep various souls in bondage for any number of reasons deemed un-contestable. I suspect that each of the devil's cases are heard. Since the triune God is completely righteous and just, I believe that Satan is granted his request if his petition remains uncontested by the saints in prayer. 7

Consequently, the emphasis of pre-deliverance counseling with mental health cases is primarily one of investigation to prepare a case bold enough to come to the Throne to seek grace and mercy for the captive. In the natural, when a district attorney has taken a case to court, this is the culmination of an investigation that has exposed the breaking of a law, requiring action to be taken by the court. Correct practices are crucial during the investigation process so as to reduce challenges and difficulties that will be presented by the opposition. Investigation primarily involves the collection and the assessment of "evidence." Evidence is any material that is relevant to proving or disproving the offenses including but not limited to witness statements, transcripts, documents, physical evidence, and the like. In a natural trial, it is necessary to prove each element of the suspected offense and to rebut any possible defenses.

My spiritual position within the investigation stage of pre-deliverance counseling is akin to that of "the expert witness," the one who receives light or "enlightenment." Enlightenment is the potential for truth to be revealed in every situation, an essential condition of vision. Every demonic wile of the religious demon and all others is set in motion to keep me in the dark about the captive's true spiritual condition. Darkness comes in all shades. It can be vague, not even noticeable until an obscure nuance is brought to the light of my attention. Accuracy in discernment is being able to perceive character, detect trends and uncover motives---the power to see what is not evident to the average mind. Darkness also produces a spiritual condition where the truth is concealed behind a spiritual fog. Consequently, a crucial key to my prayer victory is to have faith in the fact that I have been translated out of the kingdom of darkness into the kingdom of light, and therefore, the Lord "wants me to know."

Since it is the job of the Holy Ghost to reveal all truth to me, I purpose in my heart not to quench or grieve Him with my own baggage and unresolved issues concerning the case. So I must cast off my own works of darkness by putting on the armor of light. (Romans 13:12-14, James 3:16) If I myself have fellowshipped with the unfruitful works of darkness, (Ephesians 5:8), if my own heart is unclean because of any self seeking or ambitious tendencies, if I despise correction, chastening or brokenness (Hebrews 12:5, Hebrews 10:22), then I have quenched the Holy Ghost and my case before the Throne will be ineffective. God is light and God is love. If I say that I have fellowship with Him and I walk in darkness, I lie, I do not practice the truth and the Holy Ghost is both quenched and grieved. (I John1:5) Intercessory prayer is a manifestation of love and should be inspired by it. Any obstruction to love is an obstacle that stands in the way of "enlightenment", just as clouds obstruct and veil the sunlight.

Progress and fruitfulness are hindered by obstructions. For example, agreement between the captive and the deliverance counselor is absolutely essential. I cannot "come boldly" for someone who is in disagreement with me or who does not have any confidence in my authority to command. Boldness is defined by Webster as "the confidence and courage to move forward to meet danger." When dealing with demons and dignitaries, as an intercessor, I am putting myself on the front lines where the attack is focused, deliberate and concentrated. Any un-crucified or weak spot in my character as well as in my relationship with the captive is a target for the enemy. Therefore, I will not risk myself by standing in the gap for a captive who is adamantly defiant and resistant to unlearning error. For God resists the proud and gives grace to the humble. When I plead my case, my goal is to obtain grace and no one knows better than the apostle Paul how to present a case. In a book called "Ravens", the power of the Apostle Paul is powerfully explained by Paul Cox:

> "Paul was dangerous to the powers of darkness, to the rulers of this world. They met him at every turn and fought his every advance. Yet, with prayer, Paul saw God frustrate the plans and power of the enemy. What Satan intended for harm, God turned to good. Even Paul's imprisonments became platforms for preaching---all the way to Caesar's court." (Ravens, p.25)9

Another obstruction to maintaining fellowship with the Holy Spirit is doubt and unbelief. Since faith is seen in what you do and what you say, it answers the question "do you believe God?" I have found that the best way to believe God is to understand His ways and His conditions. To illustrate, the Lord was upset with the children of Israel because what they did and what they said did not line up with faith to believe in Him. I myself refuse to come against the demons and the dignities with blind faith. Therefore, I had to know that it is God's will to save those with mental illness, because natural evidence was defying the scriptures in regards to "whosoever will, let Him come."

Once I began to intensely study the doctrines of pre-destination and election, my faith to make my case before Him began to slightly waver. It was only when I found scripture to support my case that my faith became strong and solid. For example, when I read scripture that declared that God will save those who don't even seek Him, when I realized how Jesus saved the madman of Gedara and God reached out to proud, idolatrous King Nebchannezer, my faith became strong. Uplifting my courage to stand, fight the good fight and plead with an effectual, impassioned fervency, the word of God proved to me that the Lord will save anyone, mentally ill or not.

ENDNOTES

1. Sheppard, "To Curse the Root: A Christian Alternative to 12 Steps", Author House, 2005 pg. 356

2. Ibid, pgs. 360-367

3.The religious demon in Hattie Mae could not abide the religious demon in George. In fact, Hattie Mae's last act at Morning Glory church was to openly shame and disrespect

George, calling him "a dirty ole man" because he quite innocently touched her hand. As Jesus points out, a divided kingdom cannot stand. I believe that the Lord removed both of them: George, and Hattie Mae, so that the ministry could be free from the obstacles and hindrances inflicted upon it by the religious demon over several years.

4. War on the Saints, 9th edition, pg. 178

5. Ibid, pg. 176

6. Dr. Rebecca Brown, He Came to Set the Captives Free, pg. 114, 115

7. I first read about preparing a case for the heavenly court in a Chapter called "The Court of Final Appeal" in "Unbroken Curses" by Dr. R. Brown and her husband, Daniel Yoder.

8. The pictures of the dignities in the sky are located at www.healingwaterscc.com, under the sub-link called "Third book: Faces of the Religious Demon", under the main link entitled "Books/Articles and News"

9.Paul L. Cox, Ravens, Aslan's Place, 2000, pg. 25

SECTION TWO

A CALL TO PROFESSIONALISM

Chapter 9: Counseling the Captive

When the sons of Sceva tried to cast out demons, the demons declared, "Jesus I know, and Paul I know but who are you?" (Acts 19:13-16) Not only were these brothers not able to cast out the evil spirits, they were attacked by them. I myself have been astounded at how demons have left captives when I used the name of Jesus against them but I have also been disconcerted when I have come up against a situation where a captive's vocal cords were used by demons to let me know that I had a fight on my hands. I have personally found that each captive offers the counseling experience new problems even to the most experienced counselor. With each captive, you will be confronted with difficulties you have never encountered before, with attitudes that are hard to recognize and still harder to explain, with reactions which are far from transparent at first sight. Differences in culture and inheritance and in the experiences each captive has withstood, particularly in childhood, may seem boundless.

However, I have learned not to forget that the Holy Spirit is my Helper and He will reveal to me what He has heard in the Throne Room (John 16:13) and He will use my counseling skills, providing me with wisdom and revelation, as long as I don't become so spiritual that I am no earthly good. So to guard against losing my commonsense, I have learned how to cultivate some important mental tools to keep me in balance. Each and every minister or counselor has his or her own particular weaknesses. For example, I recognize that I am particularly vulnerable to the spirit of rejection. From the time I was a child, I experienced rejection. Since I refused to compromise, as a consequence, I experienced a great deal of rejection from parents, peers and the world, just for being different. Once I became born again, and thereafter a preacher of righteousness, I experienced even more rejection within the church. Therefore, I am particularly on guard when I am confronted by a spirit of rejection within a captive.

Spiritual abuse, one of the outgrowths of rejection in the church, can create or magnify a spiritual vulnerability. A few years ago, I experienced the residue of rejection within hours after I cast this demonic spirit from a captive. Almost immediately, yet rather covertly, the spirit of rejection tried to find a doorway. It was very subtle. Very sneaky. It began with a phone call wherein I thought someone with whom I had enjoyed friendship and intimacy for a long time was now nonchalant and uninterested in what I had to say. Then someone said something to me that I took as a put down based upon age. I internalized a harmless comment that was not intended to suggest that I was too old to relate to the needs of a younger generation. I started to feel mildly depressed, which is very unlike my persona. Taking heed to valuable information, in "War on the Saints" I realized that something was amiss:

> "It is essential, and indispensable for full deliverance from deception by evil spirits, that a believer knows the standard of his normal condition, for with this gauge before him he can judge his degree of deliverance---physically, intellectually and spiritually---so as to fight through with steady will and faith until every faculty is free, and he stands as an unshackled man in the liberty wherewith Christ has made him free."(War on the Saints,

abridged edition, pg. 151) 1

Consequently, I considered my normal condition which is never depressed for more than a few minutes. So I rebuked the demon of rejection and it left from me instantly.

Demons know who you are. The question is "do you know?"

I believe that it is important to acknowledge that any one who is truly born again and filled with the Spirit of God, the Lord Jesus Christ will not leave him nor forsake him. Those of you who came to Jesus with a sincere heart,--- yet because the doctrine of Christ was preached by demons---, you received "another Christ",--- the fact that you are now being tormented by demons right now is in itself a divine blessing. The Lord is allowing the demons to torment you today so as to wake you up to the reality that if you have a spirit of fear and if you do not have a spirit of a sound mind, then you are not saved. If you are speaking in a tongue, and yet you have never felt the dark night of the soul in repentance, then you are not saved. And if you are speaking in a tongue, and you are not saved, then it is not the Holy Ghost who is speaking through you. It is a religious demon.

The religious demon is extremely clever. In order to discredit the move of God in these times, this demon is also entrenched in the ministry of casting out of demons. As a part of her training, I asked one of my students to review a particular case that came into public view in the courtroom, and sadly enough, the church was ill prepared. This unfortunate horror story is that of the minister who accidentally killed an 8 year old autistic boy during a deliverance session a few years ago. Every Christian deliverance worker should be aware of such cases because the religious demon is using the ignorance of untrained deliverance ministers and the courts to sabotage the integrity of casting out of demons. In this particular case, the decision of the courts to send a professing believer to prison for five years was primarily based upon the fact that the deliverance worker was untrained. I would also suggest that in fact, the deliverance worker was probably infested with a religious demon himself.

According to newspaper reports, little Terrance Cottrell, Jr. died of asphyxiation,---- suffocation as a result of being laid upon as deliverance was being conducted upon him. Published accounts stated that Rev. Ray Hemphill, a minister at the Faith Temple Church of Apostolic Faith, who is 5 foot 7, 150 pounds "sprawled across the boy to keep him from hitting his head on the floor, because he was bucking.'" The idea to lie across little Terrance came from I Kings 17:21. Reports also mention that the boy's mother, Patricia Cooper 29, was also present at all of her son's deliverance sessions. Even though she held her own child's legs down, she was not charged in the case of his death, nor was the pastor of the church, who was not present at the time of Terrance's death. Unfortunately, such a high profile and unique case is a subtle, underhanded work of the religious demon to tarnish the true legitimacy and authority of the Name of Jesus Christ of Nazareth. This demon took ample advantage of the fact that deliverance is already considered controversial, misunderstood not only within the world, but also within the organized church.

When reviewing this case, scriptural confusion is clearly evident. For example, for the minister and his team to use I Kings 17:21 as the verse to stand upon as a deliverance scripture was serious error, as the scripture and the entire account in itself was taken completely out of context. The truth is that Elijah, the prophet was sent to a widow woman to lodge with her and her son during a three year dry season (I Kings 17:1, James 5:17). During the course of the prophet's stay, the widow's son died. Clearly Elijah could not suffocate a boy who was already dead BEFORE he laid upon him:

> And it came to pass after these things, the son of the woman, the mistress of the house, fell sick; and his sickness was sore, that there was no breath left in him.

> Therefore, Elijah cried out to the Lord:
> And stretched himself upon the child three times and cried unto the Lord, and said, O Lord my God, I pray thee, let this child's soul come into him again (vs. 21).
> And the Lord heard the voice of Elijah; and the soul of the child came into him again, and he revived (vs. 22).

In short, The Lord used the prophet to raise the boy from the dead, not to cast out demons from him. In fact, when death does occur, demons leave the corpse by necessity. It is interesting to note that Elijah "stretched upon the child three times." One newspaper reported: "prosecutors say Ray Hemphill laid on Terrance Cottrell Jr.'s chest for at least an hour to release demons' from him, before the boy died." Moreover, the "casting out of demons" is a New Testament ministry, founded upon the use of the Name of Jesus by the power of the Holy Ghost, a significant mandate of the "Great Commission" to New Testament saints. (Mark 16:17). I Kings 17:21 has nothing to do with casting out of demons as it relates solely to raising the dead. How long Elijah laid across the widow's son each of three times, the bible doesn't record. Ironically, Terrance's "bucking" might have begun with demons, but ended with him struggling for his life as he was slowly being suffocated. Skin was even found under the child's fingers and the deliverance worker still did not budge.

As the story of the Terrance's death unfolded, there are other matters which cause serious concern. For instance, according to the mother's friend and neighbor, Denise Allison, she "looked through her friend's window and saw church members taking turns striking the boy with a belt as his mother, Ms. Cooper watched." Allison added "I told Ann that it was wrong, but she said the Bible told her you're suppose to chastise your children. I told her to stop, told her what could a little kid ever do that was so wrong to beat him like that?" She said the church told her it was the only way to heal him." If such actions by the church are true, how would "striking the boy with a belt" heal him? Once again, a biblical text was taken out of context, spare the rod, spoil the child.

It is also reported that church members began to take Cooper and Terrance to the church in a van three and four times a day for prayer, three times a week (Wednesday, Thursday and Friday) for an hour and a half. Apparently, the sessions only lasted three weeks due to the boy's death. I find the boy being prayed for three to four times a day to be extreme. As previously indicted, it has been my practice in a deliverance session that if the demons don't come out in 15 minutes, either there are no demons there, or the ground was not properly prepared prior to the deliverance. The power of the name of Jesus Christ of Nazareth in the mouth of a believing saint is just that strong. For example, I have commanded demons in 15 minutes without any manifestation, yet a few hours later, they were expelled outside of my presence. Demons have also been expelled by listening to a tape recording as well as over the telephone.

This unfortunate occurrence brings me to the question: Was Terrance "disorder" demonic? Was the church correct in assessing that he had demons? Autism is a developmental disability, typically diagnosed during the first three years of life. It affects the normal development of the brain in the areas of social interaction and communication skills. Many with autism are considered to be unaffectionate and cold individuals. However, with most disabilities, this can differ based on one's personality, environment and level of disability. Called a "neurological disorder," autism effects the functioning of the brain. Although autism is neurological, I believe there may be a spirit that lodges in the brain of a person with this disease whose mission is to stunt his or her interpersonal and social interaction skills.

Therefore, the church may have been on the right track in its assessment that little Terrance had demons.   However, they were not correct in knowing how to conduct deliverance, especially upon a child. For example, the minister should have at least considered   whether or not the boy   could   hold onto his deliverance. Was his mother strong enough to be able to intercede and stand in the gap for her son if the demons would try to attack her son again? Did the mother herself have an understanding of the ministry of casting out demons? Would there have been enough spiritual authority in the home for Terrance to have kept his deliverance?

To summarize, this case is a poignant example of the need for a professional approach. If a person truly does not understand deliverance---the ministry of casting out demons and the principles that ensure maintaining one's deliverance----demons should not be cast from them AT ALL. Furthermore, the devil can certainly use an unstable mind with layers of mental illness in order to discredit this viable ministry. For example, what if a minister proceeds to cast out demons from an individual and they go to a psychiatrist claiming they feel they want to kill themselves after they had demons cast out of them? Who is to say that this secular psychiatrist would not report such a minister as a fraud, indicating that his/her patient had become worse psychologically due to this unconventional way of treatment? With lawsuits running rampant in our society, such a scenario is not out of the realm of possibility.

Even among the more trained professionals, including Christian psychiatrists and other licensed and trained Christian counselors, the religious demon's strategy is extremely clever.   For example, the new wave is that professionals are unobtrusively seeking personal glory by developing their own fragmented group of disciples, who refuse to eat from any other spiritual tables. Establishing   intimate networks among themselves, Christian counselors scrupulously protect their professional turf from those not in the network with probing questions to Christian professionals unknown to them   with "what professional group do you belong to? Who do you know?, Who is your support or your "covering?," Once it is established that you are "not connected," you will probably be excluded from their networks. If you don't drop the right name, chances are that you will be overlooked and considered to be of no consequence in the field. One name is rarely "dropped." That is, the Name of Jesus Christ of Nazareth, the only name under the sun that demons must obey.

Another trend is that some professionals are obtaining degrees in biblical studies and other religious fields that are non-related to the field of professional counseling. Yet in spite of the degree, these intelligent, even scholarly professionals are unable to obtain a license to counsel in their respective states without the practicum component that every licensed professional is required to obtain. Even so, Christian psychiatrists, psychologists, and others in spiritual ministry are lifting up unprecedented teachings. In touch with a Christian author with a PhD in a non-related field to counseling on a website where authors comment upon the work of authors, I submitted the following commentary in response to a book about inner healing:

> "I have been back and forth with your book and I must say that you had a difficult tasks that you astutely conquered: keeping it scholarly and professional with descriptive research yet making it interesting to read. This is one of the few scholastic works that I have read that I believe has made such an accomplishment. I have not read the whole book, and with a book like yours, I tend to skip around. Therefore, I must tell you in all honesty that I have somewhat of a concern about method. Women, especially African Americans and other women of color can be extremely emotional.

> Probably the most demonstratively emotional among our Christian women of color are the Pentecostals and the Charismatics. Therefore, the loud sobs, tears, screaming, falling to the floor and other outbursts of emotion that you have described herein may appear to be a spiritual cleansing, when in fact, the women may be just indulging their flesh by letting their emotions cut loose. Such outbursts of emotion appeal to all women regardless of race or color.

> Emotions are of the flesh. And as the word of God says "the flesh profiteth nothing." For example, I have seen this over and over again over my 25 year ministry in the AME Zion Church, where the women tend to be more reserved than the average black woman. What I have observed is that when they DO "cut loose" and it seems like they have been cleansed, in a very short time, the old ways reveal themselves and nothing has been "of profit" in terms of some genuine spiritual growth and healing.

> Furthermore, where sex is concerned, the bible warns us to "flee." I believe that the reason why we are to flee is very important. Someone who has been raped or sexually molested cannot flee. One of the clients within your case study y makes a very astute observation. The demons of the perpetrator become attached to them and will periodically and progressively wreak havoc in their lives, after remaining dormant for even decades."

I believe that the author's response to my review exemplifies the subtle strategy of the religious demon to use Christian professionals within the university system in general and the field of deliverance in particular, to minimize and even dilute the biblical mandate of casting out of demons:

> "Yes, it was difficult attempting to keep my book scholarly while interesting. I made that decision because of all the research I used while

writing it and found that in fact their stuff was scholarly and interesting. I also wanted major universities to pick it up as a textbook, while both Christian and secular audiences could still find it interesting. You are right in your observation that the book minimizes the ministry of casting out of demons. That was not to detract from the importance or significance of this ministry, but bear in mind that I attended a White male dominated (religious) Theology school who had problems with the whole issue of casting out demons in the first place. My goal was not to recruit them or change their mind about the ministry of casting out demons, but simply to earn my degree.

The first submission of my 400-page dissertation discussed in detail the casting out of demons. They gave it back to me and said it would never be approved in that current writing. So I spent the next year rewriting (while trying not to compromise what I'm called to do). Once it was approved by the Theology Staff, it didn't make a lot of sense to go back and rewrite the book to include the ministry of casting out demons. My current goal is twofold; to reach the masses of churches, pastors, and leaders, (many of whom don't have a clue about casting out demons, and some who don't even believe in it), to inform them of the widespread epidemic of female trauma and that it should be addressed if we're going to help our women; second is to inform those people who work in the mental health field (again, many of who do not have a clue of how to cast out demons) that there can be an integrated approach of mental health counseling and spiritual healing.

I have worked with secular psychiatrists and psychologists who have called me in on numerous occasions to work with clients who did not receive healing from just their approach alone. And our combined approach has been instrumental in getting the people healed. Furthermore, I network with reputable Christians who work in deliverance ministry casting out demons, while others are limited to inner healing and other integrated approaches; all of which they claim have worked for the past 20 or 30 years.

I hear your concern as to the method I use, but please bear in mind that we all have a Holy Spirit driven method. After many years of working directly with abused women, the only thing I can say is that they experience healing and deliverance based on the method the Holy Spirit has given me. I think you've misunderstood my perspective on casting out demons. Although it is very much a part of what I do, it is not always the number one priority. I tend to allow the Holy Spirit to lead me into what I'm to do and I just follow His lead.

Yes, the women that I have worked with demonstrated various degrees of emotionalism, (and I must tell you that I am not motivated by emotionalism), the majority of them nonetheless (even expressing their emotions) have been set free to work through the process. My follow up counsel and/or referring them to other counseling ministries have produced phenomenal results. I am extremely excited about what and how God is working in the lives of abused women. Those who have received deliverance from domestic violence, promiscuity, pornography, masturbation, shame, guilt, you name it. They know that they have been set free indeed! Though my method may appear a bit strange to you, it appears to work for the women who seek healing and deliverance from me."

I understand this Christian author's desire to promote her own particular model and that of her associates. I do the same with the model that I believe that the Holy Ghost has given to me. Yet I also believe that Christian scholars and professionals must be careful not to allow our attachment to our subjective models to cloud our objectivity. Nor should professionalism become a smokescreen to avoid facing demons upfront and personal. It has certainly been my experience in the pre/post deliverance counseling model that I have developed and implemented that sometimes with anointed counseling and teaching, the entrance of His word brings so much light, that demons will flee on their own. However, rarely does this happen with the many faces of the spirit of Jezebel. At some point in the therapy, a demon MUST either be cast out of or off of the one who has been abused.

When I originally trained several professionals with non-related degrees to Christian counseling within the School of the Prophets of the AME Zion Church, I was able to observe for myself how intelligent, well respected Christian professionals with non-related degrees had absolutely no counseling skills. My evangelistic work within the School of the Prophets first began as an itinerant ministerial training program, with networks in New York, New England, Nigeria and the Bahamas. Once I left the AME Zion Church, the Internet has caused my segment of the work to continue and expand around the country, including various parts of Africa, Australia, England and Canada.

My contribution to the School of the Prophets provided a practicum for students to learn some basic counseling skills. On occasion, I observed students in a counseling session with a captive, where the inadequacies have become clear. For example, some students without counseling background engaged various captives in a teacher or a seminar leader style, rather than allowing the client to identify his own problem. In other words, she committed the carnal sin of counseling: "She talked too much rather than focusing on engaging the captive to speak." I work from the premise that most of what the client needs to know about his problems are within his own soul, and if engaged to share, out of the contents within the captive's inner man, his mouth will eventually speak. Yet throughout several sessions that I have observed, the students taught the captives about a particular mental health disorder rather than simply sit back and "listen."

Consequently, some sessions are reminiscent of well known clinical investigations where sex therapists attempt to engage a child to find out if he or she was sexually abused, yet through probing questions, damages the child's testimony by implanting suggestive information. In a particular case, not only did the client not having any terminology for her condition, but the student did more than merely explain the general concept. She actually advised the client to give names to the fragmented parts of herself. From the client's puzzled facial expression, it was clear to me that she did not view her lack of self knowledge and her self mutilation as "cutting alter personalities." In fact, the captive's understanding of dissociative behavior was evidently non-existent, yet the student proceeded to teach her about it with an assumptive articulation that the captive is indeed "DID". Standard counseling protocol involves a simple listening to the captive's own understanding of what it means to her to be out of touch with her very soul. She very well could be dissociative. However, to train her in DID is premature and inappropriate.

Some Christian therapists suggest that defense mechanisms are God given ways of avoidance for captives who have suffered overwhelming trauma--- mental walls that safeguard a captive's way of escape. I happen to disagree. For example, If I myself were a DID captive and a therapist were to suggest to me that my alter personalities were divine, I would not be impressed. In fact, it would anger me. For if God was the One who did not provide a natural way of escape for me from the original abuse of the perpetrator who traumatized me, there would be no way that I would be able to either thank Him or glorify Him for preparing a mere internal, spiritual escape that involves a lifetime of personality fragmentation.

It seems that the professional path that well meaning Christian workers have chosen has its own set of conditions of tightly built in risks of provide a safe haven for demons. In my opinion, I suspect that the religious demon has cleverly devised yet another strategy to keep itself from being cast out. For if as some teach---that the counselor should validate the existence of the "alters" and not cast them out as though they were demons,--- then if demons are masquerading as "alters," their continued home within the captive is virtually secured.

I wonder if a subtle agenda for searching for professional alternatives is that those accustomed to spiritual warfare within a deliverance session that lasted for several hours casting out demons, proved to be more a physical battle than a spiritual one. I have heard many seasoned warriors vividly describe exhaustive deliverance sessions, where the formidable "beat downs" inherent within client restraint left the deliverance worker physically weary. I understand. So did the sons of Sceva who got beaten down when they tried to cast out demons ill prepared. Furthermore, no one wants to go to jail for casting out a devil.

Truthfully, with all of the professional scholarship inherent in the field today, I have personally heard very little about Jesus and in that observation lies the underlying answer to professionals. Unless Jesus Christ is at the center of any alternative, professional efforts will be as unfruitful as that of those without training. Too much protection against liability can stifle both the faith and power to cast out demons. As a rule of thumb, I repeat once more that if demons are not expelled after 15 minutes, either there is no demon there, or the worker needs to go back to the drawing board and search out the problem in more depth through the steps and stages of pre-deliverance counseling.

Not to suggest that my model is perfect or superior to others, but I believe that my pre-deliverance counseling program called Spiritual Boot-camp Sessions and the training program for deliverance workers called Spiritual Empowerment Workshop (the SEW Program)serve as a balance between the unprofessional and the excessively professional. On a practical level, in cases such as the death of the autistic boy, licensed counselors should generally keep abreast of litigations within their respective professions, becoming familiar with how to testify in court.

Yet I believe that the best way to avoid facing the courtrooms of the country is to conduct intense counseling before a single demon is cast out. In fact, the client is apprised prior to admission that submitting to the SEW/SBS approach is in itself an acknowledgment that they may have evil spirits working in their lives. In fact, they are required to sign an advised consent form, a disclaimer admitting to the fact that they themselves believe that they have demons.

Actually, the Holy Spirit's involvement in the process should not be overlooked. For example, ninety nine percent of those who enter into deliverance counseling have first come to me with dreams highly suggestive that they are demon oppressed---dreams that when tried, I have found to have been inspired by the Lord. So I don't have to convince my clients of the existence of demons, nor do I have to persuade them that the root cause of their torment is demonic. I also will not cast out a demon from a child, even with parental consent. However, I am willing to train the parent to cast out his or her own child's demons and provide guidance and prayer support to parents who are willing to stand in the gap for their child. Even though I view every torment or bondage as potentially of demonic origin, I do not assume that a demon must be cast out in every case. I have found that as each captive takes a stand against demons by allowing their souls to be broken through genuine contrition, demons could leave because their dwelling place has been rendered "uninhabitable." However, this is not typically the case. Consequently, my personal experience is in accord with the insights of Jessie Penn Lewis:

> "In the stress, and ofttimes confusion, of the dispossessing period, the deceived and possessed person unwittingly fights against his deliverance by covering and siding with the evil spirits who have deceived him. The will may be set, and declared to be for deliverance, yet when the truth is given, evil spirits manifest their presence in the circumference of the man, or where ever they may be located, by arousing feelings of rebellion against the very truth, or messenger of truth, which the man in his will has chosen to receive." (9th edition, pg. 270)

The Deliverance Disclaimer Form (the DDF) is proof of advised consent that the casting out of demons is not a traditional or even an acceptable mode of practice within the secular fields of psychiatry, psychology and social work. I believe that pre-deliverance counseling is crucial to captives, especially those with mental illness, in order to reveal and uncover what has been concealed. In order to convey a more specific impression of what I do as a deliverance counselor in pre-deliverance work, my general task is to equip the captive to stand "and having done all to stand, STAND THEREFORE!",

My first step in the process is assessment or what I refer to as the "plowing stage." My work in assessment can be divided into three main divisions: investigation, observation and interpretation.

INVESTIGATION

The purpose of investigation is to unravel confusion and to unfold the mystery by searching for repetitive themes. Through concentrated and intelligent inquiry, I gather my clues as to whether or not there is a demon present. Ultimately, the mystery should unfold as to what in the captive's background is a clue to demonic activity. As I progress in the case, a possible connection will appear from time to time, and a tentative picture will be formed. Not easily convinced of this solution, I test it over and over again to see whether it really congeals in all parameters.

It has been my experience   that there are innumerable strategies that various personalities will use to resist the process. Since pre-deliverance counseling is so brief, I cannot afford to waste time on people who what me to do all the work, those who use all of my energies to hide things from me so as to mislead me, or those who become hostile because they are threatened by any real discovery.   What I am looking for are the desperate captives who will cooperate in any way because they have come close to or reached their "bottom" and therefore are serious about deliverance. Rarely do I find a client who knows that there is something wrong, and commits themselves to facing the truth.

Since we can never really know with absolute certainty whether or not a church goer or a professing Christian is saved, one of the most effective strategies built into the deliverance process is the use of a tool called the Deliverance Assessment Form.   The Deliverance Assessment Form (the DAF) is a device adapted from the questionnaire found in the book entitled "Evicting Demonic Intruders" by the late Noel Gibson and presented in a book by Doris Wagner called "How to Cast Out Demons." I revised the form and made it comparable to a psycho-social tool within my own profession.

By asking the right questions in the assessment process, I use the information gleaned from the DAF to uncover the root causes for demonic doorways that left the captive vulnerable to infestation or oppression. To summarize, there are various questions on the DAF that are designed to discern whether or not a captive has been spiritually abused in some way. Some of these questions have to do with the captive's description of his church and pastor. Other questions are more subtle, dealing with the captive's self evaluation of his personality type. Here are the questions that I pay the most attention to, relative to spiritual abuse:

Part II The religion of birth, were you raised in church, denomination, years in church, church attendance, practicing a religion that is not Christian

Part III Define repentance, "born again", resurrection. Describe born again experience. Have you had supernatural experiences, speaking in tongues, fallen slain, hearing voices, seeing a spirit, played with Ouija Board, occult, witchcraft involvement, all of questions 8 and 9. Question 10: Have you been involved in a Christian church where you needed the approval of the pastor for everyday experiences, ie. traveling, visiting other churches, buying a home, deciding on having a child, etc.

OBSERVATION

As a deliverance counselor, my listening skills are very important, particularly if the primary method of counseling is by telephone and email. Therefore, I have to be particularly skillful because I will not be able to observe facial expressions and body language. However, by telephone and even email, I am able to discern aloofness, warmth, rigidity, spontaneity, defiance, compliance, suspicion, confidence, assertiveness, timidity, ruthlessness and sensitivity. As I listen to the captive, I will invariably form an impression:--whether the captive is able to verbalize freely or whether his communication is disjointed; whether he is a person who presents details or generalities; whether he volunteers information or leaves the questioning to me. As I listen intently, my goal is to try not to select any one element prematurely but to pay a balanced interest in every detail. No observation should be regarded as unimportant. The key is to search for repetitive themes.

INTERPRETATION

Repetitive themes are particularly helpful for understanding. For example, consider the captive who continues to start up projects, but never completes them, or the captive who continually ends up in relationships with controlling people. Trends such as these help me to obtain a perspective on the captive's life, past and present, and also an understanding of the forces operating in his personality. It is important to note here the importance of the Holy Spirit as the Counselor as He helps me in my assessment and interpretation of the trends. Consequently, I make use of various clues by means of my own reasoning capabilities, enlightened by the leading of the Holy Ghost. Therefore, when I have recognized some possible connection and I have gained an impression as to the unconscious factors that may be operating in a certain context, I will seek the Holy Ghost's guidance as to the appropriate time and manner to reveal my interpretation to the captive. Since pre-deliverance is a brief therapy, the issue of timing in sharing interpretations is different from long term counseling. In this regard, I generally "cut to the chase" in the sharing of my interpretation as long as I perceive that the captive not only can stand it but can also be equipped by it to stand against the demonic forces.

It should further be noted that an interpretation is merely a suggestion as to a possible meaning. Yet even though the interpretation may only be partly correct, it will often open up the door for the captive to test it out and either qualify it or dismiss it. Remember that in the arena of "spiritual strangeness", particularly where a religious demon is concerned, my interpretation may provoke anxiety or a defensive reaction. Whatever the reaction is, my responsibility as the counselor is to understand my clients and to learn from them. The particular point in which the captive turns from co-operation to defensive maneuvers furnishes another tool for understanding him. As an example, you have read about the case of Maxine. My general impression of Maxine was that she was a very compliant captive, eager to be set free from demonic torment. However, an observation that I considered minor brought forth a such a resistance that served to expose the religious demon, when both Maxine and I were focusing our attention on the witchcraft spirit.

Since this was a counseling relationship entirely conducted by email, I did not immediately sense that there was any conflict between us for almost three months. In fact, the captive's emails were filled with gratitude and praises of the various insights I continued to present to her. However, this one particular insight enraged her to the point of firing me. It seemed a harmless comment, meant to encourage Maxine. However, as a vital observation, this conflict with Maxine provided new understandings and a more enlightened interpretation. Hidden thus far, the religious demon was uncovered. It had been obscured by Maxine's mild mannered demeanor and an apparent desire to be set free. When a resistance of this kind occurs, it is my job to take the lead by helping the captive to recognize the resistance. If I can succeed in convincing the captive that a resistance is operating, significant progress will have been made. In Maxine's case, once fired, I was able to convince her to re-hire me. In hindsight, I believe that once re-hired, I should have postponed Maxine's deliverance until the spiritual cause of her resistance was further explored.

MY COUNSELING PERSPECTIVE

The term "spiritual abuse", is a relatively recent expression that was employed to describe the damage inflicted upon the sheep by the organized church. In recent times, much has been written about spiritual abuse and rather than attempt to restate what I believe to be good material, in a nutshell, spiritual abuse is defined as being the result of a spiritual leader or system that controls, manipulates, or dominates a person with its traditions and its doctrines. David Johnson & Jeff Van Vonderen in The Subtle Power of Spiritual Abuse 2 define the term in this manner:

> "Spiritual abuse can occur when leaders use their spiritual position to control or dominate another person." (p.20)

> "Spiritual abuse can also occur when spirituality is used to make others live up to a 'spiritual standard'." (p.21)

> Spiritual abuse occurs when shame is "used in an attempt to get someone to support a belief, or...to fend off legitimate questions". (p.22)

> "When your words and actions tear down another, or attack or weaken a person's standing as a Christian—to gratify you, your position or your beliefs, while at the same time weakening or harming another—that is spiritual abuse." (p.23)

> "There are spiritual systems in which...the members are there to meet the needs of the leaders... These leaders attempt to find fulfillment through the religious performance of the very people whom they are there to serve and build. This is an inversion of the body of Christ. It is spiritual abuse." (p.23)

Licensed social worker and former cult member Daniel Shaw provides some additional insights concerning thought reform, more well known as mind control in an essay entitled "Traumatic Abuse in Cults":

> "Thought reform techniques are readily found in use in any cult, yet it is my belief, based on my own exposure to and study of various cults, that many cult leaders are not necessarily students of thought reform techniques. One might argue that meditation and chanting, for example, are techniques specifically designed to control others, and they can be. But they are also ancient traditional spiritual practices. Cult leaders who require their followers to perform mind-numbing, trance-inducing practices may do so while fully believing that such practices are for the greatest possible good of the follower. In religious philosophies that emphasize detachment and transcendence, for instance, trance states are highly valued as avenues toward these spiritual goals.

> Cult leaders, however, practice forms of control, such as intimidation and humiliation, which demand submission. In Ghent's view, masochistic submission is a perversion of surrender. Cult leaders often use the idea of surrender as bait, and then switch to a demand for submission.

151

Nevertheless, in so doing, they may not actually be practicing mind control in any conscious way. They may simply be behaving in ways typical of pathological narcissists, people whose personalities are characterized by paranoia and megalomania—characteristics, by the way, that are readily attributable to one of the modern masters of thought reform techniques, the totalitarian dictator known as Chairman Mao. Totalitarian dictators study and invent thought reform techniques, but many cult leaders may simply be exhibiting characteristic behaviors of the pathological narcissist, with the attendant paranoia and mania typical of this personality disorder. Thought reform is the systematic application of techniques of domination, enslavement, and control, which can be quite similar to the naturally occurring behaviors of other abusers, like batterers, rapists, incest perpetrators, in all of whom can be seen the behaviors of pathological narcissism." (D. Shaw, LCSW, 2003) 3

I would personally amplify these professional insights and definitions with my personal belief that spiritual abuse is the result of several demons conjoining together to seriously damage the human spirit. The two lead demons involved in spiritual abuse are the witchcraft and the religious demons. However, they are also joined by others: the spirits of depression, anger, rejection, fear, and insanity, to name but a few. In Proverbs, the Holy Spirit exhorts us to vigilantly protect our human spirits. To sum up some important proverbs, we are warned to guard the spirit, for from it flow the issues of life. Furthermore, he that rules his own spirit is better than he that can take a city. And finally, a wounded spirit, who can bare it. (Proverbs 16:32,4:23, and 18:14)

Moreover, I contend that spiritual abuse goes beyond the damage that occurs within a cult or a church. Broadening this definition even further, I include any person, place, doctrine, situation or circumstance that distorts or in any way damages the captive's seeking and obtaining a personal relationship with Jesus Christ. In other words, the spiritual weapon of the helmet of salvation has been rendered powerless in a twofold process of :

1.quenching or grieving the Holy Ghost

2.hindering a Christian from baring spiritual fruit.

Unfortunately, this sort of damage not only continues to occur by people who stay home and watch Christian television or who follow behind mega preachers from one conference to another, but it also occurs in reputable churches among sincere, well meaning Christians. I believe the cause is summed up in the word of God as prophesied through Hosea: "My people are destroyed for a lack of knowledge." This lack of knowledge falls into 3 main categories, a lack of knowledge of God, of self and of the devil:

1.a lack of knowledge of the triune God

a. The captive may now have moved to an extreme of not trusting any religious organization or biblical doctrine.

b.The captive may be angry at God because he believes that the Lord should have protected him from deception.

c.The captive remains habituated or addicted to a   plethora of triggers from religious ceremonies, like being constantly slain in the spirit, personal prophecies, harmful and/or false experiences [altered states; feverish tongues-speaking; endless spiritual warfare exercises

d.The captive may still be   dominated by core teachings that he has not yet discarded. I have found that it takes a lot of time and study to challenge the content of the teachings that captives were indoctrinated with]

e.The captive may believe that he has left God when   disfellowshipped or exiting the cult, club or the church on his own. This is because the relationship between the leader, the teaching and God is very interconnected.

2.a lack of self knowledge

a. The captive has assumed the leader's purpose and therefore is far removed from knowing the Lord's   purpose for his own life.

b. The captive is filled with confusion, and wavers   between several opinions. He is often unsure about his salvation.

c. Depressed and angry over lost years, the captive is out of control of his soul, particularly his mind and his emotions.

d. The captive may have lost hope because of trials, tribulations and troubles, including but not limited to broken marriages, estrangements from family and friends, and a loss of career goals.

e. The captive's personality has been swallowed up by the   cult through mind control and demons have seized   various parts of his personality, causing him to appear to be dissociative, fragmented in his soul with various "alters."

f. Trained in religiosity from childhood, it is difficult to re-train the captive in areas that he believes he already knows.

It is my belief that captives will only become free of the mental and emotional damage incurred by the spiritual abuse afflicted upon him by others when he can accept full responsibility for allowing himself to be spiritually victimized. A captive who has not faced himself can only see or feel in the flesh because he has been blinded from true self perception in the spirit. Therefore, he may find it difficult to recognize how much his own sensitivities, his hidden hostilities, as well as his own exacting demands for attention may have interfered with his relationships and actually drew him to controlling people. Without facing his true self, when he does find a genuinely assertive leader, the captive may unconsciously set up situations to try to compel the new leader to attempt to control his life.

For example, he may tell lies and when uncovered, he may try to provoke the new leader to appear dominating and unreasonable. Nor is the self deluded captive equipped to judge the impressions that he makes on others or their reaction to him. Consequently, he is at a loss to understand why his relationships, particularly among the saints are not satisfying. His distorted view will project fault and blame upon others. In his mind, those at the church are inconsiderate, disloyal, and abusive.

3. and a lack of knowledge of the devil.

    a. Unfortunately, the Destroyer continues to take advantage of the manner in which the word of God is preached and taught as the foundation for the enactment of spiritual abuse.

    b. Both the religious and the witchcraft demons selectively choose ministers who are amenable to deception and sheep who are prone to vulnerability.

    c. The stage is then set to put the bread of life into a defiled heart who will speak it forth into damaged spirits.

What about the leaders who scatter His flock? The fact that demons are looking for doorways of vulnerability should not be surprising. Satan unsuccessfully employed this very tactic with the Lord Jesus Christ. Satan assumed that Jesus was vulnerable because He was hungry and thirsty after a 40 day fast in the wilderness. Then he confronted the Lord Himself with "the word of God out of context." Even though this strategy proved unsuccessful with the Lord, it should not be surprising that the Destroyer would continue to employ the same tactic against vulnerable sheep. For this reason, James warns those seeking to be masters or teachers that theirs will be the greater condemnation. (James 3:1) This is as it should be. Why? Those who handle the word of God are Satan's targets to bring damage and destruction upon the sheep by that very word. It is a very clever tactic indeed---so much so, that we now have the term "spiritual abuse" in our Christian vocabulary.

What about the enemy and the captive? Well, the enemy can interfere, distract, accuse, pressure, condemn, threaten, lie, confuse, deceive... but he cannot stop the captive from choosing to turn to God for the strength to make the right and healthy choices that are part of His good will and intention for him. The Lord's good intentions for the captives have been there since he was conceived in the womb and before then because the Lord new the elect in eternity. Abuse does not disqualify the captive, nor does it make null and void the glorious plan and intention of God for the captive's life. As a pre-deliverance counselor, this is the message of hope to the abused that I continue to bring. This is the truth, and all the messages and lies and accusations that sought to defeat the captive and convince him otherwise cannot change that truth. Jesus is that truth. He has nailed the ordinances that were against the captive to His cross.

I believe that spiritual abuse can also be self inflicted when a person yields to the evil emotions and desires of his own heart. As such, the witchcraft demon is attracted to a person with a soul that is predisposed to the three (3) "P"s of position, prestige and power. In other words, those who wish to dominate, to acquire fame and prominence, can become a safe haven for both the religious and the witchcraft demons. In such cases, the captive's own personality will be a secure place in which demons of a similar nature will be able to hide. This is because no one will suspect that the captive's ambitious striving for control and domination will be demonic because the captive has continued to demonstrate over time a steady pattern that propels them to seek power. Everyone just assumes that the captive is just being true to his nature or character.

The witchcraft demon will also hide within weaker personalities. For example, there are those who wear a facade of false humility, who appear to be very self effacing. However, deep within his or her soul is a striving to "be somebody." People so affected will offer up many testimonies of their inadequacies and their lack of ambition, yet when confronted, they will show in their actions that they are not at all convinced of their own unworthiness. In fact, when there is even a minor concern or question about their actions or motives in a particular situation, they will become extremely defensive and resentful. If others show a tendency to take their self-belittling attitude and recriminations seriously, a seething anger may erupt that is out of balance in the extreme. For example, while the so-called "humble" will proclaim their unworthiness, a witchcraft demon will cause them to make great demands for consideration and admiration. The witchcraft spirit will rise up and expose itself in these "low key" people, presenting a strong unwillingness to accept even the slightest degree of criticism.

Normal strivings for power in a believer are motivated by a sincere desire to want to see souls saved and delivered as the kingdom of this world become the kingdom of our Lord. What distinguishes normal inclinations from obsessions is that demonic striving for power is often rooted in fear, hatred and feelings of inferiority. For example, racism is a good example that also involves a cultural factor. When the predominant culture is in fear of losing its power and even worse, becoming extinct--- demons of fear, hatred and pride will become united with the witchcraft demon in order to control, dominate and suppress those of another race or culture. Moreover, those who feel insecure mentally and emotionally will strive for power as a means to protect themselves from anxiety and from a feeling of helplessness.

The witchcraft demon functions very covertly with carnal natures of this variety. However, the demon will be exposed when he will attempt to lead the captive to be out of balance in very common, everyday situations. For example, the captive will shun commonplace situations such as acceptance of guidance, advice, or help, including any kind of dependence on the brethren---- in short----any acquiescing or agreement with his brothers and sisters in Christ. Such protests do not always arise in full force but rather will increase gradually.

I myself have been severely abused by people who profess to be Christian. Notwithstanding., it is in my nature to fight back and to attack. Retaliation in my flesh is my middle name. My flesh is very comfortable with it. In fact I was so bold before I came to Jesus almost 30 years ago, that I would plot and scheme to destroy each of my enemies, and then I would wait a moment, and get right up in their face and say "Gotcha!!!!" The word of God teaches us that the flesh doesn't change. The reason that I have been able to overcome the spirit of retaliation and vengeance is that I actively and seriously pursue walking in the Spirit and not fulfilling the lust of my flesh.

Nevertheless, I consider myself to be a wounded Healer, similar to the manner that Jesus Himself is wounded. He still has the scars. So do I. His scar are healed. I thought that all of my scars were healed until the Lord showed me six months ago that there are still some tender spots that need to be worked on. He is doing that work by the power of the Holy Ghost. Where my pain comes from is in submitting myself to being transformed into the image of Jesus Christ. I am like Paul in Romans 7.

It is not so much a pain emanating from spiritual abuse or trauma. I have never been raped or physically abused in any way. Yet prior to Jesus, I was one hard, cold black woman. My anger served to protect me from scars. Even so, I was less spiritually abused as an atheist than I was as a Christian. People in the world KNEW not to mess with me because they KNEW what they would have to face. I am not just referring to a women. Men were intimidated by me. On my secular job, I was called "the woman with gonads." When I was in my 20's, men were afraid of me. I have torn up more suits that I didn't buy, battered more cars---ripped the tires, bashed out the windows, poured bleach on stuff----I was on the verge of killing somebody.

The only thing that kept me from jail is my daughter. I didn't kill anyone because I didn't want anyone else to raise her while I spent the rest of my life in prison or even executed. It is as simple as that. That Pam is dead and gone, long time ago. However, if I allow my flesh to resurrect, even for a moment, my flesh is still "a killer." So when it comes to Christiandom, and these phony, weak minded folk "do me like they do me", I have to allow my flesh to stay crucified because of Jesus. This struggle has brought me some deep pain over the years. There have been so many times, years ago--- when I would have to fall on my face and cry out "Lord, don't these people know who I am? Don't they know how much I could hurt them?"

I have come to understand that people have rejected me as much as they have because they have felt my inner strength and my fearlessness before I even knew how strong I myself am. Some label this quality as spiritual fortitude or simply, courage. All I know is that when people are around me, they feel power. Yesterday it was personal power. Today it is Holy Ghost power. Many Christians are scared of both. I also know that I have been hated of men because of Jesus. Even when lost, people hated me for His sake because the demons in them knew who I would become in Him. So I have definitely overcome spiritual abuse as evidenced by the fact that if I was not in Christ, I would not be hurt because it is my carnal nature to go after my enemies and topple them DOWN!!!!!

As a babe in Christ, when I restrained myself from retaliating, I have been in serious inner pain. However, the pain continues to fade. In truth, I had to force myself from retaliating. I don't experience that kind of pain anymore, as I have allowed my flesh to die to a need to "pay back." Vengeance is the Lord's and I have witnessed Him repay my enemies. For example, in my auto biographical work, the Making of a Prophet, I purposely did not touch upon the evil that the laity did to me in the three AME Zion Church's that I pastored. I KNEW that I was not ready to talk about it because the pain of my not retaliating against them might have overpowered me. What the membership in these churches did to me was just that evil. It might cause my own flesh to rise to write about it in detail.

When I was on the streets in the 60's, wheeling and dealing with the world, I never experienced that much hatred, that much evil. Pimps and whores have more integrity than many professing Christians that I have encountered. I came into Christ off of the bar stools, so I know what I am talking about, first hand. All I can say about my experiences with those that I pastored in Zion is that "they were in the Lord's hands." And He dealt with them. There is no retaliation that I could have dispensed any worst than what my enemies obtained at His hand. The cross I carry is heavy. We all must "pick it up" when we follow Him. But I'm moving toward that place of rest, where the slings and arrows don't penetrate my armor and reach my heart like they used to. As a deliverance worker, what I guard my inner being against spiritual contamination, particularly when confronting a spirit of rejection or if I am working with a person in bondage to the occult---my own areas of vulnerability.

I have learned from experience that spiritual abuse can also be self inflicted. In my case, it was a hunger for greatness that was with me from childhood. In my early years, I was always number 1 in school, all the way up to high school. I was valedictorian in an all black elementary and Junior high, and #7 in a well mixed high school in NYC, out of 1000 students in my senior class. When I was in the AME Zion Church, Bishop George Walker recognized that I hoped to be "discovered" by him in ministry but the Lord hardened his heart toward me. At first, I did not see the Lord's hand within the situation and I took Bishop's Walker's hardening as spiritual abuse, when in reality it was the Lord's doing.

My ambitious nature drove me to desire Bishop Walker to pave a way for me in Zion. When I first saw TD Jakes providing a platform for sistahs in ministry, I thought to myself "that could have been me." Yet when I was almost there in the AME Zion Church, the Lord allowed the demons in the people to "push me out." As I "went through", I had no idea how close I was to finally being recognized, but "the Lord knew." As I wrote in my second book, the Bishop who replaced Walker was my kind of apostolic leader and without a doubt, Walker's replacement would have "discovered me." He had visited our area once for a conference. As he and I walked and talked through the neighborhood, I looked him dead in the face and said "I wish you were my Bishop." He blushed and grinned, half scolding me with his eyes and half saying "YES!!!!" I want to be your Bishop also.

So with the Lord "knowing all", The truine God conferred and declared, "I've got to get Pam out of there before she gets "lifted up" in pride and in a position of human power that she will become too attached to. Even after I left Zion, the book was complete, and about to be published, the religious demon tried to tempt me. He whispered "Go back and mingle among the hypocrites and make them eat crow. The kind of Bishop you have hoped for is here. Your dreams are about to come true. Just turn the book into a novel. Forget about "blowing the whistle" for your time has come. Go back! Go back!!!!!"

Well, by this time, the fear of the Lord was on me so strong that I knew if I went back, the Lord would never use me again and my entire destiny would have been for nothing. I'd just be another powerless pastor with a big church. So it was not hard for me to say "no" to the devil "this" time!!!! Anyway, once hypocritical worship was out of my system, the thought of going back among those phonies was extremely distasteful. I just cannot stomach it anymore. When the dust is shaken from my feet, it is "SHOOK!!!!!"

Therefore, within my particular situation lies an important revelation of the ways of the Lord---an insight that I hope will comfort those who have been rejected or spiritually abused in a church or a denomination as I was. If the Lord had not blocked my climb to the top all of these years, I would be of no use to Him in these end times. Position, power and prestige requires compromise and protocol restrictions. For example, if I had fulfilled my secular ambition to become a Commissioner in state government, I would not have been able to go into a state prison and preach. I can't say how many inmates really got saved, but an average of 10 per service came forward and repented. I would have altars filled with men, coming to Jesus, some with tears rolling down there faces. In 8 years, I estimate that about 2000 predominately black men came to the prison altar to be saved. Consequently, I believe that I was restrained so as to be able to be ready for what is coming in the near future, with all hindrances removed.

If you have been rejected as a Christian by those who claim to be His, consider that Jesus may have used the rivalry, envy and ambition of others to allow the religious demon to place stumbling blocks in your way. The Lord Himself often employs the religious demon to keep us humble and restrained from either following or becoming a false prophet. In my case, the Lord saw to it that my plans for ministry in the AME Zion Church would not be fulfilled. Actually, He allowed the religious demon to ride me like I was a wild horse that needed to be broken. For a person with my soulish nature to be able to deal with not being successful and famous in anything that she put her hands to do is itself a miracle that only Christ could perform. In fact, when I consider what I evolved from to who I am today, I am utterly amazed.

For example, years ago, I received several visions of having a mega church even before I knew that such churches existed. I saw myself in a vision with 6000 members, a rather small mega church by today's standards. Even so, I have a distant membership web ministry, and as people begin to get frustrated with "church as usual", it would not be difficult for our membership to quickly grow electronically to those proportions and beyond. However, such a huge ministry is not really in my heart today and I don't believe that the mega church is the "new thing" that I am called to. I suspect that my vision was inspired by a religious demon in his attempt to derail and disappoint me when the Lord blocked my way. When I perceive my own spirit, I realize that I am truly a "one on one" person, who goes after the 1 yet still nurtures the 99. In fact, I don't particularly care if anyone knows who I am or not. I am a spiritual warrior.

Whether in failure or in accomplishment, popular or rejected, it is in my nature to feel significant. However, the Jezebel spirit is particularly attracted to a soul that feels very insignificant. Those who are so oppressed will develop a rigidity and an unbalanced "super strength" which makes them think and act as if they can master any situation in their own power. Such a person will pretend that he is leaning and trusting on the Lord's power by spouting scripture like "I can do all things through Christ who strengthens me", yet within his soul he considers any weakness as a disgrace.

Steeped in pride, he judges other saints as being weak, when in reality, he himself feels weak and insignificant. This is fertile ground for a witchcraft spirit because the demon can use the captive to intimidate the weaker brethren, followed by accusations and recriminations that cause the captive to feel condemned. The witchcraft spirit finds a special enjoyment in causing its captives to despise themselves once they have fallen. This demon is also comfortable inside of an apparently timid soul that secretly lusts to have control over others as well as over himself. A person under the influence of a witchcraft demon will want nothing to occur that he himself has not initiated or approved of.

Such people claim to want everyone around them to be free, while simultaneously demanding to know every detail of even the most insignificant situations. When such a person has not been informed of everything, he becomes extremely agitated. People with this character flaw can appear to be extremely generous. No one may even notice his desire to dominate and control because the captive is so subtly manipulative.

Usually in such cases, a lying demon is involved also. One who does not know his own personality type will become so frustrated that he may develop psycho-somatic illnesses such as major headaches or fits of depression when he feels "out of control of others." This kind of illness can occur when the person develops an unconscious defense mechanism to fight the witchcraft spirit by using his willpower to repress his own curiosity. As the saying goes, "curiosity killed the cat." When a person lies to his own soul, this gives demons the opportunity to attach the body. The desire to have his own way will be a source of serious irritation and inflammation when others do not do exactly what he expects of them and exactly at the time that he expects it. The desire to have his own way will be inflamed by the witchcraft demon's lust for domination.

When the captive's lust for domination is uncontrollable, the witchcraft demon will cause the captive to be in a constant state of irritation when others are "disobedient" or "non-compliant" to his suggestions, recommendations and instructions. Any kind of delay or necessity to wait may even lead to outbursts of temper that may also erupt into rage. Demons will also work to cause the captive to superficially restrain such outbursts so as to cause him to be ill prepared for a future eruption that will lead to an unexpected disaster that demons have secretly planned for years. In such cases, the witchcraft demon will align itself with a spirit of death. The spirit of death specializes in accidents, suicide and murder. The devil comes to steal, kill and destroy. Out of control of his temper, the spirit of death will work in consort with the witchcraft demon to cause the captive to have either a stroke or a heart attack. This is when the fruit of patience and long suffering will come to the rescue.

The demons also work well when the captive is unaware of his own bossy behavior. Even if he becomes hostile and angry when things don't go his way, the witchcraft demon will cause him to still insist that he is merely a gentle and meek soul who is provoked into anger because the brethren are so ill advised in their rebellion against him. The rage arising from the rebellion of significant others may be hidden to such an extent that the captive may not even recognize why he often feels depresses and tired. Only accurate observation can gradually and progressively uncover the connection between the captive's desire to control others and how this desire must be broken by the Holy Ghost. If the captive begins to recognize the connection between his pride, his desire to control others, and his fatigue, depression and anxiety, he will be able to successfully prepare the ground of his soul for the expulsion of the witchcraft demon.

To summarize, witchcraft demons can hide in a person who naturally has a strong personality as well as a person who appears to have a low self image. Every newborn comes into this world a sinner, tooting his own horn. Infants learn quickly how to have a temper tantrum by screaming to get its needs met. Babies have the power to control their adult parents with such screams of temper. Jesus said that the meek would inherit the earth. A meek person is one who puts the Lord's will before his own and complies and submits to the word of God in spite of his own desires and feelings. Yet, somehow, the witchcraft demon will also use the seemingly weak to inherit or "own" the souls of others.

The witchcraft demon will also use "the weak" to bring guilt trips, condemnation and accusations against those who have a strength of character that they themselves lack. This is the spirit of Jezebel at its best because the weak seem to be so helpless in their attempts to control people with "love and affection." This is the manner in which the witchcraft side of Jezebel very often enters into parent/child relationships, a situation that is discussed in more detail in other chapters.

In consideration of the personality of the soul, suffice it to say that the domineering personality trait in the pursuit of power and control does not necessarily manifest itself with open hostility towards others. In fact, it is often disguised in socially acceptable ways, like giving advice, seeking to manage other people's affairs, or taking a helpful initiative in problem solving. The religious side of Jezebel will see to it that the captive himself has no idea that he is manipulative, dominating and controlling. Even when he becomes agitated when things do not go his way, he will live under the delusion that he is simply a gentle Christian soul who is annoyed primarily because others are just too ignorant to realize the value of his investment into their lives. The following are some common types of cognitive distortions characteristic of people who have a Jezebelian influence:

All or nothing thinking: Experiences are evaluated in terms of extremes, concluding that one fall leads to complete failure is an example. Such thinking is detrimental to fighting and standing against demons.

Selective attention: Attention is given to only those facts that support the captive's preconceived ideas about the Lord, their perceived enemies, the demons and themselves. Truth that points to a different conclusion from their own is rejected.

Molehill thinking: The captive anticipates and looks for the worst possible outcome, nullifying hope and therefore weakening his faith.

These are but a few cognitive distortions. Where the religious demon is concerned, every human personality presents unique variations. Place in your mind if you would, watching a child blow bubbles with liquid soap. Picture the bubbles floating around in the air before they all burst. I am finding that with Christians who have a religious demon as well as severe mental illness, each false notion or doctrine in the mind is like a separate demon,in a long line of "bubbles." The word of God in this instance rings so true. Clearly, this type of client MUST be taught how to "cast down imaginations and every high thing that would exalt itself about the knowledge of God and bring EVERY THOUGHT INTO THE OBEDIENCE OF CHRIST JESUS. (II Corinthians 10:4,5)

I have found that a captive's thoughts are themselves like little demons in the mind, floating around like bubbles that are as solid as rocks. Through our unique pre-and post deliverance counseling approach, my task is that of a bubble buster. However, once these bubbles are burst, there may not even be a need to cast out any demons. I have found that the only demon that must be faced to be cast out is the witchcraft side of Jezebel because the power of witchcraft is connected to a claim of covenant rights. However, it is easier to cast out a witchcraft demon than a religious demon because of the client's inability to "cast down high thoughts and allow the counselor to break those bubbles!"

ENDNOTES

1.J.P. Lewis, War on the Saints, abridged edition, pg. 151
2.David Johnson & Jeff VanVonderen in "The Subtle Power of Spiritual Abuse"
3.Daniel Shaw LCSW, Traumatic Abuse in Cults", Cult Studies Review, Vol 2, No.2. 2003 101-129

CHAPTER 10: PREPARING THE GROUND

Before I plant new seed, I begin the counseling process by plowing the ground of the captive's soul. Repentance is the most essential plowing tool. Repentance will soften the hardened ground of a cold conscience and prepare the darkened spirit to be translated out of the demonic kingdom into the kingdom of God. Discerning of spirits is yet another important tool. As a supernatural gift of the Holy Ghost, the gift of discerning of spirits operates by the will of God and not the will of man. Therefore, I use diagnostic assessment tools, questionnaires, and screening devices to uncover demonic deception, influence and infestation by the use of the Deliverance Assessment Form. As mentioned in Chapter 9, I have created my own version the form found in a book entitled "How To Cast Out Demons" by Doris Wagner. Doris Wagner credits others for their input into the form.

In a search for demonic doorways, plowing is an initial and fundamental step to pre-deliverance counseling, involving the steady and painstaking turning over of the ground of the soul. A demonic doorway may be personal or generational. It involves an action or a practice that opened up the individual, and perhaps his or her entire family to demonic oppression. The pre-deliverance counselor that employs this model must develop keen listening skills during personal interviews. Virtual counseling requires excellent reading, reasoning and even investigative skills to not only be able to understand and interpret the lines, but also to "read between them." For as the Greatest Counselor of all has proclaimed "out of the abundance of the heart (the mind and emotions of the soul), the mouth speaks." (Matthew 12:34)

Plowing is an information gathering, storing and organizing phase of the work of pre-deliverance where I pose the questions of "who is this client?""what is this client the product of and who has molded him or her?" "is this client saved?" "How many demons are involved and what are their names?" "What are the most important spiritual truths that this client must receive in order to be able to actively participate in his or her own deliverance?" "What are this client's strengths and weaknesses?" and most of all, "is this client capable of standing in the midst of a deliverance, in the fight to regain stolen territory?" The information gleaned during the plowing stage will also lead to the development of a deliverance treatment plan.

Planning follows assessment in the problem solving process. Assessment sets the stage for the actual deliverance and planning specifies what should be done. The most important tool in the planning process is the client. For example, if the assessment process reveals that the client's faith is not active or that there are major issues of doubt and unbelief, then a major objective of the pre-deliverance counseling process is to build up the client's faith. As a counselor, the deliverance treatment plan will list problems, hindrances in the situation, the goals, objectives and the strategies toward building the client's faith. The question then becomes "how important is this issue of faith relative to the strength of the particular demon or demons involved? Can the demon be cast out prior to his or her faith being built up? Does this person have a strong network system of Christian elders who can stand with the client or is the client's church the source of the problem? Will the client be even further devoured because of a lack of faith?

As I prepare the deliverance treatment plan, I also examine the pros and the cons relative to what are the captive's chances of success. Demons will always come out at the name of Jesus, whether the person is saved or a believer, but I recognize a need to assess incremental steps to be taken in order to ensure that the captive is able to stand against re-infestation. This is why the religious demon is the first to "hunt" for. The reality is that if the captive is not saved but believes that he is, to cast out demons may just place the client in even more bondage. Only a saved person has the power to stand against the enemy. The armor of the Lord only belongs to those who believe on His Name.

As previously stated, a major part of the treatment plan is to also specify objectives. For example, on the Deliverance Assessment Form is a question that seeks information on whether or not the captives has tattoos. In a particular case, the captive checked the box. When I inquired deeper about it, she revealed to me that there were three large python snakes on her back. Subsequently, the treatment plan included a specific objective to remove the tattoos by either covering them with tape during the deliverance, or going back to the tattooist and have these snakes covered with "the red blood of Jesus" and blocked out with a cross.

In short, once the problems and issues are revealed, then along with the client, we prioritize them, set up specific goals, objectives and tasks to be completed in order to ensure a successful deliverance. For example, in a recent case, a young woman raised in a word of faith church continued to doubt her salvation, even though she was well trained in scripture and understood the doctrines of repentance and the resurrection. Through the plowing process, we uncovered that her problems were connected to an incident of lesbian exploration, a circumstance that involved its own set of objectives.

As an aside, through experience I know that certain demons put up the worst struggle during deliverance because it believes that it has rights, ---a lease to the house of one's soul--- based upon an act such as "giving one's soul to the devil" or tattooing the devil's mark on one's body. I myself would not put any client through that sort of strong buffeting to the body by an outraged demon that believes that it has "squatter's rights" due to the client's willfully branding of herself with a Satanic symbol. In this case, the client went back to the tattooist had him cover the snakes with red ink, signifying the blood of Jesus. The witchcraft demon did put up a fight, but it was very minor, considering what I know it is capable of.

The main objective of deliverance counseling is to set the captive free. Therefore, in order to assess whether or not the objective of freedom has been obtained, we must do what Jesus did. We must ask questions about the client's condition while in captivity. For example, in Mark Ch 9:17-18, a father describes to Jesus the condition of his mute son. He reports that the demon would seize his son, cause him to foam at the mouth, gnash his teeth, and become rigid. Jesus then asked the father an important question BEFORE He cast out the demon in question. He asked , "How long has this been happening to him and the father replied, "since he was a child." Even more information is obtained. The Lord finds out that the demon often threw this man's son into fire and into water to destroy him.

A demon that tries to throw a captive into fire or water for the sake of killing him is what is called a spirit of death. However, the demon of death was not addressed. Jesus spoke directly to the two most powerful demons in this case: the deaf and dumb spirit. In this regard, the importance of gathering information and forming objectives is for the major purpose of providing a means for measuring whether or not the objectives have been attained. In other words, have the demonic manifestations stopped? The only way one would know if freedom has been obtained is to clearly describe the typical demonic condition. Has the fear and anxiety ceased? Are the voices gone? Even so, from experience I have learned that demons can "play possum." The symptoms may disappear but since the doorways that gave them entrance may not have been addressed, the release from torment may merely be a smokescreen.

> "When evil spirits are able to give visions, it is an evidence that they have already gained ground in the man, be he a Christian or an unbeliever. The 'ground' being, not of necessity known sin, but a condition of passivity, ie., non-action of the mind, imagination, and other faculties. This essential condition of passive non-action as the means of obtaining supernatural manifestations is well understood by spiritist mediums, clairvoyants, crystal gazers, and others, who know that the least action of the mind immediately breaks the clairvoyant state."

> "Believers not knowing these main principles can unwittingly fulfill the conditions for evil spirits to work in the life, and ignorantly induce the passive state by wrong conceptions of the true things of God. eg., They may (1) in seasons of prayer, sink into a passive mental condition which they think is waiting on God, (2) deliberately will the cessation of their mind action, in order to obtain some supernatural manifestation which they believe to be of God (3) in daily life practice a passive attitude which they think is submission to the will of God' (4) endeavor to bring about a state of personal negation which they have no desires, needs, wishes, hopes, plans which they think is full surrender to God and their 'will' lost in God." (J.P-Lewis, 9th edition, pp. 149-150)

Simply put, captives may unknowingly develop mediumistic opportunities for the religious demon in their quest to be pleasing to God. Recently, a blind woman was at one of my seminars and I thought that I should pray for her healing. However, when I asked her what she wanted, her response was "I want to have the level of sight that I ONCE had, wherein I could see shadows." She had no expectation or even a desire to see normally. So I prayed for what she asked for. This is as far as her faith would take her.

Where deliverance is concerned, you must first of all assess the relationship that the client has with the demons and what are the emotional factors that would cause the client not to want to be completely delivered. Believe it or not, some people like their demons. The demons are accepted as a kind of "company of friends." It is only those rare times when they are being viciously tortured or tormented that they seek help. The reality is that they do not want to do what it takes to be completely delivered. All they want is for their demons to be appeased.

I believe that the more thorough the training, the greater will be our usefulness in God's work. Likewise, the more I spare myself,--my pride, my narrowness, my happiness— the less my usefulness. If I refuse to face the truth about how the religious demon has deceived me, I cannot uncover his elusive tactics with others. According to Watchman Nee, a proud person cannot deal with another with the same condition; a hypocrite cannot touch the hypocrisy in another, nor can one who is loose in his life have a helpful effect on one who suffers the same difficulty. How well we know that if such is still in our nature, we will not be able to condemn such particular sin in others; we in fact can hardly recognize it in others. A doctor may cure others without curing himself, but this can hardly be true in the spiritual realm. The worker is himself first a patient; he must be healed BEFORE he can heal others. Where he has not trodden, he cannot lead others. What he has not learned he cannot teach others. (Taken from "the Release of the Spirit" by Watchman Nee (p 41)

Watchman Nee also wrote:

"We must see that we are the instruments prepared by God for KNOWING MAN. Hence, we must be dependable, qualified to give an accurate assessment. If you want to know what ails a person, you need to first recognize his most prominent feature. It will stand out so conspicuously that, try as he may, he cannot hide it." (W. Nee, p 42)

Along these lines, I perceive my role in deliverance counseling as akin to a trainer who prepares a prizefighter for a boxing match. The trainer lays out the training strategy, and once in the ring, provides the boxer with those aspects of his opponents strategy that causes him to be vulnerable as well as advises the boxer on how to handle an aggressive battle. However, the battle itself belongs to the boxer. Once a deliverance is scheduled, I myself will face the demons and command them in Jesus name, but I must do so with the complete cooperation of a captive who is not only willing to fight, but one that I myself have diligently prepared for battle.

Therefore, as a trainer, the emphasis of any strategy is to implant in the captive a willingness to fight in cold blood because "we wrestle not against flesh and blood but against principalities and powers." (Ephesians 6:12)When we fight in cold blood, we are able to recognize how demons habitually attack us through our significant relationships. In order to empower them to do so, we must be able to teach the sheep how to prepare a counter strategy. Some of the training techniques that I employ include behavioral rehearsal, role reversal, managing self talk, and confrontation and challenge. Behavioral rehearsal is a strategy that prepares the captive on how to handle a specific interaction with a "significant other" for which the the captive feels unprepared. My goal is to reduce anxiety and teach him to use his spiritual armor, particularly to emphasize his "shield of faith." Equipped to anticipate and therein to handle unexpected situations , I prepare the captive to quench the fiery darts of the enemy that come at him through significant others.

Essentially, this is a form of role play. Until the captive has been sufficiently prepared to stand his ground during his own deliverance session, the overall purpose of this strategy is to assist the captive in learning how to bind the demons through practicing new behavior to better cope with demons that use others against him. Whether used during a one-on-one session or during group, the steps are basically the same:

1.The captive identifies the demonic situation, the significant others who are involved and then describes or demonstrates how he or she would ordinarily behave in the situation.

2.The pastor, group leader and/or group members make suggestions on how the situation might be handled according to the word of God and the fruits of the Holy Spirit.

3. The captive is given an opportunity to provide additional information about the problem or concern and to ask the deliverance counselor and or group members to further explain the suggestions.

4. A role-play is used to demonstrate the behavioral changes suggested to the captive. The counselor or group members will usually take the role of the captive. However, the captive may enact the behavior if he or she feels ready and understands the changes being suggested.

5. After the role-play, the counselor or group members first identifies those aspects of the captive's performance that will lead to victory, with suggestions for improvement.

6. When the captive understands how he or she ought to operate, the captive will practice the behavior until he or she is satisfied.

7. The counselor or trainer should arm the captive with scripture that is suitable to the particular situation.

The major limitation of all of these strategies is that even though the captive may successfully learn what to do in the presence of the pastor, counselor and/or the group, he may not be able to generalize it to the real life situation. Sometimes the real situation poses problems that cannot be anticipated during a practice session. Even so, failure is an important aspect of growth through practice. For example, whatever the captive shrinks from hearing about will ultimately stifle his productivity. Since demons will not retreat unless the cause is removed, I train the client not to take back ground from the enemy by learning how not to avoid truth or to shrink from reality.

Role reversal is similar to behavioral rehearsal in that its goal is to prepare the captive to not allow demons to be victorious in shaping the captive's behavior through provocation. In role reversal, the captive learns to prepare for the significant other's interaction in a particular situation and plan a counter strategy. Whether behavioral rehearsal or role reversal, the ultimate goal is to prepare the captive to meet an invisible foe by learning through experience how to take and use his spiritual armor for the battle. Each role play should emphasize a particular demonic strategy: seduction, temptation, distraction, accusation, division, confusion, persecution, tribulation, deception, vexation, oppression, depression, and provocation.

Another important facet of preparing the captive to stand in spiritual warfare is to arm him with the spiritual knowledge of the nature of the fight. Demons most often use those that we are close to in an attempt to break down our defenses and cause us to act out in ways that are not becoming our Christian witness. Along these lines, a very basic spiritual truth is that the soul of the unsaved has been conditioned by his life experiences in the world with significant others, who themselves have unwittingly been led by demons. Each unsaved soul has become accustomed to "practicing sin." Some people have lived most of their lives by lying, gossiping, and by not walking in the truth. Before Christ, most of us are filled with lies and walk very naturally and comfortably in the midst of strife and confusion.

This kind of behavior is soulish or carnal, a doorway for demonic infestation. It has its roots in pride, lust, desire, a need for approval from others and vanity. It is crucial for us to know that as soon as someone is born, the main strategies of the "evil one" are to plant negative seed into the ground of the captive's soul and his spirit so that his assigned demons can produce a negative harvest in that person's life. As recorded in Matthew's gospel the 13th Chapter, Jesus used the symbols of harvesting to describe the power of words, particularly the word of God, to nourish and develop you from within. Those who have been placed in authority over each of us--- whether parents, relatives, teachers or peers, ---and particularly those who have not submitted to the Lordship of Jesus Christ--- have been unwittingly used by demons to form us, as they unknowingly have planted negative seed into our souls.

Moreover, a crucial factor to consider in the realm of spiritual abuse is the recognition of the spiritual importance of parental authority. Demons have worked behind the scenes in early childhood, using the authority of parents and relatives to create demonic doorways. For example, demons continue to use parents to encourage a child to develop an unhealthy competitive spirit that will ultimately lead to jealousy, pride and strife throughout life. None of us have been exempt. I can personally remember that getting high grades in school had such a fixation on my young life, that I would even cheat to maintain an "A." Why? Because I was looking for favor from the world of education and approval from the world of my family. I lusted after the positive strokes obtained from such an achievement.

Let's face it. Demons specialize. Other children did things that sought favor from the world of their peers. Like joining gangs, lying, stealing, fighting and boasting---whatever it took to be popular. It is all the same. Whoever owns your soul, you will attempt to please. Excelling in school for the teachers appears so wonderful and noble. However, we must be cautious of those things that seem righteous, yet whose motives are unrighteous. I remember how I was trained to look for favor from the world. I used to study and wave my hand in the classroom, looking for the praises from my elementary school teachers. Is that wrong in itself? No, it isn't. It is an acceptable norm in the world to do well in school. However, an ungodly habit formed in me from what seemed to be a positive thing. In a broader sense, my behavior could have subtly been motivated by a philosophy that "the ends justifies the means", particularly if the results appear to be positive, such as getting high grades in school. Put another way, the captive's mind can become accustomed to perceive and react to life in "worldly" ways.

In order to put on the new man, there are some basic steps we must follow as we are guided into all truth about ourselves by the Holy Spirit. Suffice it to say that the ideal situation for a believer is to allow his mind to renewed by the word of God so that the spirit will have more of a direct influence on the soul than will the flesh. This is a difficult task to accomplish. When a person becomes "born again", the spirit is made new but the soul has remained basically the same. Consequently, renewing the mind or "putting on the new man" involves dealing with habits that were formed in us by our interactions with the world. Take my childhood cheating to impress the teachers as an example. This was a pattern of behavior developed in me over time, wherein the act of cheating to obtain favor with others became a repetitive form of manipulative behavior that I adopted as a young adult, in order to remain in good favor with others. Consequently, unless issues of this kind are dealt with BEFORE deliverance, demons will ultimately enter into that doorway again, in the very near future.

I personally do not believe that a demon can enter into the spirit of a truly born again believer and possess him. However, demons can and DO obtain access to the soul. Since the spirit and the soul are wrapped together tightly, ie. like joints and marrow, (Hebrews 4:12) a person who is born again in his spirit can manifest the same behavior as a demonized unsaved person. In such cases, the demons in the soul have grieved and quenched the power of the Holy Spirit that resides in the temple of the saved person's spirit. Demons will leave both the saved and the unsaved when called out in faith in the Name of Jesus Christ of Nazareth.

The difference between the demonized saved and the demonized unsaved is a matter of covenant rights. In the book of Isaiah, the Lord refers to two different kinds of captives: the prey and the lawfully captive. I believe that the prey are the unsaved. The lost are like helpless rabbits ensnared by a fox---consumed, devoured and destroyed without Jesus. This is the condition of an unsaved demonized captive. Furthermore, I believe that those who are lawfully captive have been taken prisoner by demons because of mitigating factors that have led to the captive's breaking of the covenant made in blood by Jesus the Christ. In this regard, the most important element of deliverance is for both the deliverance counselor and the captive to gain an understanding of the nature of the captive's relationship with the Lord. As the assessment process unfolds, I seek to uncover predictable patterns.

Therefore, it is crucial to ascertain whether or not the captive has covenant rights obtained only by salvation. Since I can never be 100 percent sure of an individual's salvation. I require the captive to sign and notarize the Deliverance Disclaimer Form (the DDF) so as to free myself from all liability. (See Appendix) For example, suppose I cast out a demon from someone whom I thought was saved, and it turns out that their condition worsened because several more demons entered his soul due to the fact that he did not have covenant rights---was not covered by the blood--- to stand and to remain free. Only God really knows who is saved but Jesus said that it is possible for us to know the saved " by their fruit."

I have discovered that when a person has been seriously oppressed by demons, it is not easy to find fruit early on. The best thing to do is to ask the captive to describe his conversion experience. I pay particular attention to the captive's understanding of repentance, rebirth, and resurrection. These "3 R's" will generally reveal whether or not the person has a clear understanding of salvation and if their soul is "good ground." For as Jesus said, good ground is determined by understanding the gospel and baring fruit. (Matthew 13) The first fruit of the salvation experience is repentance.

Those who are demonized and unsaved should be led to the Lord prior to deliverance. Sometimes this is not possible because the demon that has them bound has blinded their minds from understanding and receiving the glorious gospel of Jesus Christ, the major cause for their own particular darkness. In such a case, the religious demon, or a spirit of confusion should be cast out first. Once the demons have been expelled, it is my practice to immediately present the "3 R's", and lead the captive into the kingdom.

Personally, I believe that a person who is saved will generally know that he is saved. There should be no doubt in his mind about that. He definitely will need his helmet of salvation to be fixed and immovable. With the saved captive, the next step is to determine whether or not the captive already had demons prior to rebirth. This is usually the case.

Very seldom has the demons of a new convert been dealt with, particularly if he was saved at the altar of a church. Most of the time, the pastor and the church will write the new converts name down for the roll book and give him the right hand of fellowship. There is no place in the order of worship to "cast out demons." If a new believer's demons were dealt with within days or weeks of his conversion, he would definitely be able to avoid demonic pitfalls in his effort to grow up in the Lord.

So I highly recommend that the pastor and/or the deliverance counselor be prepared for this reality. In cases where demons were not immediately dealt with, the captive will find that once he became a believer, his problems of the past not only persisted, but in most cases have intensified since he received Jesus as Lord and Savior. This should be expected. Demons hate Jesus. If the flesh by nature wars against the spirit without demons, then it is predictable that the warfare will intensify if demons also inhabit the captives' soul and body. Consider the person whose family is involved in some form of witchcraft, whether it be Catholicism, Santeria, or Voodoo. Let's face it. Manipulation, intimidation, coercion, extortion, threats and fear have been indicative of the predominant lifestyle of his dysfunctional family.

In my own practice, I have uncovered in counseling that the root of obsessive-compulsive behavior is quite often the undercover work of the witchcraft spirit. Similarly, a person whose parents were alcoholics may have been exposed to a lying spirit in his childhood in his attempt to cover up or hide his parent's addiction. The addiction demon rarely stands alone but is also in league with demons of perversion, depression and the spirit of death through the suicide demon. In any event, once the information that has been gathered and gleaned from the DAF has been reviewed, the assessment process begins with the initial interview and continues with the first 4-8 weeks of pre-deliverance counseling. In this context, the strategy involves assessing the number and nature of the demons, determining the personality traits of the soul that give place to demons, and designing a treatment plan that will prepare for pitfalls.

COUNTERFEITS OF DELIVERANCE MINISTRY

I have recently read in an article on the web about a form of spiritual abuse that has occurred within deliverance ministry. Those among the remnant church must be particularly cautious in not falling into a trap set by a demon who specializes in counterfeit deliverances. One thing I do know by the word of God and by my own experience: Where casting out of a demon is concerned, if the Christian captive is sufficiently prepared and armed with spiritual knowledge to fight the good fight, the expulsion itself should not take more than 15 minutes, if that long. An hour's session should be about 45 minutes of counseling, prayers and confessions, with about 15 minutes or less for the actual demonic expulsion.

The following horror stories of spiritual abuse in deliverance will help you to understand why I warn you to proceed with due diligence:

"One picture which I can remember from the early days of ministry at Ellel was that they said I had been a twin (that was what they felt) and that my mother had aborted it herself. They then got me to name it. For months I was in a state of grief. They said I had been carrying part of my "twin" brother's spirit in me. You can only imagine the panic and grief that such an idea can cause you. I don't believe for a moment that I ever was a twin."

"When I had my ears pierced in Brighton, they said that I had received the spirits of thousands of babies that had been thrown over cliffs in the Norse period as they thought I was related to them. They had seen these people doing it because I was blond and my ancestors had come from Northern Europe many hundreds of years ago. They asked me to take off my earrings so the screams of the trapped souls could come out. I was devastated with the screams they all made. You really do get into all of this when you are there because you are taken on journeys with pictures you see of your ancestors doing things. This is really horrible. Then you have to forgive them and get set free from the demons. To think that you had the spirits of people, your ancestors plus your own brothers, was enough to make you go insane. I didn't though, by the grace of God."

It should be noted here that during a deliverance session, manifestations could occur. Demons generally leave through openings in the body, most often the mouth and the ears. They are frequently located in the stomach or belly area. This too should not be a surprise since the belly is noted in the bible as the place where the human spirit dwells. Since the spirit and the soul, though separate in function, are wrapped together tightly like bone and marrow, the soul is also located in "the belly." Since the belly or the diaphragm are close to the stomach, the captive may experience some vomiting because of the struggle the demons exert upon leaving the belly. However, demons also play possum type games with manifestations so we should not depend upon them to validate whether or not a demon has been cast out

Because of the potential for vomiting, the captive should be advised to fast for several hours prior to the deliverance. Coughing is another common manifestation. Furthermore, the captive should be comfortably seated in a chair or on a sofa in a private session. The purpose of pre-deliverance counseling is to strengthen the captive so that he or she will not "pass out", but actively participate in his own deliverance. The captive should first come to you rather than a traditional Christian counselor or a secular counselor because he is convinced BEFOREHAND that he is demon oppressed. I am not in the business of trying to persuade the saved or the unsaved that they have demons. The following quote taken from the same article that describes a deliverance counseling ministry called "Ellel" is definitely NOT the kind of deliverance counseling session that my deliverance training programs are all about:

"I should say that most people who go to Ellel for ministry have to go on a 3 day healing retreat BEFORE they start the actual ministry and this is what this man who ran away was on. I too went on this. The sounds that used to come out of this building were horrible. Screams and retching all the time. It is horrible to think about it. Ear piercing sounds. Their bodies behaving in bizarre ways. Always going down in the spirit when being prayed for. Splat! Falling backwards on the floor. Some would start trying to rip off clothes and jewelry. There would be many people ready to hold them down. Very bad cases would be dragged off to the many bedrooms away from public viewing. Eventually, after my 6 sessions in 1998, they said that I was free from all demons. They had ministered inner healing too. Basically praying for my soul to be cleansed from any spirits and emotional holds. The problem with this ministry is that you rely on pictures that you see or they see. They can be very wacky or disturbing to your soul.

During 1999, I went to all the healing meetings. I went up for prayer regarding a hip pain I was getting. A different person ministered to me. She said it was freemasonry and it was "Jacobs Hip." She said it was something one of my ancestors had done in freemasonry. Then she got someone else to help. (This is when you know it's going to be heavy.) They started cutting me off from freemasonry, going through various degrees. It took too long because they went through the ceremonies at each degree, asking me what I could see, and then I had to forgive my ancestors for taking part. The problem was that, as far as I know, not a soul in my family has been a Freemason."

To well meaning but untrained deliverance workers, allow me to impress upon you that deliverance is a very important mandate for this hour. Consequently, you can see why demons have already entered into this viable ministry in an attempt to contaminate it. Satan is aware of what the Lord has in store where deliverance is concerned and so he has very skillfully developed a counterfeit by deceiving well meaning people who became enthralled with seeking after demonic manifestations and other signs. The professionalism of my method of counseling in no way overshadows the anointing of Jesus Christ to cast out devils. However, in the complicated society that we now live in, I believe that today we need to be prepared to stand in power in the courtrooms around the world.

Depression, Victimization and Rejection

Depression is common to survivors of abuse. The depression I refer to is more than having just a bad day or feeling occasional sadness. As a deliverance counselor, I must know the difference between dysthymia, a despondency in mood, and clinical depression. Major Depressive Disorder is a serious condition that needs to be recognized and treated. I encourage captives to take advantage of medications for depression that are prescribed by a psychiatrist or a doctor. As Christians, we should use good sense and thank God for those who not only discovered medication for hypertension and diabetes but also for those who have provided us with mental health medications.

I also train each of my depressed clients to learn what triggers depression in them and I prepare them to take necessary precautions. For those who have suffered with such a condition for long periods of time it may not be easily recognized. Depression may just appear to be a common personality characteristic. Episodes may come on without notice - especially during difficult and highly stressful times. I encourage the depressed to take extra good care of himself physically. Proper diet, exercise, and medication when merited, will all help to alleviate the symptoms of depression. Allowing himself to become overtired and exhausted in the healing process will only add to it.

Where victimization and spiritual abuse are concerned, I make every effort to learn what I can do to diminish its affects upon the captive. The captive may manifest an inability to make simple decisions without spiritual leaders being consulted. The hunger for spiritual guidance and relief from varying degrees of despair and fear are often what impels people to explore religious and secular self-improvement groups. Yet the leaders of these groups typically do not attempt to help the captive explore and make sense of the difficulties that have led him to seek spiritual consolation or self-improvement in the first place. Rather, the cult leader tends to exploit the seeker's emotional vulnerabilities and seduces the captive into a state of dependence. Promising the acquisition of success and power, salvation and redemption, or relief from frustration and inhibition, the leader persuaded the captive that the leader's self-proclaimed perfection can belong to the follower as well. All one must do is totally embrace the leader's ideology. (Shaw, 2003)

In cults, this generally translates into securing the leader's favor by enthusiastically agreeing to recruit others to the leader's church or to tithe or give offerings into the leader's ministry so as to obtain a 100 fold return. Eventually, the captive may become frustrated, confused, and extremely passive. Often, the captive becomes so overwhelmed by what he believes that he cannot do about a situation that he does not do what he can! One way the captive can begin to break the frustration of feeling so out of control of his circumstances is to intentionally exercise his will power's ability to choose.

The first step is that he must refuse to remain in bondage. He should also actively fight victimization by allowing his mind to be renewed by the word of God to reject maintaining a "victim mentality." Sometimes a captive who has been spiritually abused is so stuck in a particular mindset that he needs someone to help him discern and recognize what is actually going on because he has become habituated to the same attitudes and behavior patterns. During the counseling sessions, I spell out for him exactly what victimization looks like and what victim mentality actually is, with lots of practical, everyday examples on how to identify it.

Unfortunately, traditional church polity and politics create fertile conditions for being ostracized when ones behavior does not conform to group norms. It is important to point out that once the captive realizes that the care and love that he once experienced within a fellowship group was merely conditional, bitterness will have to be dealt with prior to deliverance. In addition, when the captive discovers that his relationships within the abusive cult or church were based upon a dysfunctional family model, the captive will experience deep feelings of rejection.

Where spiritual abuse is concerned, rejection may manifest itself in the following ways:

a. The captive feels empty, lonely and unable to trust people; it is hard for him to make a commitment to others

b. The captive may believe that he will never find a place to belong again;

c. The captive may be angry, bitter and resentful, thereby he rejects all authority

d. The captive may demonstrate a lack of trust with the therapeutic community, including all Christians

e. Realizing that he was defined by success or lack of it, his self-worth has been seriously impaired by group rejection. Therefore he is now socially shy and immature.

Recovery begins with this first: Be not conformed to this world, but be ye transformed by the renewing of your mind, that you may prove what is that good and perfect will of

God,---FOR YOU, OH CAPTIVE. Renewing of the mind includes the entire renewing of the soul----the thoughts, feelings, emotions, and most important of all, the will. In other words, recovery comes when the captive can choose how he will and will not live, who he will and will not live with, what he will and will not allow to happen to him, what he does believe and does not believe, what his soul desires and does not desire, whom he will serve and whom he will not serve--- not so much in himself, but in Christ who has formed him and created him for a purpose.

RENEWAL OF THE SOUL

Many of the captives that I see as a counselor grew up in dysfunctional families, particularly those suffering from cultural witchcraft, substance abuse, and other abuses. The captive has probably learned how to suppress his true feelings. Often they were criticized or emotionally punished for expressing emotions. The captive may also have been exposed to childrearing that invalidated or discounted the feelings that he did express. Therefore in his adult life, the captive may carry with him a tendency to suppress, misinterpret, or mistrust his own emotions and feelings. He also may not be sure of his true feelings, unable to distinguish one from another and can speak of feelings only in broad terms, like saying "I was upset." A counseling practice technique to help the captive to identify and express his feelings involves encouraging the captive to review a list of feelings as an aid to finding the words to describe and express his feelings. 1

While discussing feelings, the captive should be able to understand that feelings and emotions are a normal experience of the soul. Since feelings are barometers of the soul's condition, they should not be hidden or denied. Although some feelings are pleasant and some are unpleasant, the captive should be counseled to realize that having an unpleasant feeling is not a sin. Yet, to indulge an unpleasant feeling by hiding it or trying to suppress it is to allow sin to have dominion over his soul and to give the demons grounds to operate in his life. This will cause the captive to use the willpower of his soul to cause him to "act out" in ways that are unhealthy to his spirit, soul and body.

THE CASTING DOWN IMAGINATIONS METHOD:

Not only can thought be "an imagination", but feelings can also be the same. Therefore, the captive should also be taught at this time how thought guides feelings and how feelings also influence thought. One of the primary strategies of a religious demon is to damage the captives ability to think logically. Therefore, rational thinking can play an important role in counseling. This approach focuses on a client-centered analysis of particular life events and behaviors, using the word of God to either confirm or refute the captive's reasoning. Helping the captive to focus on particular life events or behaviors, analyze them from traditional cultural beliefs versus revelation knowledge and then guiding the captive to use his freewill to choose the will of God as revealed in His word.

As a part of the process, I attempt to guide the captive to objectively examine his emotional state and to bring the entire situation into perspective by making a rational assessment. It will take time, but I look for areas of agreement and build my rational thinking approaches around points of limited contention. It is important to note that the captive cannot begin to solve his problems or take control of his life until he has taken the responsibility for defining the situation that he is facing and seek deliverance with his whole being. In this regard, the captive needs access to all of the available information relevant to his own particular form of oppression from the religious demon.

THE EMPOWERMENT METHOD:

As a deliverance counselor, I view myself as the captive's helper with a small "h." If the client is saved, the Holy Ghost is his Helper with a big "H." I view the born again client as having access to the real definition of his problem because within him, he has "an unction from the Holy Ghost and he needs know man to teach him" about the true nature of his situation. This is the way that you I empower the captive to become an active participant in his own deliverance. My goal is to help build not only his self confidence, but also His faith in God. I present the captive with a view of his life that unfolds meaning, even the demonic activity itself is a source of purpose and victory.

In this way, the captive will be empowered to take the personal risks necessary to break out of self-defeating, self-limiting patterns, and build a Christ centered support network. Although I would like to encourage the client to become involved in a church, unfortunately, with the infiltration of demons of all kinds within church walls and at times, the church itself being a major source of the captive's victimization, I proceed with caution. I am more inclined to serve as a resource as to what the captive should look for in a church than to recommend that he attend any church while he is preparing for deliverance. Experience has taught me that people who have been continuously oppressed by the religious demon in all of its several faces tend to be drawn to churches that are legalistic, spiritually controlling and abusive. Also charismatic witchcraft is prevalent in the church. Once I have gotten to know the captive, I myself have established support groups through teleconferences.

Other empowerment methods include recognizing and building on the captive's strengths, encouraging the captive to make decisions and to follow through on decisions, and help them to understand that trials, tribulations and trouble can be beneficial if it pushes him to reexamine his situation and take actions that are necessary to be delivered from oppression of all kinds.

THE EQUALITY METHOD:

Where cultural witchcraft is concerned, I affirm that ALL cultures have sinned and fallen short of the glory of God. This reality encompasses the idolatrous living of all cultures as well as diverse forms of rebellion in each of them, a rebellion which is akin to witchcraft. Racism and ethnic superiority defy the uniqueness of each ethnic/cultural group. Those who are culturally insensitive will not be able to understand or relate to the captive within his cultural setting. Such an exclusive view ignores the scriptural mandate that as we walk in the spirit, we do not fulfill the lust of our flesh to be either superior or judgmental, for all have sinned and fallen short of the glory of God.

Moreover, it is important to realize that every culture has been impacted by the unseen demonic world. Satan does not discriminate. He is an equal opportunity employer where it come to killing, stealing and destroying God's creation. I make every effort to a impart in my deliverance counseling approach that the Lord is no respecter of persons. Yet, I do not ignore the multi-cultural diversity of the Jezebel spirit. The diverse geographic and cultural backgrounds notwithstanding, I familiarize myself with the common facets and attributes of the captive's culture, followed by designing a broad based outline or profile that highlights basic elements of cultural witchcraft in each particular case.

REPLACING OLD SEED

The captive has been used to words of bondage. Words of bondage have to be replaced with words of freedom. Captives find it helpful to receive feedback regarding the progress they are making. Therefore, every verbal appraisal that I make supports freedom. Since faith comes by hearing, the word of God in my mouth is very important. A deliverance session can set a captive free from demons but if the captive still maintains the same mindsets, another authority figure in their immediate environment, whether it be a job supervisor, a friend, even a pastor or strong church member can put the captive right back into bondage. Put another way, demons know how to travel. They will find someone in the captive's immediate environment to use to continue to send "seed that binds."

Therefore, in my counseling sessions, I make every effort to enable the captive to know how to guard his spirit. In the world, there are colloquial expressions that have become a part of everyday speech. Expressions like, "Go Girl." "I respect your gangsta", "Don't Go there!" "Forget About It", and an oldie but goodie, "Right On!"For example, for "Go Girl", there are many scriptures in the word of God to attached to it, like "you can do all things through Christ who strengthens you. For "I respect your gangsta", let us not forget that the captive has an unction from the Holy Ghost and therefore he needs no man to tell him how to live his life. Whom the Lord has set free is free indeed. "Don't Go There," is yet another necessary expression to use when one is guarding his spirit. Why? Because a wounded spirit, who can bare it? Out of the spirit flows the issues of life. Binding words penetrate the spirit. Therefore, I teach the captive how to assert himself with overpowering people, with role play and role reversal.

Sociologists use the term "cultural theme" to refer to broad, guiding principles that serve to control human behavior. I call them "binding words." For example, there was a prominent false religion among black people prevalent in my mother's time called "The Father Divine Movement." In this movement, the theme was "it is better to be celibate than to marry." This theme pervaded the entire organization. Faithful followers of Father Divine did not believe in sex, marriage, or family. Married couples could join the movement, but they had to separate. In this example, it would be difficult to replace these "binding words" because they are taken out of context from scripture. However, in that same scripture, you will also find some "freedom seed" which goes, "it is better to marry than to burn." No one can be celibate without receiving a supernatural gift from God. Sex is as normal as human appetite. Therefore, someone who has been bound needs to fill his spirit and his soul with words that will set him free.

As a counselor, I cultivate "freedom seed" in my mouth.

CHAPTER 11: THE DYSFUNCTIONAL FAMILY AND CULTURAL WITCHCRAFT

Cultural witchcraft is a phrase that I believe that I may have originated. Defined from a scriptural perspective, cultural witchcraft relates to a dysfunctional family's interactions and collective lifestyles--- subtly linked to an ancestral sin of idolatry and/or witchcraft, passed down to subsequent generations. Ancestral idolatry and witchcraft will generally appear in the form of issues of family control and competition, including but not limited to sibling rivalry, domestic violence, verbal abuse,--- in other words, controlling behaviors or "power trips". Intimidation, manipulation and domination are repeatedly enacted within a family that has been oppressed by demons from generation to generation because of ancestral idolatry, false religion or witchcraft.

The old testament warns that those who practice idolatry and witchcraft will pass these demons down to their descendants, at least for four (4) generations. (Exodus 20:5, 34:6-7, Numbers 14:18, Deuteronomy 4:9-19, Jeremiah 32: 17-18, and Matthew 23:31-35) For the most part, generational curses become operative if any of the Ten Commandments are broken. Where idolatry is concerned, God the Father warned the children of Israel that since He brought them out of Egyptian bondage, they should not make a carved image to bow down to it. The consequences for disobedience is a warning that the iniquity of the fathers will be visited upon the children to the third and fourth generations.

Although Jesus Christ has redeemed us from the curse of the law, having become a curse for us, this does not mean that the warnings of the 10 Commandments no longer apply. The curse of the law is physical death for anyone who breaks the law. We have been redeemed from the consequences of physical death in that Christ died for us, paid the price and went into hell on our behalf as our substitute. The Lord's sacrifice provides us with eternal life. Even so, the cross does not automatically redeem us of the consequences of idolatry and witchcraft. The wages of sin is still death. In his book entitled "Blessings or Curse",1 Derek Prince identifies seven (7) signs that a curse may be operative, as derived from the "blessings and curses" outlined in Deuteronomy 28:

1)Mental and/or emotional breakdown
2)Repeated or chronic sickness
3)Barrenness and miscarriages
4)Breakdown of marriage and family alienation
5)Continuing financial insufficiency
6)Being "accident prone"
7)A history of suicides or unnatural or untimely deaths.

The way to victory is that known sins of previous generations should be identified where possible, repented of and confessed. For example, King Asa demonstrated repentance from his father's sin by destroying the idols in the land and serving the Lord.(I Kings 15-14). Following this scriptural precedent, in every instance I lead the captive to confess the cultural witchcraft of his or her ancestors and remove its damaging affects. By reminding the spirit of Jezebel of the redemptive power of the blood of Jesus Christ of Nazareth, I actively pursue forgiveness, cleansing and restoration for the captives whom the Lord Jesus Christ entrusts me to deliver in His precious name.

I believe that cultural witchcraft is at the root of the dysfunctional family. Within a dysfunctional family, children are vulnerable and demons take advantage of them. Just as a father's blessing has measureless potential for good, so a father's curse has a corresponding potential for evil. Sometimes such a curse may be uttered deliberately. More often, perhaps---as in the relationship of a husband to his wife---a father may speak words to a child that are not deliberately intended as a curse, but nevertheless have exactly the same effect. The undermentioned examples consist of a composite of elements that I have encountered in real life situations. The following quote from "Blessing or Curse" is descriptive of how cultural witchcraft can manifest itself in a family:

> "A father has three sons. The firstborn is welcome just because he is that--- the firstborn. The youngest has unusual talent and an outgoing personality. But the middle son has neither of these factors in his favor. He broods over misunderstandings, but tends to keep his feelings to himself. Furthermore, the father sees in this middle son aspects of his own character that he does not like, but has never been willing to deal with in his own life. He finds it less painful to condemn them in his son than in himself. As a result, the middle son never has a sense of his father's approval. In the end, he no longer tries to win it. His father interprets this as stubbornness. More and more frequently, the father vents his disapproval in words such as 'you don't even try!' You're lazy! You'll never make good!" Little does he realize that he is pronouncing an evil destiny that demons will perpetuate against his son throughout the rest of his life."2(Derek Prince, pg. 111)

could not count the captives I have encountered personally whose lives have been blighted by negative, critical, destructive words spoken by a parent. Out of these encounters I have learned that such words, are, in reality, a curse. The passage of time does not diminish their effect. Men and women past middle age may still find their lives blighted by words a parent spoke to them in childhood. The only effective solution is to deal with them specifically as a curse, and to apply the remedy God has provided.

A mother, too, has authority over her children, which is either shared with her husband or delegated by him. Sometimes, however, a mother is not content with the exercise of her legitimate authority. Instead, she exploits her children's affection and loyalty to gain illegitimate control over them and to direct the course of their lives. Another example of 'witchcraft!' For the most part, I have found that black people in this country are less familiar with occultic practices such as hypnotism, yoga, and other forms of mysticism. However, the less intellectual, indigenous black folk have embraced cultural witchcraft through familiarity with roots and root workers.

As a result of American slave trading, African Americans brought the practice of witchcraft with them to this country. As dealt with in more detail in the next chapter, the Yoruba religion of Nigeria has had far-reaching affects through the slave trade both in the Caribbean and in America. Consequently , there remains a demonic mixture within the black church, a Christian religiosity that falls under the stronghold of cultural witchcraft. The culture with which I am most familiar is my own as a Caribbean descendant.

The Caribbean islands are well known for the practice of witchcraft, often called "obeah." Where Caribbeans are concerned, the spirit of witchcraft within a family will manifest itself as power struggles characterized by envy, rivalry and an unhealthy competitive spirit. Furthermore, Africans also brought with them their religious beliefs and practices which ultimately were influenced by Roman Catholicism and spiritism, as well as by other religious traditions and superstitions. Voodoo, often called Hoodoo by African descendants is still practiced in many places in the world today, particularly in the Caribbean, Haiti, Cuba and even in the South as well as in the inner cities of the North where there are heavy concentrations of black people who were raised in either the deep south or the Caribbean.

As a case in point, my grandparents came to this country on boats that sailed from the Caribbean--my father's people from Antigua and my mother's people from Barbados and Trinidad. There was no evidence that either my grandparents or my parents ever practiced witchcraft in any form that I am aware of, and yet the Caribbean witchcraft spirit passed down to me. With knowledge of only two generations, it is quite possible that witchcraft and/or idolatry was practiced by my grandparents' ancestors. It is even more plausible when you consider that I became an astrologer and a psychic medium in spite of the fact that I had no interest at all in anything considered "spiritual." Furthermore, I rejected all religion. My point is that even though I knew nothing of witchcraft from my grandparents, and I was close to all 4 of them, witchcraft may have passed to me because my roots are Caribbean.

Some black people will be highly offended at this remark, but I believe that the practice of Yoruba and other forms of witchcraft in Africa is the underlying reason why the Lord allowed slavery and racism to occur in America. As I study the scriptural consequences of cultural witchcraft in the curses listed in Deuteronomy 28, I understand how only by the grace and mercy of God that my people have not been completely annihilated by racism, addiction, poverty and black on black crime along with a plethora of other destructive forces that Satan has used against an entire race of people. It is important to reiterate that the one who counsels has to be ethnically sensitive, be willing to become familiar with the cultural traditions of the captive, as well as understand the dynamics of how the rituals and celebrations, language and cultural institutions may provide an open door for demons to oppress the captive with stress, discordance, strife and envy.

I could use any number of Caribbean families as an example, but since I am most familiar with my own, I present my own family as an illustration. On the surface, I come from a family that appears to have overcome racism, poverty and inner city life. Practically all of my elders own property and have a modicum of success in adjusting to the challenges of assimilation. My point is that my family knows nothing of the things that are obviously demonic and yet both the paternal and the maternal sides remain dysfunctional families, ruled by the witchcraft spirit. With consistent and pervasive underlying struggles with control issues, the way that the witchcraft demon has entered into my family is through a witchcraft dysfunction which the therapeutic community has labeled "sibling rivalry."

Sibling rivalry is the parenting tool and childrearing strategy of cultural witchcraft that permeates most West Indian families, including the descendants from Barbados, Trinidad, Antigua, Jamaica and other islands in the Caribbean. Even my native African clients report widespread sibling rivalry throughout the Mother Land. Implicit to sibling rivalry is the parental attempt to maintain control by causing siblings to be talebearers, and thereby encouraging gossip, lying, and backbiting. Those who gossip and snitch the most are rewarded with parental favoritism. Early on in a child's development, parents try to crush any sign of independence or free thinking within their children. Those who conform grow up to be narrow minded conformists while those who rebel are often considered the family's "black sheep."

When the parents', particularly mothers are pleased with a child's choices, the mother is all sweetness. But if the mother disapproves, a totally different side of her character will manifest itself. She will turn her other children against the child that she is displeased with, using fear of rejection as a tool to intimidate, manipulate, dominate and control the one who refuses to make choices acceptable to the mother. Furthermore, both parents will try to control their children by praising one to the detriment of the others.

This parental strategy of "divide and conquer" is the root of the Caribbean style of cultural witchcraft---where children will begin to build up deep seated resentments against a brother or a sister who has been "thrown up constantly in their face" as an example of success. Daughters and sons suffer for many years from the negative, demoniacally inspired effects of constant criticism and negative words. Sometimes matters are made worst by humor that pokes fun at a certain sibling. Words spoken as a joke have the potential of making a permanent impact upon a captive's self esteem, to the extent that demons of rejection, pride and bitterness have taken over the captive's soul.

As the children grow into adulthood, the parents have subtly trained their offspring to idolize them as parents by diminishing their loyalty to each other as brothers and sisters. It is not unusual in a West Indian family to discover that adult siblings continue to hold mutual grudges, not even speaking to a brother or sister for 20 years or more. Once the parents die, from the grave they continue to control their offspring. For example, on both sides of my family, there are brothers and sisters who have not spoken to each other for longer than 20 years who would pass their siblings on the street and haughtily walk by them and not even nod their head. My aunts and uncles have even viciously fought over parental grave sites—praising themselves for making the most grave site visits. This is the power of cultural witchcraft. Parental deification will cause siblings to despise each other, and even go to their own graves as embittered captives whose unforgiving souls are in danger of eternal damnation.

Where cultural witchcraft is concerned, the two most outstanding words are condemnation and competition. In the manifest picture of cultural witchcraft, guilt feelings caused by intra-family condemnation plays a significant role. Demonic activity is suggested by the captive's behavior, attitudes and ways of thinking and dealing with his or her personal life. In some cases, even if the family, particularly the mother has blatantly abused the captive, he will still manage to defend the mother, and blame himself instead. When the witchcraft demon has established a stronghold in the captive's soul, guilt feelings can remain unconscious. Unconscious guilt feelings can manifest itself in an overall malaise or in a depressive condition.

Generally speaking, the root of the problem is not so much the guilt feelings as it is the fear of disapproval that condemnation received from parents and relatives has created within the captives personality. The fear of disapproval may appear in various forms. Sometimes it manifests as either a fear of annoying others or a fear of being "found out." As a counselor, I have discovered that this character trait hinders the counselor/client relationship because even though the captive may desperately desire to be delivered, he is afraid that myself as a counselor will disapprove of him once I know the truth. Since only by truth is freedom attainable, deliverance has had a better chance to be long lasting when

I have first deal with the captive's fear of disapproval. With every cause, I am prepared for the captive viewing me, the counselor. as an obtrusive intruder. Even worst, at times the captive will consider that I am his judge, that the captive will be to himself as a criminal, and therefore will do whatever he can to deny my help or to mislead me.

As a case in point, it took a year of getting to know one of my church members for the Lord to reveal that she was oppressed by demons. Raised by a mother from Trinidad with an extremely critical and judgmental personality, Winnie developed what appeared to be a perfectionist spirit. Whenever questioned on even the most trivial of matters, she became very defensive to the point of rebellion. In truth, Winnie manifested a subtle unwillingness to accept even the slightest degree of correction or criticism. Once she became more comfortable with me, she confessed that after a word of even minor correction from me, she would go off to herself and scream and curse---literally have a temper tantrum to offset one of my comments that I personally considered to be minor. When the Holy Spirit knew that Winnie was ready, He set up a deliverance that was most shocking. On the surface, no one would ever expect that this outgoing, jovial soul was captive to several demons.

Sibling rivalry within the perspective of cultural witchcraft is a form of competition that remains active within the Caribbean family from the cradle to the grave. As a result, the fear of failure is connected to the captive's self image: he amounts to something when he is successful and he is worthless when he is unsuccessful. Success is generally based upon a rigid standard that has been engraved upon the captive's soul from childhood by the words of parents, siblings and other relatives. This situation represents fertile ground for the oppression of cultural witchcraft. As a result, the captive's soul is characterized by either a low self esteem or a false persona of a high self esteem, pride, envy, jealousy, stress, "a short fuse", moodiness, destructive impulses and an excessive need for affection that is often hidden by a false bravado, particularly among West Indian boys and men.

The spirit of competition will also lead to the soul's need for self justification. For example, when faced with failure, the captive will rationalize and become defensive and even aggressive. For example, it is not the captive who desires to cheat, steal, exploit or humiliate but others who want to do these things to him. It is not the mother who is trying to ruin her daughter merely because her daughter refused to receive her advice. No, it is the daughter who is disrespectful and unappreciative of the mother's concern and dedication. A Caribbean personality trait that is often uplifted and admired is the trait of stubbornness. However, since stubbornness is akin to rebellion, I often must make the captive aware of the scriptural warning that "rebellion is as the sin of witchcraft."

I have been faced with challenging issues about how to address the deliverance needs of those captives who have been exposed to cultural witchcraft. I anticipate that my future research efforts will concentrate on studying in more depth various cultures. I have discovered that with each case of deliverance, it has been crucial for me to expand my knowledge of demonic strategies within the cultures of my particular client base. In one of ,u training modules, students are provided with descriptive knowledge of those aspects of cultural witchcraft that affect Caribbean people, including the West Indian island of Puerto Rico. It is my objective to use descriptive knowledge toward the assessment process as well as to explore approaches on how to effectively intervene to set a captive free. In this way, I hope to develop strategies and ways to neutralize the influence and affects of dysfunctional family relations so as to enhance the captive's social functioning.

For example, having the wisdom to rightly divide the word of God is crucial to addressing such issues as unquestioned loyalty to traditional cultural belief systems, even though there is an indication that they are demonic. I emphasize the preparation of each captive to allow the sword of the Spirit, the word of God, to challenge these belief systems. The captive must learn how to negotiate between two (2) opposing systems: the family system and the kingdom of God. Suffice it to say that how I assess the dynamics of cultural witchcraft upon a captive's ability to stand and persevere during deliverance is crucial. Therefore, the following summarized list consists of some basic principles in addressing cultural witchcraft during the pre-deliverance counseling process:

1.Build a knowledge about cultural witchcraft. Making wrong assumptions by simplistic misinterpretations of events, explanations, rituals, and traditions. can be costly to deliverance.
2.Assess the duration and the urgency of the presenting problem and the extent to which it has oppressed the captive. Simply put, is the situation life threatening.

3.Examine personal vulnerability. I am careful to set personal boundaries so that I am not drawn into the center of a family confrontation.

Culturally competent counseling will seek to reveal to the captive's "significant others" those underlying problems in communication that serve as doorways for demonic infestation within the captive. I have found that equally important is an assessment of the impact of cultural witchcraft on the captive's mental and emotional state well before I have scheduled a deliverance. It is imperative that a Christ-centered supportive environment is established prior to deliverance. A crucial component of the counseling process is to ensure that the client does not return to a chaotic environment after deliverance. For example, no client should return to a home where a relative is openly practicing witchcraft.

The following are a few methods, strategies and approaches that have helped me to enhance my competence and effectiveness:

THE REVELATION METHOD

In practically every case, captives have been led to seek my services by the Holy Spirit, most often in dreams. As counseling progresses, it is my job to bring clarity to a situation that may never have been fully examined by either the captive or the captive's family. In such cases, my strategy is to guide the captive into a process that clears his mind to receive revelation from the Holy Spirit. I have personally found that an enduring deliverance is secured when the captive can hear directly from the Lord for himself. In counseling, I function as a probing facilitator, helping the captive review the issues and problems that are directly linked to cultural witchcraft by finding the solutions in the word of God. When the religious demon is in full control, the captive has already been bombarded with a plethora of dreams, revelations and signs of all kinds, and it will take wisdom to lead the client to see that he has not been hearing from God. Therefore, this is the more favored method when a religious spirit is not the controlling demon. It emphasizes the analysis of particular life events and behaviors that either confirm or refute the captive's reasoning. My goal is to help the captive:

1. focus on particular life events or behaviors, analyze them from both the traditional cultural believes versus revelation knowledge from the word of God

2. assist the captive to examine his emotional state and to bring the entire situation into an objective, rational assessment.

3. guide the captive to use his freewill to choose the will of God as revealed in His word.

THE "SOUL STRENGTH" METHOD

Truth presented in a spirit of peace is very powerful. This approach focuses on the transfer of soul power from the dysfunctional family to the captive. My goal with this strategy is to work with the captive to develop a healthy sense of self that is compatible with the word of God. From this perspective, I seek to discover the elements of the environment the captive is in. In this regard, I ask "What is the interplay between the captive-in-environment that is causing the imbalance in the captive' life? What elements should be changed that would help restore balanced functioning for the captive? " I concentrate on viewing the captive in his particular situation. As the cultural witchcraft issues emerge, I assess the captive's strengths and attempt to build the captive's strength of identity, strength of his born again spirit, and strength of determination to be set free, delivered and to be fruitful in the Lord's kingdom . My goal is to:

1. lay the foundation for the captive to develop skills of self examination.

2. provide a base from which to proceed in evoking the potentials for the captive to gather the data of his own life, and objectively assess it.

As a method of edification, the focus is to address the issue of the captive's internalized self condemnation, negative attitudes and self destructive behaviors that have been promoted by the spouse, parents, siblings and relatives. I also identify the conflict that results from self hate as it relates to cultural witchcraft and its impact on the captive's soul.

THE BELIEF SYSTEM METHOD

The goal of this approach is to expose what the captive truly believes. Examining the captive's belief system is important to deliverance to determine whether the client will be able to stand under a demonic crossfire. In this way, I develop an understanding of the power dynamics within a dysfunctional family and how powerlessness is reinforced by the captive's belief system. Within this framework, I try to remain keenly aware of and willing to candidly discuss cultural,ethnic, and racial issues. This requires sensitivity, compassion and skill. I also strive to have self knowledge and a deep, abiding respect for self and for people who are different. This method also begins with identifying the problem as perceived by the captive. The belief system method also helps the captive focus his or her own definitions of the problem and gives me insight as to how the captive perceives and processes information as well as submits to the word of God. Out of the abundance of the heart, the mouth will speak. Therefore, language constitutes the single most important factor to assess whether or not the captive is adequately prepared for deliverance.

Moreover, the belief method also exposes the captive's tolerance for stress and allows for cultural witchcraft beliefs to be exposed and challenged prior to deliverance. From experience, I have learned that progressive questioning enables the captive to become more involved in his own deliverance and helps to equalize the relationship between myself as the counselor and the captive. Since certain cultures have a tendency toward cultural witchcraft, there are questions on the DAF aimed at collecting information that will serve as focal points of inquiry. They include but are not limited to: country of birth, places of birth of relatives, and whether the captive has ever lived in another country, There are also questions that indirectly target the problem of cultural witchcraft.

These are questions that would indicate that the family is under a curse--- questions about family addiction, incest, sudden accidents, deaths in the family, murder, abortions or suicide. There are also questions concerning membership in cults and various faiths or organizations where the witchcraft demon is prevalent—questions concerning freemasonry, Eastern Star, Hinduism, Buddhism, and transcendental meditation. As a part of the initial assessment interview, I also address issues of rejection as it pertains to the role of the captive in the family, whether or not he was an out of wedlock child or adopted. The DAF also seeks information as to who in the family is most influential with him. It should be noted that hereditary rejection is generally accompanied by physical, emotional and/or sexual abuse.

THE SURVIVAL INSTINCT

Many Christian captives have experienced various forms of violence and abuse including physical, sexual or emotional abuse. Such trauma has the potential to be devastating. Yet consider that each survivor has gone on and found ways to get through each day in spite of some very difficult circumstances. Most oppressed people have overcome difficult odds. Captives benefit from exploring the ways they have survived. My purpose is to present the lessons of the captive's trials, tribulations and troubles in a way that will set him free. Moreover, I assist the captive in a twofold way. First of all, when the captive appears to have no more fight in him, I point him to the Lord and use the counseling sessions to build up the captive's trust.

Then when the captive has become complacent because the cultural witchcraft demon's clever strategy is to reduce the attack to dissipate the momentum, I focus my attention toward being a nonjudgmental, objective carrier of the truth. Unlike secular counseling, as a deliverance counselor I am involved in the captive's life at a more deeper level. One thing I have at my command is intercessory prayer. Here is where I most definitely am extremely careful. I have found that many of the captives who have been a victim to cultural witchcraft have also been subjected to demonic prayers and rituals that have been employed to keep them in bondage.

For example, the main character in the TV movie entitled "Real Women Have Curves" is a prime example. This is a movie about a demonic struggle between a controlling latino mother and her young adult daughter. The mother's binding words were, "if you are not married by 25, then you are an old maid", "you are a very pretty girl but you are too fat. Lose some weight and you will find someone to love you." "You don't need a career because you are a woman."

    Besides the "binding words", in her spiritual ignorance, the mother also employed various demonic rituals from her idolatrous belief system. It appeared to be a mixture of Santeria and Catholicism where various idol relics were used in the exact same manner as a voodoo doll. The girl in the movie was strong in spirit and from a worldly perspective, won freedom in the battle for her soul. It should be noted that in cultural witchcraft, idolatrous practices are relatively common. They are employed to control the life of a significant other. In intercessory prayer, I bind such curses with prayers for freedom. What I am vigilant to avoid as a counselor is to falling into the same pattern with prayers that people employed within cultural witchcraft to control the captive's freewill in the first place. Prayers that are sent forth to control the captive are also demon inspired and I make sure that my own prayers are not motivated by my desire to control the captive's destiny.

    As a case in point, Ola is a prime example. As previously indicated, this case is significant on several levels. Actually, Ola's case is the first outstanding face or profile of the religious demon that I have encountered. For this reason, Ola is also referenced in the profiles of other significant cases. Considered to have great promise in the kingdom of God, this young Nigerian woman spent most of her life in a family that is still involved Yoruba and Catholicism. Presented in detail in upcoming chapters, all outward signs suggested that Ola was saved. When I met her in the Bahamas twelve years ago, I assumed that she was saved. When I spoke to her pastor before enrolling her in the School of the Prophets, he informed me that Ola was his best member in terms of commitment, tithing, church attendance and outward manifestation of demonstrative worship. As Ola's case relates to cultural witchcraft, she had not dealt with one particular "binding message" that she had heard all of her life--- that a Nigerian woman who is 21 or over and unmarried is not a real woman, in danger of spending the rest of her life alone.

    However, I found a way to stop Bobby's mouth. The key was that I stopped falling into the demonic trap of treating Bobby like he was the enemy. Wrestling not against flesh and blood, I took a spiritual warfare stand against the spirit of Python. My greatest victory is to convert a chosen vessel of the enemy to the Lord. Therefore, I will not return slander for slander. My goal was not marriage counseling in this case. I cannot and will not counsel an unsaved addicted man who is also actively using drugs and who on occasion, is both a physical and emotional batterer of a woman younger than his own daughters. I also did not lose sight of my only goal which is that the captive will learn how to fight for freedom to become the person whom the Lord desires. Where the enemy is concerned, he is defeated every time I return good for evil, praying for and witnessing to people like Bobby of the kindness of Jesus Christ that will call the abuser himself to repentance.

    Another important consideration in cases of this kind is that demons often incite people to enslave one another through stirring in them the witchcraft spirit that will form their personalities. By transforming people who seek out opportunities to control the lives of others through manipulation, coercion, domination and intimidation, the demon of cultural witchcraft will prepare its vessels well. However, when a person's freewill has been restored to seek God and His righteousness as well as to choose God through obedience, demons lose power. Breaking is therefore crucial, because the process will set the captive free from obsessive behavior and from unhealthy soul ties. In each case, an alienation from the true self is often disguised by a false religiosity.

Furthermore, as pride goes before a fall, the conflict centers within the client's pride system. At times the client may experience himself as a superior human being and at other times as his despised self. When these two ways of experiencing himself operate at the same time, the client will feel like two people pulling in opposite directions. This conflict could be of sufficient impact to tear the client apart. Usually, if the inner conflict is intense, the client will automatically seek solutions to alleviate the tension. The role of deliverance is to find the true self, because very often a demon or demons have so infiltrated the client's personality that the demon involved is well hidden by lies and deception. As Jesus said "the truth shall set you free." Therefore, deliverance counseling is always directed toward uncovering truth, not only in uncovering the true meaning of life's apparently insignificant messages, but also in exorcising the demonic influence from the client's personality. Those who are frustrated in their personality type may manifest solutions of self glorification, self abasement, or a combination of both.

SELF GLORIFICATION

In this solution, the captive glorifies and cultivates in himself everything that means mastery. Religiosity and charismatic witchcraft play a significant role. Mastery with regard to others entails the need to excel and to be superior in some way. The captive tends to manipulate or dominate others and to make them dependent upon him. This solution is also reflected in what he expects the attitude of others toward him ought to be. Whether he is out for adoration, respect or recognition or the 3 P's of power, position and prominence, he is exalted when others subordinate and humble themselves to him as they look up to him. He strongly resists the idea of compliance, appeasement or dependency. The solution of mastery includes the captive's striving to accomplish and achieve. Helplessness may make him feel panicky and he hates any trace of weakness or insufficiency within himself. Those who seek mastery through religiosity may manifest jealousy and envy when others appear to maximize their spiritual goals.

THE SELF ABASEMENT SOLUTION

Self abasement can be seen among those in Christiandom who tend to subordinate themselves to others so as to prove by their behavior that they are "suffering for Jesus." Such a person will fight any inward feeling of being superior to others to such an extent that he is often overlooked both in the world and in the church. This is that one who would hide his talent in the sand, with all kinds of excuses for not using it. He is uneasy when he receives any admiration or recognition, as he rejects being put in a superior position. What this captive longs for is help, protection and surrendering love. In his attitude toward himself, the captive lives with a sense of failure to measure up to his own personal "ought to's", the "ought to's" of others as well as biblical precepts and mandates. He tends to feel guilty, inferior, or contemptible. Passivity, a doorway for demons, becomes his solution, where others are either accusing or despising him at times when he can find no fault in his own behavior.

Although self pride is not consciously felt, the captive becomes proud in secretly belittling others for not being as forgiving, understanding and as "humble" as he is---in other words, for being self centered and selfish in comparison to his own self effacing ways. Pride will also manifest in the opposite direction, where the captive will secretly admire pride and aggressiveness in others, and thereby passively submit to being dominated and controlled by self seeking people. The need for company is all the greater since being alone becomes a pride issue---proof that he is unwanted and unpopular and is therefore a disgrace, to be kept a secret. Consequently, those who belittle themselves are usually not very discriminating where it comes to their relationships. As a rule, this captive will not be able to recognize the difference between genuine friendliness and its many counterfeits.   In fact, captives like these may be too easily manipulated by any show of warmth or interest. In addition, his inner dictates tell him that he should like everybody, and that he should not be suspicious.

Furthermore, his fear of antagonism and possible fights makes him overlook, discard, minimize or explain away such traits as lying, crookedness, exploitation, cruelty and treachery. Religious Christians find solutions to not facing such realities by claiming that they must "always walk in love." Their definition of love is often connected to suffering abuse in relationships. To uphold such a premise creates a vulnerability to demonic soul ties.   The personality type that seeks this particular self effacing solution makes for a greater subjective feeling of unhappiness and depression than the others. The genuine suffering of this solution causes the captive to feel most miserable because of his commitment to suffering. In this sense, his concept of love is the only thing that gives a positive content to his life. During assessment, the captive may appear to be very cooperative in searching for demonic doorways that may have led to his present torment. However, as I have entered into deeper stages, I have experienced resistance from the captive's who has acclimated themselves to self abasement.

THE SOUL'S BONDAGE

For various reasons, the soul's resistance to the truth is the result of the captive's development over time an intricate subliminal strategy that will hinder his ability to face his problems "head on." Therefore, the process of transformation and renewal of the mind by the word of God is blocked, even though the client believes that he has actually presented his body as a living sacrifice. (Romans 12: 1-2). His sacrifice was not holy because of his own self deception. Renewing of the mind is not just an intellectual process but it is also an emotional experience. In other words, the insights that he receives about himself ought to be felt in his gut or belly. When all things have truly become new in salvation, the believer who has remained bound in various areas of life may respond to insights or truths about himself in unexpected ways. Just as a 30 minute outdoor swim may be refreshing and invigorating to some, it may be exhausting and even fearful to others, depending upon the intensity of the sun, the temperature of the water , the physical condition of the person and several other unforeseen factors.

Similarly, a nugget of truth may be extremely painful or it may immediately bring joy, exhilaration or relief. If received as pain, the captive may feel that the insight is a threat. He might also perceive any new revelation as "opening a can of worms", and thereby become discouraged or depressed because he perceives that he is facing too many changes, too soon. As a pre-deliverance counselor, I align my stance with that of the Savior's. Jesus Christ declared that once truth is known, it will set one free. Yet He did not guarantee that the price of freedom would not be painful. Even so, for a captive to become free to express who he really is, relieved from having to repress his emotions for so long, I believe that the pain is worth it. I believe that even if the insight or revelation received is not flattering, the truth will remove the tensions generated by the captive's former tendency to hide or to deny his true feelings. In addition, knowing that demons have been secretly manifesting their own thoughts and ways into the captive's soul can serve as the catalyst for change and a call to action. For example, once a captive discovers that his hostility toward others was inspired by demons, I find that I can then prepare him to know who he is in Christ Jesus and then guide him to "put on the whole armor of Christ."

Besides being saved, the freewill of the captive is probably the next most important element to deliverance. Once the captive decides that he or she wants to be free, even though both the religious demon and the spirit of Jezebel will put up a formidable struggle to remain in his body, it will eventually be expelled by the power and authority of the name of Jesus of Nazareth. However, the religious demon's power lies in the fact that there is an unbrokenness in the captive's soul that provides the demon a permanent dwelling place. As long as the captive is committed to even a half truth, the religious demon is comfortable. This was the problem with Saul of Tarsus. He had a zeal that was not according to knowledge. What saved Saul, was his call to become "Paul, the 12th Apostle." Though not in the scriptures, I suspect that Paul's religious demon fled immediately upon his personal confrontation with Jesus Christ through his visionary, supernatural experience on the Damascus road. (Acts 9:1-30)

As previously shared, this is how the Lord called me to Himself also. I was an atheist who believed that Jesus Christ was a myth, similar to Santa Claus. To draw me to Jesus, the Holy Spirit confronted me with the cross. Everywhere that I turned, I saw a cross both in the natural and in the spiritual. I could be riding down the street and the cross on top of a church steeple practically tripled in size. If two leaves fell from the ground in front of me, they fell into a design of the cross. I even went to sleep at night and dreamed that a newborn baby spoke to me and said "Give me my cross, please." This was how the Lord drew me. I was literally bombarded by the cross. Because these occurrences were so "urgently supernatural," they could not be ignored. Peter was the same way. I do not mean to suggest that Peter had a religious demon. However, he was operating in a half truth for 10 years after the Lord's ascension because he did not believe that the gentiles could be saved. Therefore, the Lord had to come to Peter in a supernatural way and give him a vision of Cornelius, instructing Peter to go to the home of Cornelius and preach the gospel. Peter even argued with the Holy Spirit by saying that he would never eat anything that was unclean. (Acts 10:9-23)

ENDNOTES

1 and 2. Derek Prince, Blessing or Curse: You Can Choose, Chosen Books, 1990 pg. 111.

SECTION III:

MORE FACES AND CASE PROFILES

CHAPTER 12 : The Python Spirit

Beyond a doubt, I know the witchcraft side of this demon rather well for I myself was once its captive. Yet, when I consider how challenging it has been for me to cast the spirit of witchcraft out of others, I marvel at how no human being ever cast this demon from me. When I got marvelously saved from my strong involvement with the python spirit of divination, the Holy Ghost overshadowed me Himself. So my own deliverance is a testimony that what may seem impossible with men is possible with God. In recent years, I have been surprised to discover that witchcraft is only one side of Jezebel, as this demon's primary side is religious. Since I myself was an atheist, I only experienced the witchcraft side of Jezebel.

When considering the demon Jezebel, we generally think of a female seductress and therefore sexual images are foremost in our minds. It is true that where idolatrous religions are concerned, sex, lust and worship are intricately intertwined. But make know mistake. The distinguishing characteristic of the spirit of Jezebel is in itself "religious." Jezebel is the religious style of this face of the spirit of the Anti-Christ, an overwhelming narcissistic pride that has an arrogant self image of perfection. Mainly caused by a refusal to accept their own imperfections, the pride of the Jezebel demon unrealistically denies its sinful nature. For built into the soul of such a captive is a strength of will that hinders a captive so afflicted to be able to submit his will to the Lord.

Consequently, captives to the Jezebel demon find it extremely difficult to repent. Like Satan himself, the plight of those afflicted with this demon is akin to that of an eternal rebel. As Satan cannot accept his final judgment, Jezebel's captives cannot even submit themselves to the demands of their own conscience and therefore willfully refuse to accept responsibility for their own actions. The cases included in this chapter consist of both my successes and my failures at attempting to cast out religious, charismatic demons. Over time, I have found the failures to be extremely valuable because of the truths about charismatic witchcraft that have been uncovered and that I now choose to expose operating with in the last days church. I treasure failures because there is frequently a priceless nugget of truth hidden within them that comes from the grace of God. In the words written to the Corinthians, Paul explains the power of failure much better than I do. Paul believes that failures are even worth bragging about. "Therefore, most gladly I will rather boast in my infirmities, that the power of Christ may rest upon me. Therefore, I take pleasure in infirmities, in reproaches, in needs, in persecutions, in distresses, for Christ's sake, For when I am weak, then I am strong." (II Corinthians 12:9,10)

When I myself entered into the New Age occult movement, I was so ignorant of the spirit world that I didn't even know that demons existed. Once I found out, it took years for me to develop my spiritual senses to be able to distinguish the Lord's voice from demonic revelations. I wasn't saved when I became a necromancer and consequently, I was not completely removed from its grip as a babe in Christ. Once I received a knowledge of the truth, I burned my occult books and sought baptism by immersion. I continue to thank and praise the Lord Jesus Christ that even though I was deceived, I was virtually unknown and therefore, I have led very few astray. I am blessed to have been allowed to share the truth of my spiritual error with virtually everyone whose lives I had influenced prior to my own complete deliverance. Unfortunately, today there are several well known television evangelists and mega pastors who are in serious error regarding the realm of the spirit---persons who influence countless people on a daily basis. The spiritual damage that has been incurred is beyond any human being's ability to estimate. Only God knows. If those who mislead are truly saved, they will have to give an account at the Judgment Seat of Christ.

For example, the religious demon used the ministry of Benny Hinn to play a significant role in yet another face of charismatic witchcraft, a 32 year old Asian woman whose name I have changed to "Amala." Amala is a former Hindu, presently residing in Durban South Africa. I have never met Amala personally, and so I present her profile here, in her own words:

"My mother was a Hindu, saved long before I was born and my father is a Christian. I was born and raised in a Christian home. I attended the church of the Nazarene and then we joined a pentecostal/charismatic church when I was 25. Therefore I have been an active churchgoer for 30 years. In spite of the fact that I was born Christian, since my mother was a Hindu, I was dedicated at birth to Hindu gods, as is the Hindu tradition.

Falling slain in the spirit used to be such a beautiful experience for me. As a child, I went with my grandfather to temple. A power used to come over me, my knees would go weak and I could not stand upright. I would fall back to the floor and never get hurt. I remember one time, when this presence was so strong. I landed a few feet away from my chair and again, never got hurt. I did not need anyone to lay hands on me to be slain. It used to happen even while I worshiped.

I also experienced travail. I was told that the spirit of intercession had come over me and I literally felt like I was giving birth to something. I was told that I was giving birth to souls. You are on the floor when this happens and you scream because the pain is so bad. I also experienced speaking in tongues. I also sang in the spirit. A spirit would enter me and take over my voice, singing and reaching high notes that I could never reach in my natural voice. It sounded like angels singing---the most beautiful sound you ever heard. I even prophesied once and had dreams that came to pass. I also danced in the spirit. A spirit inside of me would appear to dance before the Lord through me. You should know that I am a naturally reserved person but when this spirit manifests itself, I would dance in front of the whole church--- something I would never normally do.

I got deeper and deeper into word of faith teachings, particularly Benny Hinn. I believed every teaching literally until I used my faith to believe for something that did not come to pass. I prayed, fasted, confessed the word, stood on the word and my loved one still died. I began to doubt God, refusing to read or believe the bible. I have since repented for doubting God as this was my fault. I was helped by websites like yours that expose false doctrine. I prayed and asked God to show me if I had received anything that was not from Him. I soon began to dream of snakes (the python spirit) and

I began to go to a different pastor for prayer. He prayed a very simple prayer and suddenly I fell to the floor, writhing and twisting like a snake.

I was horrified because I believed that my life in Christ was okay. I am still finding it difficult to have a relationship with God because of this spirit that refuses to leave me. My current pastor has spent hours praying for me but it has still come back. My pastor has counseled me that I need to be stronger and not allow myself to fall into depression as it has come back, hoping to gain control over me. I am really trying... During deliverance, a spirit of laughter manifested and refused to leave, saying that Lucifer is watching and that it had followed me from my previous word of faith church.

I believe that the travail I experienced was the gateway for spirits of the dead to live in my body---spirits of family members including my uncle are living inside of me. When they manifest, they behave like they did in life. Their mannerisms manifest through me, one by one. They were all removed during deliverance, but I find deliverance is very tiring and really drains me physically."

I believe that Amala clearly and accurately describes her own experience with the religious demon yet she is incorrect in her assessment. By dedicating Amala to a Hindu god, her ancestors are definitely the original source of her captivity. However, the spirits that have her bound are merely demons, masquerading as her deceased family members. A faulty assumption can lead to wrong decisions. Until Amala allows her mind to be renewed with truth, I suspect that she will remain bound. The words of Dr. Rebecca Brown in " Unbroken Curses" ring true:

"When a child, or even an unborn offspring, is dedicated to the service of Satan, demon spirits are assigned the task of insuring that the child remains in Satan's service all of his life. Such dedications may not be worded so specifically, but this fact is inherent in all such rituals. For instance, children dedicated in the Mormon church are endowed with the spiritual power of the prophets to insure that they remain good Mormons all of their lives. Oaths taken by members of various lodges contain statements which dedicate their offspring and descendants to the service of the lodge, which is the same as dedicating them to the demon gods of the lodge or to Satan. All children of American Indians are dedicated to their gods. The same is true in African tribes and around the world." (R. Brown, D Yoder pg. 40)

The written words of Susan clearly demonstrates how the abandonment to supernatural power which is believed to be of God by those who refer to themselves as "Spirit-filled" can bring confusion and bondage. Although the manifestations were periodical in this case and the captive appears to be comparatively of a sound mind, her fruitfulness in Christ has been successfully hindered by a religious demon. In what is described as periods of "attacks", this particular woman is being persistently destroyed for a lack of knowledge. Countless believers find themselves in this sort of bondage simply because they have not tried the spirits to see if they be of God. Also in Susan's case, it is apparent that those who are untrained in deliverance are being duped by the religious demon into believing that they are operating in the gift of casting out of devils:

> I know this may sound crazy, but I went through a deep healing where I had 7 demons cast out of me. I am a spirit-filled Christian and love Jesus with all of my heart. I had been abused as a child. When the final demon which was a generational spirit was being dealt with, he spoke the words, "we'll get her". This spirit called himself 'Destroyer'. He was then cast out. I was actually going through the training program of Deep Healing which is a new ministry in our church and all of us who went through training received deep healing. I move with a prophetic gifting which I am in school being more equipped for, I believed that I received a word from the Lord as I was journaling that my daughter would be an only child. I received this word and was at peace with it.
>
> Then 2 months later I found out I was pregnant. At the same time in our small church 2 other women became pregnant. I questioned at this point whether I heard from the Lord at all that night. In my fourth month I began to bleed, ultrasound confirmed that I had a slight placental abrasion and the baby was dead. Our baby was a boy. It's been hard watching the other women progress in their pregnancies, they are having boys. My would be due date is approaching . I am confused. My husband wants another baby but I feel afraid. Did this demon 'get me'? or Did God decide? Will I fall into judgment (I am anchored in my heavenly father's love and know He is for me not against me!) if I get pregnant again, because I believe the Lord told me my daughter would be an only child, then this baby died.
>
> I feel caught in something and I can't seem to get clarity on it. I can't seem to get an answer from anyone around me either. Please pray for me. I've received personal prophecy about being called into ministry in which my children would not suffer my absence but would be taken care of. I'm just wondering how all of this ties in together. I know my spiritual authority and exercise it in the spiritual realm, but our baby wasn't protected for some reason.."

It is very sad that this woman is bound up in confusion over a false assumption that the prophecy she received concerning her daughter being an only child was from the Lord. She only questioned whether this "word" came from the Lord when she actually got pregnant and not at the moment that she received the word while journaling. It could even be that the training that she is receiving in her "prophetic gifting" is in itself inspired by the religious demon. This particular example exposes the subtly of the religious demon and how it works first to deceive through charismatic leanings and then gains access to the mind or body, or both.

Recently, an increased amount of cases are coming to my attention of people who actually received a Jezebel spirit at a church altar. Take Delores as an example. A former heroin addict at the age of 22, Delores was prepared to go into a substance abuse detox program when a friend took her to an apostolic church where a meeting was being conducted under the apostolic authority of a visiting revivalist whom I will refer to as Rev.

Monica. Not knowing what was going on, once hands were laid on Delores, she fell out into a state of unconsciousness and laid on the floor, arising with the notion that she had "just died." Rev. Monica declared "you have just been born again." Then Rev. Monica called on the Holy Ghost to come and fill Delores and immediately, Delores spoke in another language. When questioned 20 years later, Delores admitted that she had been an atheist and had absolutely not understanding of the cross, or repentance or of resurrection.

Even so, Delores became a consistent churchgoer over the next twenty years because of this supernatural experience with a few instances of "backslidding," Then unexpectedly a spirit began to manifest, causing Monica to burst out in a menacing laugh, particularly if she was praying or reading the bible. At our first telephone contact, it became clear to me that Delores not only did not get saved, but that she picked up a demonic soul tie from the spirit of Rev. Monica. Within one session, I was able to identify the root cause of the problem and obtain agreement with Delores that she did not get saved through the ministry of Rev. Monica. As I pointed out, the key to salvation is mental assent and understanding. Delores had been deceived into believing that because her craving for heroin completely left her on the day that Rev. Monica laid hands on her, that this had to be a clear sign that God had touched her.

I have run into several other cases of this kind, where unsaved people have gone to either a word of faith, Charismatic or Pentecostal church, been immediately delivered of either a nicotine or a substance abuse addiction, and assumed that because they were no longer addicted to the substance that this was an indication that they were born again. In each case, the religious demon entered them, overshadowing the spirit of addiction. Apparently clean in the flesh from intoxicants, these captives are not clean in the spirit because they climbed up into salvation "another way" and not by the godly sorrow of repentance and faith in the resurrection.

The zeal that overtakes them to witness, testify and even preach the gospel is a counterfeit anointing that will endure only for a season. In fact, most of these captives admit to several drug relapses over a span of time as well as backsliding from the faith more than once. Continual wavering in the faith is a clear sign that many who came to Jesus as a result of a supernatural manifestation never got saved in the first place, for according to the Apostle John, "they went out from us, but they were not OF us. For if they have been OF us, they would have no doubt, continued with us; but they went out, that they might be made manifest that they were not all OF us." (I John 2:19) Therefore, the practice of re-dedication within the organized church overlooks the truth in John's warning. According to this scripture, those who walk away from Christ were never OF Christ, in the first place. To rededicate them is to provide an open door to the religious demon as the spirit of Jezebel and the spirit of the Anti-Christ.

Ola: THE LANDMARK CASE

Those captives with backgrounds in the occult very often become tormented by a witchcraft spirit for being regular church goers as unlike Jezebel, the spirit of the Anti-Christ detests all aspects of Christian worship and if this demon lodged in the flesh of the captive, it will torment the captive for "taking it to church."Besides the spirit of Python, the divination face of the religious demon, I believe that the captive that I refer to as "Ola" is a landmark case--- as she is dually victimized by various facets of the spirit of Jezebel and the spirit of the Anti-Christ.

To illustrate, Ola's rather subtle refusal to submit to the authority of any minister is a significant sign of Jezebel's presence. The demon Jezebel can be a classic backstabber----soft spoken, smiling, her mouth gushing with religious blessings and words of encouragement, yet simultaneously conniving and vicious. People are really pawns with these captives, motivated by the demon Jezebel's love of power trips and seductive games of control. In this regard, I consider the case of Ola to be very important to understanding the religious demon in general, and charismatic witchcraft, in particular---demonic fruits of the Jezebel spirit.

As revealed in the previous chapter, the case of Ola has its original roots in the indigenous practice of Yoruba by Ola's Nigerian ancestors. The religion of the Yoruba people in West Africa, who live in Nigeria and Benin, is a thousands of years-old tradition of nature worship and ancestor reverence. In addition to the worship of one God named Olodumare, the Yoruba worship dozens of deities known as "Orishas" who are personified aspects of nature and spirit. The principal orishas include Eleggua, Oggun, Ochosi, Obatala, Yemaya, Oshun, Shango, Oya, Babalu Aiye, and Orula. Yoruba has spawned several branches of religious witchcraft where its gods are synchronized with Catholic saints, with the creation of Santeria in Puerto Rico. In Brazil, Cuba, Haiti, and Trinidad, Yoruba religious rites, beliefs, music and myths are evident even in present times. In Haiti, the Yoruba's were generally called Anagos. Afro-Haitian religious activities give Yoruba rites and beliefs an honored place, and the pantheon includes numerous deities of Yoruba origin. In Brazil, Yoruba religious activities are called Anago or Shango, and in Cuba they are designated Lucumi. It is no accident that the Yoruba cultural influence spread across the Atlantic to the Americas. Yoruba slaves were sent to British, French, Spanish and Portuguese colonies in the New World, and in a number of these places Yoruba traditions survived strongly.

One of the insights that continues to emerge is that when a person's ancestors have practiced any form of witchcraft, the witchcraft demon will form a partnership with the religious demon in an attempt to block future generations from worshiping the Lord Jesus Christ "in spirit and in truth," followed by the birthing of charismatic witchcraft into that family. In spite of the powerful influence of ancestral witchcraft in this case, I still believe that the case of Ola is an indictment of the word of faith, Charismatic movement on several levels. First and foremost, for almost two decades, Ola spoke in tongues, praised and even "prophesied" in a word of faith churches in the United States and she wasn't even saved!!! Therefore, in spite of my own failures where Ola is concerned, I certainly thank the Lord for this one!

Since my interactions with Ola, I have experienced several cases of a similar kind. I believe that each case is a serious warning to the word of faith, non-denominational charismatic movement, that since they are not preaching the gospel of Jesus Christ in a fullness, they are empowering the charismatic witchcraft demon and the religious spirit to create false births. Consequently, people who believe that they are saved are headed for hell. As the Lord has used the intimate details of my own life to serve as an indictment against the AME Zion Church in "the Making of a Prophet," if not an indictment, Ola's case is a powerful warning to the charismatic, word of faith movement THAT SOMETHING IS DEFINITELY AMISS. As in the case of Amala, I also believe that Ola's captivity is an example of how the practice of witchcraft by either a parent or a grandparent can empower a religious demon to hinder the salvation of their children and grandchildren.

In Ola's case, she was led by a friend of the family to a word of faith church in her native village. Once a member, Ola learned to "praise and worship" and she became very adapted to the utterance gifts of prophecy, discerning of spirits and speaking in other tongues. By the time we met Ola, she had been involved with various word of faith and Pentecostal churches in the United States for several years. Born and raised a Catholic in Nigeria, Ola was also familiar with Catholic Christianity with it adoration of the saints and with the practice of Yoruba by her ancestors. Ola appeared to be a mature Christian, having a good grasp with scripture, committed and extremely faithful to her church . It was January in the year 1994, when Ola first visited my ministerial training group called "School of the Prophets" held in Nassau Bahamas.

At first glance, it seemed as if Ola was in some kind of daze or trance. A native Nigerian, Ola was very self confident as she boldly captivated everyone's attention, drawing all eyes to herself. From the moment that I laid eyes on her, I hoped that my first encounter with Ola would be my last. Not only was I turned off by her intrusive, attention seeking ways, but my spiritual eyebrow was raised when I heard her prophesy. I personally observed that her prophetic style too closely resembled that of a psychic reader or a medium. Rather than just come in and quietly join a meeting in progress, she entered the classroom as though no one was in the room except herself and the person she was prophesying to . Interrupting my teaching, Ola proceeded to "read" one of the members about her past life. Her actions were not only abrasive, but they could have been considered embarrassing, other than for the fact that our class was small enough, where we were not normally uncomfortable with personal intimacy. As Ola publicly laid out this woman's past before the entire group, she was about 50% accurate.

As she proceeded with this "reading", sentences and phrases poured out of Ola like a water fountain that could not be turned off. When I interrupted her and remarked "that is incorrect. She is not like that", Ola continued on like she had not heard my comment. In retrospect, I don't think that she did. She gushed forth the words without even a pause. Finally she slowed down, gave a deep sigh, a satisfied gasp, and she was finished. She looked around at everyone as though she was seeing us all for the first time. With this impish smile on her face, I got a sense that she was about to stand and take a bow. From the beginning, I sensed that this young woman would be trouble. However, when I went home that night, I had an outstanding dream that showed me that Ola would be around awhile. In the dream, Ola was standing at a bus stop, waiting on the bus, when several buses pulled up. When each bus stopped in front of her, one by one, each of several buses had the word "Sheppard" printed as its final stop. When I awoke, I could not discern whether this dream was from the Lord or from a demon. All I knew then was that I need to "watch and pray." It turns out that for the next several years, Ola would become an integral part of my life. It would be through Ola that the Lord would open my eyes to the truth about how the religious demon and the Jezebel spirit conspire together within charismatic witchcraft.

Since Ola joined "the School of the Prophets" in her home state, she was never officially my client in private practice nor was she a member of my pastorate. The counsel and guidance that she received from me was strictly as a mentor who happened to be professionally trained and licensed in the secular world. Even so, from the onset and from a psycho-social perspective, I wondered if Ola suffered from borderline personality disorder. Most people with this kind of diagnosis cannot maintain relationships with two people at a time who are close to each other. Friction and strife will eventually manifest, as the BPD will create tensions and confusion within a social triad . The subtle attacks that continued throughout the years always seemed to have me as the target. One bit of strife that Ola attempted to set up was between myself and my ministerial colleagues. As most of us are licensed professional therapists in the secular world, we have learned how to defer to each other's expertise.

Where counseling is concerned, my associates and I function separately, each as a sole proprietor of his or her own independent counseling enterprise. I often will seek clinical consultation from various members of the ministerial connection , and where we may differ on rare occasions. At those times, I very often will concede to a staff member's area of expertise. Our love for each other as brethren in the Lord, professional therapists and co-laborers in His vineyard is so strong that our relationship is impregnable. However, this did not stop the spirit of Jezebel. Ola went to one of my colleagues and whispered, "I have a lot of issues from my childhood and I know that I need psychotherapy. I would like you to be my counselor. By the way, I don't want Pastor Pam involved in our counseling relationship." Ola was informed that such a counseling relationship would not be possible within the School of the Prophets since we each consult with each other on every case, and I am the ultimate authority. Furthermore, Ola was apprised that our professional practices were separate from our pastoral ministries and that the colleague of her choice had a full caseload.

As we continued to dodge several more bullets of strife sent our way, our relationship with Ola continued to evolve over the years. Since I recognized her spiritual side, I gave Ola many opportunities to minister publicly by traveling with me on evangelistic tours as my assistant preacher in training. In this regard, I called upon her to deliver public prayer as well as extended her opportunities to preach and prophesy during my conferences and revivals. The first few years, she consumed countless hours of my time on long distance telephone calls and in person with endless questions about the word of God and various spiritual matters. Like a leach, she seemed to try to suck up information and knowledge of various subject matters. As time passed, I began to suspect that all she really wanted was stimulation to fill her hours and her days. The enemy certainly used her to drain energy and to usurp valuable time. The real truth was that the demons in her compelled her to try to avoid being alone at all cost.

In short, Ola was definitely "high maintenance." Even so, her need for constant human contact caused me to believe that a real closeness was being established. Ola seemed so eager to become a strong Christian soldier and eventually I began to believe that she really cared for me. As I continue to grow in discernment, I can't help but repeat that first impressions are often the best. When I consider the first time I heard Ola prophesy, even then, my knowledge of the word of God caused me to suspect that she at least had a python spirit of divination. Nevertheless, I had to also remember my own past as a charismatic witch. For several years, I too remained under the deceptive influence of divination and the occult. My personal lack of knowledge and spiritual understanding caused me to dabble in divination after I was saved, until the Lord opened up my spiritual eyes and revealed the truth.

Therefore, because of my own experience, I never consistently doubted Ola's salvation. Ever so grateful to my bible study teacher Steve for recognizing that I was saved, I thank the Lord that Steve prayed for me. Likewise, as Ola's mentor, I believed that she was born again also, yet perhaps misguided as I once was. In this regard, I believed that once Ola was taught the truth about demonic strategies and deceptions, she would naturally and progressively be delivered from the spirit of divination. I was even more convinced of Ola's salvation, primarily because I wrongfully judged various personality attributes and behaviors as "fruit of the Spirit."

Since Jesus declared in the gospel that we would know His people by their fruit, in my mind, no one had more spiritual fruit than Ola. No one could preach the cross like Ola, not even myself. The first time she ever preached, she did it without any notes, a feat that took me years to attain. Nevertheless, there were recurrent problems that kept me dismayed and frustrated. For example, just when I would feel encouraged because of a revelation or an incident that seemed to demonstrate that Ola had made some positive strides in her spiritual growth, nonsensical and sometimes serious events would transpire to cause me to wonder "who IS this person that I am dealing with!?" Times too numerous to count, I would find myself speechless with my mouth opened wide, in a state of awe and bewilderment. Most of these incidents and situations are too numerous to mention here. Suffice it to say that the up and down swings of Ola's spiritual life caused the "the School of the Prophets" to nickname Ola "the Drama Queen."

At any rate, life with Ola was never boring. Notwithstanding, I never questioned her salvation mainly because of her strong word of faith background and my own confidence in the charismatic movement. I rationalized that like other Christians, Ola was merely striving for perfection and not completely matured. While in the United States, Ola had been a member of various reputable word of faith churches across the country. While associated with the school of Prophecy, Ola remained an active member of a very reputable Pentecostal denomination. Even though I wondered from time to time if she was saved, I made an erroneous assumption that there was no way that she could have fooled mature Christians---Charismatic believers who had pastored her for so many years. After all, no one loved to pray, praise the Lord and worship Him with outstretched hands, or watch Christian broadcasts more than Ola. Even more, no one I knew had the issues of the organized church and the propagation of the gospel on their hearts more than she did. For example, she even went out to soup kitchens, preached the gospel as well as served the food to the homeless in her home state. Ola also ministered on dangerous streets and crack dealing corners, witnessing to the lost, as an apparent light in the midst of darkness. How could this young woman not be saved?

After I had known her for several years, Ola approached me with a dream. In this dream, she saw three large snakes wrapped around her, emanating from her chest. She claimed that the Lord told her that these 3 demons were a lying spirit, a spirit of death, and a spirit of torment. Ola claimed that the Lord advised her to come to me and to ask me to cast these three demons from her. I was shocked to further find out that for most of her life, Ola had been relentlessly tormented practically every day since she was a child by hearing the voices of accusatory and condemning demons. Sometimes these demons would threaten her and cause her extreme vexation and even fear. However, Ola thought that most Christians experienced this kind of demonic harassment, and so she trained herself to adjust and to "suffer for Christ" by learning how to live with these voices without complaining. This explained why Ola needed constant attention. She was afraid to be alone with "the voices." She also confessed that she often had suicidal thoughts. Therefore, I suspected that we needed to cast out the spirit of death as one of those 3 demons.

After much prayer and supplication, I was obedient and I proceeded to cast these three demons from Ola. As soon as I opened my mouth to call the demons by the names identified in her dream, Ola began to vomit and convulse. I did not have time to be afraid, but when I thought about it after the session, fear set in. What if this poor girl had died on me? This was what it looked like was happening to her. The demons took over her facial expressions so that she no longer looked like Ola in the face. When the spirit of death came out, it looked at me with fearful, pleading eyes, as if it was saying "leave me alone. Let me stay here." The lying spirit was very angry in expression, while the spirit of torment convulsed and tore at her. Finally the manifestations stopped and the demons appeared to be gone. What was even more disconcerting was that once the session was over, Ola did not have any awareness or consciousness of what had just transpired. She was even shocked to see the vomit on her clothes and on the floor. She just laughed and squealed like a little kid who was at a horror movie.

Once Ola returned back to her home state, the torment stopped as well as the voices. Then about a year later, Ola met Bobby on one of her visits to my community and the lying and the deception resurfaced. It was evident that the lying demon was back because Ola continued to insist that her relationship with Bobby was merely platonic. Ola wanted to talk to me about her relationship and so we arranged to meet. She caught a flight and came to the area for a prolonged visit. I picked her up at the motel and as I was about to let her out of my car, I said "Let's pray." The motor was still running, because I thought that my prayer would be a short one. It was also cold outside, with snow on the ground. I remember tucking my head, but thank the Lord, I did not shut my eyes. I now take literally to "watch and pray." When I pray, I do not close my eyes any longer. As I spoke to the Father, I found myself making reference to the spirit of rebellion. It was not my intention to call forth a demon. I merely sensed that Ola, though respectful outwardly, was filled inwardly with outrage and rebellion that I had brought her to task about the potential dangers of a relationship with a man like Bobby. So I didn't think I was talking to a demon.

All of a sudden, Ola's face turned into the most hideous grimace that I have ever seen on any human being, outside of a monster or a werewolf in a horror movie. Her lips were twisted into a crooked, ugly grin, like a version of the cartoon, Casper, the friendly ghost. She began to growl and hiss like a snake, raising her little scrawny arm in the air like a club that was about to come down and hit me on the top of my head. I grabbed her arm, and began to pray for her even harder. I could not believe my eyes. When the demon backed off, Ola broke into tears, sobbing and yelling, "I don't want to hurt Rev. Sheppard. You can't make me hurt her. I love Rev. Sheppard. I will not hurt her." I was moved with compassion for her, so much so that after driving off, I went back to the motel where I found Ola sitting in the lobby, trying to look calm and composed. She looked like a scared little child. Once we entered her motel room, I began again to pray for Ola. Ola looked up at me with helpless eyes and whimpered, "I just had a vision. I saw myself with my nails in your throat and you were heavily bleeding."

What could I say? I knew that Ola's vision was projected into her mind by demons. Demons were so angry with me for setting out to deliver Ola, that they lusted after my death. Even so, as various scriptures flashed through my mind, I refused to conclude even then, that Ola was not saved. Nevertheless, it is clear to me now that as rebellion is "as the sin of witchcraft", the spirit of divination responded to my prayer. Once my own shock lifted from me, I was determined to be used by God to deliver Ola in the mighty name of Jesus Christ of Nazareth, regardless of what might happen to me. Things seemed to settle down a bit. I advised others in the School of the Prophets to back off and give Ola her privacy. Although Ola was the one who could not stand to be alone and my ministerial associates were merely trying to keep her occupied through Christian fellowship, we could now all see that Ola had her own personal reasons for wanting everyone to back up and give her some space. She wanted to explore an intimate relationship with Bobby.

Ola continued to catch an airplane and make frequent trips to our community to pursue her relationship with Bobby. Finally, one day in the spring, Ola came to me and announced that she was attracted to Bobby and that she was dating him. Though sick at heart, I wished her the best, and decided to leave "bad enough alone." Both she and Bobby were surprised, Ola pleasantly and Bobby suspiciously. Ola was thrilled that she could have her cake and eat it too,---her ministerial mentor and her man were not in conflict. However, shortly thereafter, Ola called me up in tears, confessing that she was no longer a virgin. She had slept with Bobby.

I remember the anger that I had to subdue at how this unconscionable man had finally spoiled her. I did not know it at the time of this phone call, but I was informed later that Ola had bragged about her lack of virginity to several of the trainees in the school of Prophets for quite some time. Yet her problem now was that since her menstrual period was late, she confronted Bobby and asked him if it turned out that she was pregnant, would he marry her. Bobby responded with an emphatic "no!" He basically retorted something like, "little girl, don't try to trap me off. I've got a lot of kids and a lot of child support to pay. If you are pregnant, then you'd better get an abortion. I am already financially strapped and I can't even give you and your kid the crumbs from my table. All the crumbs are spoken for."

Outraged at this rejection, Ola contacted me for prayer to be restored from falling to the sin of fornication. I immediately went to her hotel room, counseled and prayed with her to bring her to repentance, and to restore her back into right relationship with the Lord. Later that night we would have a deliverance session that has provided insight into so many scriptures---insights into the religious and the witchcraft demon and how they operate. I learned first hand how the witchcraft demon will use a human spirit in a demonic soul tie to enslave another human spirit. It stands as one of the most significant moments of my life. I still don't know why and how the tape recorder was running. It is a good thing that the tape recorder was on, or I myself would not have believed that what happened--- DID happen!

THE DEMON THAT WOULD NOT LEAVE

I began Ola's deliverance session with some pre-deliverance counseling that was tape recorded. My preaching and teaching messages are routinely recorded . Somehow, the recorder did not shut down on its own and most of the deliverance was transcribed. To my dismay, it was as if the hours that I had spent with Ola earlier in the day had not even occurred. Not only was there no longer a desire in her to repent of fornication, but just before the deliverance, she was wavering as to whether or not she was going to remain in this sinful relationship. It seemed to me like she was dissociative, slipping in and out of awareness even though she was fully conscious. Then it came to me that demons often oppress a person through the soul ties that have been established with a sex partner. I was reminded of those scriptures that refer to the one flesh relationship of sex, particularly in I Corinthians 6:16—he that is joined to a harlot is one flesh. I believe that it was the Holy Ghost Who caused me to know that through sex, Ola's soul was now connected to Bobby's soul.

I had never done this before, but I spoke to the spirit of Bobby and I commanded him to come out of Ola in the name of Jesus Christ of Nazareth. Suddenly and instantly, Ola left and the demon appeared,--- ranting, raving, and cursing in a masculine, guttural voice that was unearthly. The demon's voice was like a roar. To make a long story short, a 100 pound frail young woman was empowered with so much physical strength, that she had to literally be wrestled to the ground and restrained by those present. The power of witchcraft caused Ola to pick up a bible that was sitting on the table and strongly swung her hand and arm in an attempt to bash me in the head with it. Avoiding the blow, I leaped from my chair and yelled out "It's ON!" Then the demon in Ola headed for me, screaming obscenities. Once she rose from the chair, I was too much in shock to say that I was actually afraid.

Whether moving in the spirit or propelled by sheer instinct, I cannot tell. I just continued to confront it with the Name of Jesus but it kept on walking toward me in Ola's strengthened body until I was backed into a wall. Not able to go back any further, someone grabbed Ola and wrestled her to the floor. Restrained and angry, the demon cried out in a wailing, unearthly voice, words that I will never forget. "She is mine. Ola is mine. She does not belong to Christ. She belongs to me. I birthed her. I birthed her through her grandmother. Her grandmother gave her to me!"

Finally the demon seemed to have left, but I knew that even though he retreated, he was not cast out. It was evident that this demon was standing his ground based up Ola's grandmother's practice of Yoruba. The witchcraft demon believed that he had rights based upon a covenant established with the grandmother, and he would not be denied. By the grace of God, the tape recorder was not disabled in the hassle. I myself would have been in disbelief if I did not have the opportunity to hear this demon roar once more, as its voice was clearly recorded on the audio cassette.

When Ola returned into her own body, she had no recall of what had happened. She seemed to be in her right mind and she was determined to break off her relationship with Bobby, particularly after she heard various segments of the tape. Ola also agreed that she would simply stop paying for Bobby's airline tickets to visit her and that she would stay away from our area for an extended time. In short, she was going to repent and flee fornication. She began to share with me the details of her sexual experience, which she reported in a way that suggested that not only was sex not gratifying, but that Bobby bordered on being sexually perverse and abusive to her--- a virgin before he had spoiled her.

The next day, while conversing with Ola over the phone about faith, it finally dawned on me that Ola was not saved. She murmured quietly: "Rev. Sheppard, I am tired of not knowing. If God is real, then He is going to have to prove Himself to me without a doubt. He will have to appear or I can no longer go on." Many hours, too numerous to mention, I had grown accustomed to talking over the phone with Ola. Yet this one statement served as a trigger that reminded me of other conversations and discussions and I realized that Ola could not possibly be saved. I began to reflect over various comments that Ola made from time to time that caused me to realize that after several years of attendance in a word of faith church, Ola did not really understand faith. This realization was so shocking that I put down the phone and hurried to Ola's motel room once more.

As I recall, that first night that I met Ola in the Bahamas, and how I thought to myself "I hope I never see this young woman again" I realize that one of the reasons that Ola was sent to me by the Lord Jesus Christ was to serve as a testimony of the kind of spiritual fraud charismatic and religious demons are continuing to perpetuate in the word of faith movement. As previously stated, on that very night, I received a dream. In the dream, I saw Ola at a bus stop waiting . Now I understand the meaning of why at the top of every bus that stopped in front of her, its final destination read "Sheppard". In the beginning, Ola and I both thought that the Lord wanted me to mentor her in ministry. However, early on, I began to perceive that Ola's top priority was not her ministry. The ultimate longing of her heart was really to have a husband. Ola also shared how the rejection of her natural father had negatively affected her.

Her most vivid memory was being all dressed in a beautiful native garment, waiting for her father to come and pick her up. She recalled sitting on the front steps from early morning to late at night and he never came. The anger and hatred that she expressed toward her father was almost frightening. I believe that the rejection of her father was at the root of her desire for an older man. Her search for a father image was successful as she and Bobby eventually married. However, after three turbulent years involving drugs and domestic violence, they divorced.

I have learned from experience that when God is moving, we will interpret His purpose according to our own will and desires. His ways are clearly not our ways and His thoughts are clearly not our thoughts. As it turned out, the significance of Ola's story is really the doorway to uncovering charismatic witchcraft in general, and the religious demon in particular. For no one seemed more saved than Ola. No one loved church more than Ola. No one loved to worship and praise the Lord more than Ola. No one could preach the cross like Ola. No one could prophecy like Ola. Yet to my utter amazement, not only was Ola not even saved but she was praying, prophesying and preaching under the power of a religious demon.

Her dream of the three snakes emanating from her chest and wrapping around her spirit really told the tale. Ola's divination was inspired by the spirit of python. The spiritual influence of the python is portrayed in Acts 16:16-19. This chapter is an account of a slave girl possessed with the spirit of divination, who prophesied that Paul and his companions were sent to preach salvation. In the original Greek, the spirit of divination is literally translated as the spirit of Python. Divination is the ability to obtain secret or unknown natural knowledge of past, present or future events. In charismatic witchcraft, the spirit of python operates usually in women who go about with "I have a word for you" here and I have a word for you there."

A compatible name for the spirit of python is the Jezebel spirit. In retrospect, while Ola was on tour with me at a particular revival at a host church, a young woman came to the altar after the service. Raised in Charismatic, apostolic/Pentecostal circles, this congregate was so impressed with Ola, that she thought she had found the right church. The reason was that Ola immediately began to "utter" in a similar fashion as she had done on that first day. She poured out of herself an assessment of this young woman's past until my spirit could not take any more of it and I interrupted this "oration" with a decisive "stop." Then I explained, "we don't do that here." I found out later from the host pastor that this young woman eventually joined a church where readings of this kind are prevalent.

The Python is a snake that crushes its victims and cause them to gag as if suffocated. This also explains why at the first deliverance session, the demons caused Ola to cough and choke when it appeared that it was coming out. I believe that it actually DID come out. However, since Ola was not really saved, they returned with a vengeance. Python is also linked with the spirit of death. Here is a direct quote taken from an Internet article written by Todd Bentley before he became famous:

> "Many times when casting out the demons of addiction, it is necessary to break the spirit of python controlling them. At times when we have cast out spirits of additions, we have had to break the power of the python, especially when the spirits manifest and come out with choking and gagging, some even feel a constriction or tightness in the chest and feel like they are being choked. Even when I received deliverance on one occasion from the spirit of sorcery because of my involvement in drugs, especially with hallucinate drugs like LSD (acid) or magic mushrooms and PCP also called angel dust. I was bound by a spirit of death and manifested the spirit of phython. The last demon to be cast out of me was death."2 www.etpv.org2002/python.html---

I believe that the last deliverance session with Ola made it all clear. The outcome of this session also provided clarity on how Ola could actively participate in charismatic, word of faith churches for 10 years and not understand the resurrection, believing that Christ was raised when His spirit merely "flew away." It also explained why in spite of all of her good works, there were no real fruit of the spirit. Once I realized that Ola was not saved, I decided to approach this subject with her in a rather low key manner. Because of her determination to have Bobby in her life regardless of sin, I suggested to her that perhaps we needed to ensure her salvation by going through the rebirth process again. This deliverance session with Ola proved without a doubt that she had never been saved. I was left speechless.

As a part of the pre-deliverance counseling process, I reasoned with Ola to consider that perhaps she had not been previously converted as an eleven year old and as such, I suggested that she repent and confess the Lord now, as an adult. Ola agreed. However, just as she was about to repeat the sinner's prayer, the charismatic witchcraft and the spirit of the Antichrist took her over. I began the session by asking Ola to repeat after me. She repeated that she believed that the Lord died on the cross for her sins, but when I asked her to say "and Jesus Christ was raised from the dead," her countenance changed.

She grabbed a piece of paper from the table and with fear in her eyes and wrote "I can't speak. My jaws are locked." I shouted "and "Jesus Christ was raised from the dead." The demon's looked menacingly through Ola's eyes and rapidly shook her head back and forth to emphatically deny the Lord's resurrection. There was a wry grimace on her face as if the demon was saying "are you kidding!!!"

The demon very strongly and clearly manifested his rebellion all over Ola's face. I repeated. "And Jesus was raised from the dead." Her head continued to shake back and forth, in an emphatic "no." Now I spoke directly to the demon and commanded it to turn Ola loose and it screamed at me "no, she is mine!!!" This went on for awhile until Ola seemed to finally come back to herself. In "Unbroken Curses," Dr. Brown provides the following account of similar cases of professing Christians once they came to understand that they had been dedicated to other gods by their ancestors:

"As they started to confess the sins of their forefathers and specifically renounce the dedications placed on their lives, they suddenly found that they could not do so. They became confused. Their minds blanked out every time they started to say the words. Some found that their tongues became so twisted that they stuttered and could not say the simplest of words. All of them were unable to remember even one simple sentence renouncing their dedication in the name of Jesus. Just a few minutes previously while discussing the situation, they could easily recall whole paragraphs of information! Clearly, the demons involved were strenuously fighting against the breaking of dedications and curses. The battlefield was in their minds. (2Corinthians 10:3-5) (Unbroken Curses)"

After a few aggressive demands and commands that the demon come out of her in the name of Jesus Christ of Nazareth, it appeared that Ola broke through the bondage. She yelled "and Jesus Christ was raised from the dead and now I am saved."   Once this utterance of apparent faith was expressed, Ola began to shout uproariously, praising the Lord with smiles and tears flowing down her face. However, in spite of all of this shouting and praising, let's not forget that the Lord warned "you shall know them by their fruit." Well, suffice it to say that since I have not seen any fruit manifesting in Ola's life, I believe that this outburst itself was not Ola. Once again,   I believe that it was yet another masquerade of the religious demon. A few days later, Ola was living in sin with Bobby and shortly thereafter, together they moved out of the state to a location unknown to me. Her telephone changed to an unlisted number, her name changed three months later when she married Bobby.

Furthermore, I should clarify   that the fluidity of Ola's prayers and preaching was almost astounding. Words flowed from her in a rush and a gush, without even a pause. Most of her messages were convicting and extremely compelling. However, there was always a serious doctrinal flaw within them that she learned either from Catholicism, Pentecostalism or the Charismatic Movement. When these flaws would flow forth in her preaching,   I would counsel her privately and rightly divide the word with her. As previously indicated, I was shocked to learn that after so many years in a word of faith church, Ola did not understand the resurrection. She thought that Jesus rose as a spirit and not as a physical body. Consequently, early in our acquaintance, it vaguely crossed my mind that Ola might not be saved, since salvation is directly based upon believing in the bodily resurrection of the Lord Jesus Christ. Since she did not even understand that He was raised in His body, how then could she be saved?

Most people who are acquainted with me are very careful not to dishonor me. I am known to be a very strong woman, and though perhaps not popular with most, I am rarely disrespected to my face by anyone, even my most ardent critics or enemies. Therefore, I don't know whether or not Ola would have been as strong in her confrontation if it was presented to me face to face. Nonetheless, by telephone, she was formidable in her attempt to kill my spirit. Throughout this subtle attack, Ola presented herself as beyond reproach, attempting to make me a scapegoat, projecting her own evil and even her failed marriage to Bobby upon me.

Where her own sin was concerned, she minimized it by casually excusing her fornication and other two faced and deceitful actions against myself and others as merely the folly of youthful trial and error. She even blamed me for her "indiscretion" with Bobby, for if I had not been upset with her and allowed them both to perceive my obvious disapproval of their relationship, she declared that she would never have married him. In other words, that she married Bobby in rebellion to prove me wrong. Therefore, in her warped mind, I am responsible for their failed marriage, forgetting that when she actually married Bobby, she had been out of contact with me for about 6 months.

Control is what the spirit of Jezebel seeks in the lives of those it targets. Ola's tactic is to seduce the needy in the Body of Christ with her financial resources in order to gain support from them later on. Furthermore, even in the good times, I always had the feeling that in spite of my love for Ola, that she did not particularly like me, but merely tolerated me for the ministerial exposure and opportunities that I provided. So as I look back on my final contact with Ola, it is logical that the focus of her verbal attack was the thing about me that she most envied---my ministerial authority and my integrity as a Christian. After she unleashed the bitterness and resentment that she had been harboring against my spiritual mentoring for more than a decade of our acquaintance, she finished with the final blow.

"I like the School of the Prophets", but unfortunately, I cannot recommend you to anyone because I do not see you as a loving, compassionate mentor. I don't think that you are tolerant and I don't perceive you as a good ministerial role model. I won't go out of my way to disparage or belittle your ministry but if I am asked, I must express my concerns. I simply do not trust you with the Lord's sheep because of the way that you have spiritually abused me." As this final fiery dart brushed against my shield of faith and nudged my breastplate of righteousness, my heart remained guarded against the accusations of this demon. The spirit of Jezebel did not kill THIS prophet!

At this point in time, I don't really know whether or not I will ever see Ola again. It depends upon whether or not Ola can humble herself. About a year ago, Ola left me a message on my answering machine expressing her desire to refer clients my way for telephone counseling, "so that I could make myself some extra money." Her voice was soft, yet nasal in its attempt to ascend and condescend. She indicated that she was now operating her own telephone counseling practice and that in essence, she was in a position to "throw some business my way" by referring her surplus clients to me, acknowledging that she was contacting me due to my professional expertise as a secular social worker. I could hear Jezebel's unspoken put down. "I do not respect or uphold you as a minister, but you are a capable professional in the secular arena."

Needless to say, I did not respond to this call. Six months later, Ola phoned me for a ministerial reference and we spoke cordially. However, I declined her request. I informed her that in spite of her commitment to ministry and her dedication, that in good conscience, I did not believe that she was ministering under the power of the Holy Ghost. In fact, I suspect that the spirit of Jezebel is even more entrenched within her than it was a decade ago. In the words of Jessie Penn- Lewis, "There are religious demons, not holy, but nevertheless 'religious' and filled with a devilish form of religion which is the counterfeit of true, deep spirituality."(War on the Saints, pg. 226)

From such, I turn away.

ENDNOTES

1. Taken from Derek Prince, Blessings or Curse: You Can Choose, Chosen Books 1990, pgs. 11-113
Brown, R. and Yoder D. Unbroken Curses: Hidden Source of Trouble in the Christian's Life, Whitaker House, 1995, pg. 40

2. The supernatural ministry of Todd Bentley in the spring of 2008 is an indication to me that the spirit of python never came out of him but masqueraded as a healer and a miracle worker. You know them by their fruit.

CHAPTER 13   Demonic Soul Ties

I don't believe that there is any area more conducive to demonic deception than in the area of love and marriage, particularly in the lives of women called to the fivefold ministry or to female leaders within the laity. The most popular demonic strategy is to present individuals of either the same sex or the opposite sex in either a seductive or intriguing form, with the object of arousing various dormant thoughts in the captive, which he or she does not realize exist within. The deceived believer will become smitten with thoughts of a particular person, as masked as for the purpose of prayer, of increased fellowship, and where the opposite sex is concerned, for ministry and communion in the things of God. When the soul tie is romantic in nature, the religious demon will work in the realm of the passions and the affections of the captive, causing the captive to believe that the party upon whom his or her affections is fixed is also equally affected. This is accompanied with a counterfeit "love" or drawing to the partner, with a painful craving for his or her company which almost masters the captive.

Certain personality types are more conducive to captivity to a demonic soul tie than others. Therefore, the Jezebel face of this demon has to devise more elaborative strategies for those of its targets who are not self effacing. The key to captivity for both the aggressive and the passive personality types is the extent that love, passion, sex, and romance is a major priority, central to life itself. Where the expansive type of personality is concerned, pride may be an entrapment factor for those whose vanity and presumed irresistibility will be their primary stronghold or doorway to demons. I have found that the general attitude of a person who is conducive to this kind of captivity is basically destructive. Some have pride in being a superior lover, while others are drawn by vanity and an irresistibility that leads to a vulnerability centered in trying to master relationships that are unattainable. For example, the vanity of the aggressive and the passive-aggressive personality types may cause them to stay in an unfruitful relationship in an attempt to master it, while instead, becoming entrapped by their own personality defect of pride and vanity.

On the other hand, passive types may be afraid of confrontation, preferring to "give in" to avoid conflict. In each personality type there will be Christians who have not rightly divided the word of God relative to being a peacemaker, where forgiveness and meekness are taken for weakness. Acclimated to the general role of peacemaker, captives may live a life of pretense, where they habitually hide and deny justifiable hostility and anger so as to "turn the other cheek" religiously. In this regard, the religious demon will cause passive saints to become spiritually crippled in their counterfeit moral purity, predisposing to a shrinking process that stifles their ability to strike back---not so much at the people who have wronged or harmed them but from taking a stand against principalities and powers. They end up feeling like one of my clients who dreamed that she was a back seat driver in her own car and the person whom the Jezebel spirit has manipulated to keep the client in captivity was metaphorically "behind the wheel" of her very soul.

Most of the women that I have either pastored, mentored or counseled as a clinician have been captive to a demonic soul tie at various seasons in their lives. In Ola's case, in particular, African cultural belief systems established a strong influence on women becoming enslaved to carnal love. According to her inner dictates, Ola, a native Nigerian, withstood Bobby's exploitation, humiliation and degradation out of the cultural cues that an African woman is not complete without a man, a phenomena that I refer to as the "Adam's Rib Syndrome." True to form, I have recently learned that Ola has once again married, this time to an African American with a graduate degree in religion, someone that she has only known for a few months. The religious demon will capitalize upon a Christian woman's desire to serve, joined to Adam's hip.

Counterfeit humility is another character defect that empowers the religious demon's advantage in tightening a demonic stronghold as highlighted in the Making of a Prophet:

> "False meekness also manifests itself when professing Christians who have low self concept develop techniques and processes whereby the self is placed in the background by losing self regard. In an attempt to avoid anger at any cost, the captive will repress hostility and will become self effacing.
> Some captives will merely adapt to the stronger personality, while others will allow their personality to be changed by stronger people.
> People like this are often wrongfully perceived as having the fruit of meekness." (Sheppard, pg. 191)

Other captives sustain a demonic soul tie for a grander purpose. For example, consider Tawanda. Tawanda, a strong, aggressive personality type has been in ministerial training with me for the last two years. One of her major character flaws is that she has placed too high a premium on passion, romance and on finding a husband. Tawanda convinced herself that she should endure hardship so that her young daughter could be raised by her biological father. Even though she is a strong and aggressive, Tawanda was prepared to marry an insensitive, passive-aggressive, mean spirited man apparently for the sake of their child.

Yet over time, I discovered that an even more powerful motive for Tawanda's decision to marry Raheem was her fear that she would never find a mate and her subsequent impatience to have her own immediate desires and needs fulfilled. In spite of the fact that it was very apparent that Raheem was clearly not her soul mate made in heaven, Tawanda was able to grin and bare the grief of Raheem's obvious hatred and jealousy of her intelligent mind and her independent spirit. For a rather long season, Tawanda endured oppressive behavior. As Raheem continued to alienate all who came in contact with him, and then conversely became depressed by the exclusion and rejection that he engendered from people whom he himself offended, he made Tawanda the scapegoat upon whom to vent his blind and wild rage. Tawanda was perceived as the sources of all of Raheem's social and economic failures.

In order to break a demonic soul tie of this kind, I presented the truth of the word of God rightly divided, with counsel, guidance and prayer applied to every aspect of this situation. Tawanda stood her own ground and the demonic soul tie was eventually broken without the need for hands on expulsion. Tawanda came to experience truth through the revelation of the Holy Spirit---that the positive gains that she had anticipated within this, a demonic soul tie, were not obtainable. Raheem's hatred of her very soul was revealed and exposed, even though he had passionately pursued her.

For example, to shame and belittle her, he watched Tawanda plan a wedding and then made every effort to spoil her plans by claiming at the last minute that "he was not ready for such a commitment." Hoping to crush her through the disappointment of a wedding postponed and eventually cancelled, he briefly withdrew. Yet, once Raheem perceived that Tawanda's strength was not abated, the vicious cycle re-occurred. Explosive, destructive and seemingly dangerous elements surfaced, where it became apparent that Raheem's hatred is truly the spirit of Jezebel's hatred of all who belong to Christ and particularly of those who serve him in the fivefold ministry.

The Jezebel spirit will also attempt to destroy its partner through domination and control in a form of spiritual, soulish and even physical battering. This demon will belittle its captive in an attempt to diminish soul power by seducing a Christian woman into a marriage to someone who professes to be saved, sanctified and filled with the Holy Ghost, only to find out after the marriage that the spouse has a Jezebel, witchcraft spirit. My second husband was of this sort. Deceived into believing that he was a born again Christian prior to the marriage, the Jezebel spirit immediately manifested and continued to harass and torment me with ever increasing frequency until I finally obtained a divorce eight years later. Since I had been set free from the occult years before, to discover that my husband's Christianity was a counterfeit mixture of New Age occultism and witchcraft was extremely grievous to my soul.

With a sinister grin and a chuckle, my second husband would repeat to me often that he had "chains and gates" on my soul. On May 16, 1990, he predicted that I would have a car accident in less than two weeks. On Thursday, May 24th, eight days after his prediction, I had left work early to go to the emergency room to check out why I had been having a constant headache for several days. Less than two miles from Memorial Hospital in Albany NY, I was hit in the back of my car, while driving on a 4 lane highway at about 65 miles an hour. My vehicle turned around in a circle, but I did not hit anyone else, nor did the car sustain another impact. In fact, a supernatural power came over me in spite of the headache, and my fingers gripped the steering wheel like a race car driver. Even the car that hit my vehicle was totally destroyed when it hit an embankment. However, I was able to resume my trip, ---driving my slightly damaged vehicle to the hospital.

The Jezebel spirit periodically used my second husband to zero in on my shortcomings, as this demon is adept at discovering potential weak spots. Taking every opportunity to relentlessly point them out with a merciless, derogatory mocking kind of criticism, he was armed toward crushing my self confidence. Unable to find any weakness of spirit, he focused on perceived failures in my life to bring various life goals to fruition. What he did not know was that these very failures were orchestrated by God Himself, as the enemy was using my worldly ambitions to derail me from the will of God. Moreover, the Jezebel spirit in my ex was not prepared for the fact that the Holy Spirit was on a mission to purge me of esteem, pride and vanity. Actually what my second husband meant for evil as well as other circumstances and situations were used by the Holy Ghost as His pruning tools.

To illustrate, here is a segment taken from a damnable letter dated August 25, 1995, sent to me in his handwriting. A physical batterer, he is the only man who not only struck me about my head and body on several occasions, but his emotional battery was even more diabolical. This segment from one of his final letters to me highlights the nature and strategy of those who try to destroy their spouse's soul:

> "The second part of my dream is the most significant I believe, for it shows the spiritual poverty in you...within you there is no actual spirit life, only an outer superficial facade having only the appearance of spirituality, but none in reality...You have no mind or spirit. You are lost because of your inability to recognize the Spirit of God presented to you through me. I question whether or not you are good for anything other than contention, strife, debate and discord as your father the devil is. ....The causes of your behavior have been surmised and you have been analyzed. Your behavior stems from a complex conglomeration: demon possession, glass ceilings, thwarted ambitions, hypocrisy, personal short comings, failures, self doubts, insecurities, low self esteem and poor self image."

Once my freedom from my second man was obtained, the Holy Spirit inspired me to put the fruit of my trials and tribulations in this marriage contracted by the religious demon into words:

> "It is foolish to lie to ourselves. As vanity is excessive pride, a vain person's conceit will bring about self deception. Self deception is a doorway to failure. Others will recognize our weakness and flatter us to our disadvantage. Vanity is foolish because it anchors itself in features of the flesh that are impermanent and transient. It causes us to live in the past, by placing value on that which is empty and fleeting. In matters of the heart, a vain man or woman will take such pleasure in his or her own physical attributes that he or she will be blinded to what is truly valuable to maintaining a lasting relationship with a significant partner." (To Curse The Root, pg. 67)

And such was the case with how the religious demon attracted me to my second husband. I was originally seduced by flattery for about six months---a conniving, surreptitious praise for my spirituality in general, and my relationship with Jesus, in particular. Then once married, the religious demon in him could not restrain its hatred for the Lord, consequently causing my ex to frequently bite the hand that fed him and so he lost a good wife. One hundred years ago, Jessie Penn-Lewis hit the spiritual nail on the head with these words:

> "Deceiving spirits carefully adapt their suggestions and leadings to the idiosyncrasies of the believer, so that they do not get found out, ie., no leading will be suggested contrary to any strong truth of God firmly rooted in the mind, or contrary to any special bias of the mind. If the mind has a practical bent, no visibly foolish leading will be given; if the Scriptures are well known, nothing contrary to Scripture will be said; if the believer feels strongly on any point, the leadings will be harmonized to suit that point and where ever possible, leadings will be adapted to previously true guidance from God so as to appear to be continuance of that same guidance."
> War on the Saints pg. 123, abridged edition)

My personal testimony is a poignant fulfillment of these very words. My particular religiosity was that I was susceptible to anyone who appeared to hold my spirituality in high regard. This same vulnerability remained an open door for the religious demon to try again to enslave and destroy me with my third husband. My relationship with Richard was very strange. We had absolutely nothing in common but Christ and our mutual attraction for each other, or so it seemed. Different ages--me the elder by 17 years,--- different cultures---he, a Puerto Rican--- different educational backgrounds, different interests, different work ethics---all we literally had in common was Jesus. However, he had a serious religious demon, whose primary task was to take me down, by bringing shame upon me through the consequences of his drug addiction. Of course, he did not know his own motives. He was just being "himself."

The first 5 years of the relationship, I believed that he was deeply in love with me and so would anyone who saw us together. There can be a lot of romance and emotion in a co-dependent relationship. I struggled to help my third husband overcome his addiction to heroin and he appeared to be helping my daughter and I to establish the ministry. However, at crucial times, the religious demon would use him to try to bring shame and degradation upon me, to no avail. Once he was subsequently arrested for a petty crime. Ordinarily, the average person might not have even been incarcerated but because of his prior record, the district attorney's lowest offer was 16 years to life.

Arrested in June, I was shown in a dream later that very night that he would be released from jail before the snow fell. In spite of the circumstances, I never lost faith. In fact, I prayed him out of it. In short, a legal miracle occurred and my third husband walked out of the court room a free man on December 10th, a day in 1999 where the temperature in New York was 70 degrees, and no snow had yet fallen. However, when I looked back just this year, once I accepted the fact that both the prophetic dream and the miraculous deliverance from life imprisonment were both demonic, I have obtained much freedom and much release. My error was in assuming that the grace and mercy that I believed that the Lord extended to Richard with this apparently divine escape from a lifetime in prison would changed him forever. But in less than a month, he was back on heroin. I also assumed that because of its supernatural nature, that it was divine. Today I wonder whether or not it was the work of the religious demon to release Richard to finish his destruction of me and my ministry.

So when I could literally "DO NO MORE" once my husband resumed his use of heroin, I fell on my face before God and cried out "Lord, take this man out of my life. His drug addiction is beyond me and I can't handle this situation not one more minute." Within days, ----less than a week----Richard was arrested in another part of the state on a petty drug charge and got 1-3 years. I stuck by him for the two years that he was incarcerated. Just to show you how the devil works, there are at least 50 prisons in this state he could have gone to, but he was sent to the prison where I myself had been preaching for 8 years. It is self evident that it was the enemy's intention to use his imprisonment to discredit me, but once again, the religious demon's plans were blocked. I even preached there for 6 additional months without anyone knowing that my own husband was among them and then the Lord spoke to my spirit and told me that it was time to leave prison ministry. I obeyed and I have not looked back.

The day that hurt me the most was July 23, 2003. It was the day of Richard's release from prison . Down to the last day, Richard lied and caused me to believe that he would be coming home. Since he   did not tell me that he was being released to a rehab for a year, I drove to the prison to pick him up. Once I arrived at the prison, I learned that he was already shipped out to a rehab and I had no idea where he was being sent. I was almost devastated that day. When we spoke later in the day, he was cold and hard, still not letting me know where he had been sent.   That is the day I found out how strong I really am.   I myself didn't know that the marriage had been over for two years,on that very day in July 2001 when I cried out to the Lord to release me from my captivity, and Richard was arrested in less than a week. The marriage was over but I held on to my marriage in my heart for two more years. For a total of four years , the religious demon gave me false prophecies, visions and dreams, suggesting that I hold on to Richard.

Locked away from me for two years in prison, one year in a residential rehab and another year in independent living, we did not live together for a total of 4 years. While incarcerated, we spoke often over the telephone the first two years apart. However, once released to rehab,   we only spoke a handful of times on the phone. Over the next two years, my third husband was as cold as ice. Upon his release from rehab a year later into his own structured living apartment , our contact was extremely minimal. I continued to pray for a reconciliation and when we reconciled the first week in April 2005, I presumed that the Lord had answered my prayers. Nevertheless, it became very clear to me within one month, that our marriage was finally over. Can you believe this? He was clean from drugs for 4 years, but when he came back to live with me, he immediately started to use heroin once again!!!!! By June 20, we were divorced.

On more than one occasion, I believed that I was walking in faith and trusting God but my crucial, spiritual mistake was that I maintained the false assumption that the Holy Spirit was leading when in reality it was the religious demon. Its goal was to divert me from the Lord's real purpose, mission and calling on my life. Moreover, since I was adamant in my false belief that the only way I could minister to the sheep was to be married to a shepherd, this "religious" assumption provided the ground for religious demons to send me visions, dreams and intuitions that harmonized with this false assumption. The result? Well, the religious demon led me into two unsuccessful marriages by sending me two husbands from the pit of hell and therefore I myself was in bondage to the religious demon for a total of 16 years.

I suspect that those reading these words with a religious mind would quote scripture at this point with "the marriage bed is un-defiled" and "what God has joined together, let no man put asunder." I believe that implicit within these particular scriptural quotations is that God is the one who joined the marriage. When I was an unsaved, atheistic heathen, God joined my first marriage to the late Garry Springsteen and we were not even married in a Christian ceremony. More than 3 decades later, it is self evident because I can see the fruit of my first marriage in the most important blessing that I have ever received: Garry's daughter conceived in my own womb. Although Garry and I were both Christ haters at the time of Zonnita's conception and birth, the Lord used us both to create not only a daughter, but the person who would know me best of all, in spite of my spiritual ignorance When our daughter was born, I was completely without knowledge of my call to Christ and my charge to ministry but the religious demon knew everything it needed to know. By the time I became born again in 1977 and then heeded the call to preach in 1981, the religious demon's blueprint to destroy me through demonic soul ties with AME Zion ministers had already been devised and implemented. (See the Making of A Prophet, Part 1) I must admit that it was a clever plan. Once I overcame falling to the sin of fornication with AME Zion ministers, the religious demon implemented plan B and plan C with my next two husbands, using the same strategy with both of these men, with a slight divergence.

Simultaneously, the religious demon successfully used church folk to convince me that the sheep were so resistant to my calling, that the only way I could minister would be to "co-pastor" with an ordained minister as my husband.   Once the deception about men in the clergy was no longer reliable bait, the religious demon appealed to my occult roots. First I was given a mission—substance abuse and prison ministry. Then the I was subtly convinced since I was neither a recovered addict or an ex-offender myself---that it would be impossible for me to fulfill this arduous calling without a mate, preferably one who was also an recovering addict and an ex-offender.

So in 1985, I was sent a being in a dream who declared that he was "an angel sent from God." It was an angel, for sure---but this angel was not sent from God. I know without a doubt today that I was sent a religious demon sent by the spirit of the Anti-Christ to present me with a counterfeit ministerial assignment. This demon claimed that my ministry was to serve along side my "husband to be" to establish and run a Christ centered residential treatment center for drug addicts and ex-offenders. In order to provide a doorway for husband number two and husband number three to enter into my spiritual life, the religious demon cleverly presented this counterfeit mission that both of these men would fit into perfectly: drug addiction and incarceration. This one dream was used as a two for one counterfeit. As soon as I refused the physical and emotional abuse of husband number one, husband number 2 was in the wings to bring me down by deception, degradation and debauchery.

Assuredly, it was a step by step process to create the demonic soul ties that I suffered, endured and finally was set free from after 16 years of struggle. First of all, my personal aspirations and preferences where a mate was concerned had to be drastically changed. Since my original heart's desire was to find a believer with comparable and preferably higher educational and professional attainments than my own---perhaps either a doctor or a lawyer--- and since the religious demon was aware of my ministerial dedication, to complete the deception was relatively easy. The process involved persuasion with continual dreams and spiritual leadings of the goose bump variety by skillfully drawing me off of God's will for my ministry through these highly religious, demonic counterfeits.

When a supernatural experience of this nature is assumed to be God without trying it, the voice of the religious demon as an angel of light is more difficult to detect, especially when it comes with specific instructions about one's mission and concrete information about a prospective mate. "As long as the believer thinks it is God who is directing him, so long the deceiving spirits are safe from exposure, and they can lead him on into more and more deception."(War on the Saints, unabridged edition, p. 59) It took almost 20 years to expose the source of this angelic visitation.

The way that I obtained freedom was to come to terms with the fact that in spite of my spiritual advancement, I too had been deceived. In my particular case, I was was not demon oppressed, nor was either husband successful in captivating me through seduction and domination, nor was my anointing blocked from casting out demons from others. Nevertheless, I myself was not able to become completely free from the religious demon until I fully accepted the fact that the dream that I received in 1985 was a counterfeit. Then, I had to come to terms with the truth--- that every other supernatural experience that was directly or indirectly linked to the 1985 supernatural episode were also counterfeits.

If I had continued to believe that angelic visitation was from the Lord, then I would probably be looking for husband #4 today. Not that I am against marriage but I do not believe that I was joined in marriage by God. My commonsense tells me that if God was the one who revealed to me that each of two husbands was sent by the devil with the goal of destroying me and my ministry, God Himself did not send either one of these men into my life. Therefore, I have come to perceive that my second and my third marriage were unholy alliances.

Traditional church folk may strongly disagree with me on the subject of divorce, but the assumption that God joins ALL marriages and secondly, that anything God joins together cannot be put asunder by man is in itself, religious bait for demonic entrapment. It is not divorce that God hates. What he hates is that a woman be "put away" without giving her a bill of divorcement so that she can marry another. Women in old testament times were dependent upon having a husband for their livelihood and any woman who was not allowed to marry would have starved to death. For this reason, financial care for every widow was mandatory for the religious community to provide. The following definition of the difference between "putting away" and "divorce" provides much clarification to the issue of divorce and remarriage:

> "Putting away is because of sin and giving the bill of divorcement is a merciful act allowed by God to dissolve the marriage so that the ex-spouse is free to marry another person. In Moses' day it was a very burdensome thing for a woman to be put away without being given a bill of divorcement so that she could marry another man. God made a provision for women who were put away so that they could be supported. It was because of men's hard hearts (Mt. 19:8) that God, through Moses, allowed men to put away their wives. And it was God's mercy that provided for a man to give a bill of divorcement so that "she may go and be another man's wife" (Deut. 24:1-2). Notice in Deuteronomy 24:4 that the Scriptures refer to "her former husband." Her first husband is no longer her husband, he is her former or ex-husband. The first marriage has been absolutely dissolved. Otherwise the divorced woman would be in adultery if she became another man's wife."[2] (Harry Bethel of www.bethelministries .com)

I also remind "the religious" that God's will is not not being done on earth. Therefore, when the scriptures are wrongly understood because of a strong adherence to a wrong assumption, deceiving spirits are skilled at using scripture effectively, particularly when rigidity and religious bias have clouded ones thoughts and mind. In my case, I personally believe that divorces from both my second and third husbands were not only mandatory, but I perceive both divorces as a blessing sent from God to help me to be set free to help others similarly bound. Even though I do not believe that I would be misdirected by the same kind of trap again, and even though my spiritual growth through 16 years of trials, tribulations and troubles was immeasurable, I have made a conscious choice to live without a "husband #4." Simply put, I have no more time to give to finding Mr. Right. I must work while it is day and I will not risk the precious years that I have left to provide yet another doorway for a religious demon to usurp my energies and in any way lessen my value in the Lord's service.

The scriptures declare in the book of Daniel that in the last days, some of the teachers shall fall. I believe that we are in the last of the last days and I am one of those teachers that has been blessed "to fall" yet to rise up wise and strong in order to be a blessing to others. In Daniel 11:35, we find these words "some of the teachers shall fall, to refine them and to purify, and to make them white, even at the time of the end." About this particular verse, Jessie Penn-Lewis writes:

> "The elect may be deceived, and from Daniel's words, are apparently permitted to be deceived for a season, so that in the fire testing they may be 'refined' (the word refers to the expulsion of dross by the smelting fire): 'purified' (the removal of dross already expelled), and made 'white' (the polishing and brightening of the metal after it has been freed from its impurities)." (War on the Saints, unabridged edition pg. 24)

I myself have been freed from the impurities of counterfeit supernatural experiences and leadings that led me to put myself in the captives' hands through demonic soul ties. I relish in truth that cuts and humbles and so to admit that I have been deceived at various times and seasons in my 29 years as a born again believer is in no way painful to my feelings, my emotions or my pride today. I have learned that spiritual experiences have not made me spiritual. Only walking by faith and trusting in Jesus Christ has made me spiritual.

So when I heard in the spirit, that George, a church member (See Chapter 6) as well as my third husband Richard were sent to me by the devil to destroy my ministry, of course I did not want to believe this word about either one of them, particularly not about my own husband, a man that I loved more than any other in my life. In fact, I truly believed that the Lord had brought us together and that our marriage was ordained by Him. Furthermore, once the Lord revealed that not only was my legal marriage bed "defiled", but that I had also been delivered from a a demonic soul tie which the Holy Spirit had sovereignly cast from me, I could do nothing but praise His Name. In fact, He revealed that I was not ready for the full work He has called me to until I was divorced from my third and last husband. "What God has joined together let no man put asunder" does not suggest that man cannot put a marriage asunder, simply because "God's will is not done on earth." Nor does this scripture suggest that every marriage that occurs has actually been joined together by God.

As previously indicated, I believe that my first marriage was ordained of God because it has been proven to have been within His will, even though both Garry and I were unsaved. I have judged it by its fruit. Without a doubt, Zonnita is my strongest supporter, and my usefulness to the Lord is in large part, her victory. Yet man did put my marriage to her father asunder, first through Garry's adultery, followed by Satan's victory in his premature death at the age of 38 of a massive heart attack. Even so, I am an overcomer because I have spoiled the religious demon's efforts to keep me bound. The word of my testimony as an overcomer was built into my spirit by words that I myself penned in 1996:

"Once we decide to humbly receive the results of the Lord's breaking, through the crucifixion of the flesh, the Holy spirit will be able to flow through us unhindered, and we will be able to accomplish all things through relying on His power. By losing all confidence in our self esteem, we will gain His esteem. We will not be tossed to and fro by pride and vanity because He will cause us to be immovable, unshakable trees that are tooted and grounded in Him. His acts of consolation will serve as a confirmation that He can be trusted in every crisis, every temptation, every trial. Then He will fulfill a general purpose that He has for all of us: that we become consolers of others that are living through the very things that the Lord Himself has delivered us from." (See To Curse the Root)

I have no personal axes to grind or struggles with forgiving my last two former husbands who have allowed the devil to use them to try to destroy me. It should also be pointed out that I am as passionate as I have always been. Nevertheless, my primary reason for desiring to remain single is that I just don't have any more time to waste with the "getting to know you" stage or the "I'm gonna make you happy" commitment. So as I teach the young girls that I pastor and mentor that "you don't need sex to live", I have taken my own advice and have decided to remain both celibate and solo. The reality is that I have to be about my Father's business. Nor do I need a husband to do what I am called to do. My ministerial partner is my daughter. I don't knock the "co-pastor" thing for other women in ministry but like they say in baseball to the batter at the plate, "three strikes and you are out." I am out. Out of time to devote to a pursuit for husband number four. I must use the remainder of my years in complete dedication to my Father's will, as I work while it is day.

In truth, as a consoler to countless women who have been held captive to a demonic soul-tie, I believe that I am moving in an important aspect of my calling. Unfortunately, some women are too deluded to be consoled. Here is an example, taken from one of several email interactions with a women who are bound in a demonic soul tie. Her name have been changed to "Lois." After reading Lois's email, the deception of the religious demon will leap off of the page:

The Lord revealed to me who my mate was on 1/21/2001. At the time, I was in love with another man when the man I was in love with married another woman on 1/28/2001, exactly 7 days after the Lord revealed to me who my real partner and husband to be really is. Coincidentally, the man I loved who married is now divorced and he has remarried. God is so faithful, gracious and patient with us. After some time, I accepted God's will for my life. However, I tried to help God out because I saw my husband to be talking to another woman who I found out later was just a friend and then I asked him to come and cut my grass. Well, I have had to repent for trying to accomplish the plan and purpose of God for my life in my own strength.

Well, we started building a friendship for a season. During that time the Lord allowed me to see some very serious character flaws in him (lying, deception, rebellion, pride, etc." He is a spirit filled believer and powerfully anointed of God. But as we know, the gifts come without repentance. I wrote a letter to him speaking the truth to him in love concerning what I saw, character flaws that could be detrimental and devastating to a marriage. We had not talked in over a year and a half. Just recently he brought another woman to church and this past Sunday, they started pre-marital counseling. He and I are both African Americans and she is white. From what I have heard from the Elder that is over Premarital Counseling, he is not in agreement with this inter-racial relationship and is praying about how he should deal with it.

I went to speak with my spiritual father who is an elder and presbyter over prayer in our church concerning the situation and he sees in the life of this individual the character flaws that I see. My spiritual father confirmed what God had shown me, even with the same scriptures that I had been studying that wee. The Lord had me studying Jacob and His sovereign will that very week. God really wants to use him and He has such great plans for the both of us to work together in ministry. But my husband to be is so deceived. He really believes that he is walking in the will of the Lord. That's the part that is somewhat frightening. Also, a fact confirmed by my spiritual father.

I know that God will not transgress a person's will, but I want the will of the Lord to be done concerning God's destiny, purpose and plan for me and this individual. This is not about me or him. This is about the will of the Lord. As I stated previously, when God showed him to me, I didn't want him. I wanted someone else. Even though I submitted my concerns to my spiritual father and to my elder, I seek your wisdom and counsel because we can all be deceived and there is safety in a multitude of counsels. My prayer request at this point is that God would break the the bondage and deception over John's mind. (His name is John) The Lord has a purpose, plan and work for us to do as a couple---kingdom business. Its about Jesus and souls, deliverance, breaking shackles, etc. The will of God is serious and this is serious business. I hope to hear from you soon. God bless you."

I basically wrote Lois and suggested to her that it was not the Lord who identified this man John as her mate. This is her response.

"Thanks—but I do not believe that my elder and my spiritual father would tell me a lie. He too is a prophet, prayer warrior and intercessor, not a false one---and spends several hours a day in prayer. He would speak the truth to me in love, even if it hurts me, and he would not lead me astray. He would not lie to me as he has the gift of discernment, word of wisdom and word of knowledge in his mouth. He has been walking with the Lor for many years. Many years. I appreciate your input, but I cannot accept it. My pastor is very good friends with one of the best friends of President George Bush who is the Pastor of a spirit filled, tongue talking, demon busting AME Church. My pastor and his wife were just in Washington at the White House with the President and first lady for the National Day of Prayer. My pastor is also a prophet---not a false one. I too have a prophetic anointing on my life, though I do not call myself a prophet as you do. I suggest that you read the following books by Jonas Clark. Seducing Goddess of War and

Exposing Spiritual Witchcraft and also the Religious Spirit. God bless you and keep you but I would prefer no further correspondence or communication with you. Be blessed."

In summary, Lois wrote me for advice and when I did not agree with her own thoughts and the opinions of her spiritual leaders, then she basically implied by her book references that I myself am under the influence of a Jezebel spirit and a religious demon. Her behavior is typical of a person who is deceived---intolerant and irrational---declaring that "God said this to me and God said that!!! Unable to reason without running for cover, Lois is so spiritual that she is no earthly good. She is also hypocritical, blessing me on one hand, and then dismissing me on another. It was very clear that she did not "appreciate my input" but indeed was offended by the suggestion that she did not hear from God. Spiritual snobbery and pride oozes from her pen because in her mind, I am an unknown "nobody" but her spiritual leaders have fellowshipped with the President of the USA!!!

It is all so foolish. If it were not for the fact that I am crucified with Christ and the world is dead to me, I would be too embarrassed to expose my own folly. Nevertheless, I believe that my testimony will help yet another deceived woman like Lois and therefore, I can accept humiliation and expose myself in this way. In fact, for 30 years, I myself believe a lie because when I was a young woman, I could not accept that there was "no dream man." I thank the Lord that 30 years have not been wasted and that the religious demon's handiwork has been significantly exposed. For example, I do not need a revelation from the Lord to know that Lois will become ever increasingly deceived as the religious demon steps up the pace to mess with her head. Been there, done that!!! Lois is at the stage where she already interprets every statement, every glance from John as a word from the Lord. In addition, her own personal racism is showing. The demon of racism and the demon of religion have been partners throughout the centuries, the very demonic duo that enslaved African Americans for 400 years.

To religious women like Lois, I pose the following questions. "When you were in the world and you still had your commonsense, did you not know when a man wanted you from when he did not? Would you have been like Lois, surprised and shocked to find out seven days before your man's wedding that he was about to marry someone else!? Would you not have read the signs suggesting that he was not in love with you? Furthermore, what makes you think that the Lord would force you to be with yet another man who you claim that you "could not stand", for the sake of saving souls for Jesus?" Get a grip!!! If you and your husband cannot stand each other's flesh, how many souls do you think both of you will be able to save together? I'll answer that question myself. NADA!!!! NO, not one!

The religious demon continues to overwork the Christian"soul mate deception", simply because it works. It worked on me more than once, a fact that I attribute to my false notion that a woman in ministry must serve with an husband in a co-pastoral team. Deceiving spirits are very skillful at planting its victims with visions, dreams and other supernatural leadings and revelations suggestive of the co-pastor, co-ministry belief. Actually, in 1974, three years BEFORE I was born again, the soul mate concept was surreptitiously planted in my mind by an astrologer, who called himself Norvelle. Norvelle predicted that in my astrology chart was an unusual phenomena: the planet Venus was in an exact conjunction to my 10th house of career and spirituality in the sign of Scorpio, and that my 7th house of love and marriage was also in conjunction to the Moon in Leo. He gushed with lots of ooo's and ah's, particularly in regards to this very powerful, special man that Norvelle predicted I would marry and "work with."

In Norvelle's understanding, the powerful man would be someone famous like a senator or prominent like a doctor or lawyer. I hate to admit it but in the beginning of my search, I set my eye on a well known New York politician. I even went to his campaign headquarters, hoping that he would look my way. Well, the competition was too steep and I soon gave up, primarily because politics was not my playing field. However once I became saved, Norvelle's prediction caused me to assume that "the man" was a prominent minister.

Then once I received the counterfeit charge of prison ministry, I believed that the man must be a former addict and an ex-offender. Like Lois, I too threw away all common sense regarding a mate. The truth is that the real reason why I myself entered into witchcraft in the first place is by becoming an astrologer myself, I hoped to learn more about my future with my "mystery soul mate." Since this prediction of Norvelle's, 33 years have gone by. The irony is that I have no mystery soul mate. The Lord delivered me from it all, praise His Holy Name. I tremble at the thought of how many women have died, still deceived by the religious demon. So I consider myself blessed to have escaped, even though it too decades to do find freedom.

Women are not only captive to a religious demonic soul tie, as demonstrated by a man that I call Ronald. In this particular situation, two months after Ronald married Cynthia and moved his bride a thousand miles away from home, Cynthia returned to her hometown for a visit, never to return. According to Ronald, Cynthia began to date an ex-boyfriend and proceeded to file for a divorce. He writes to anyone on the Internet who will listen:

Hello dear friends in Christ!~

I need to let all of you know my updated situation in regards to my new bride of 2 months that moved home and is involved (probably) with an 'Ex-Boyfriend' and has gone off deep end with mad spending and rebellion towards me, & God (I really fear!), her stubborn streak of getting HER way and and 'associating' with the unsaved (bar crowd) that she calls 'friends'!!!I spoke with Cynthia early this evening re: health insurance/doctors bill...What had started off rather peaceful, kind and non-confrontational soon turned into Cynthia flying into bursts of anger, frustration and points of outrage! Some tears as well! I still wish I knew why she is SO hateful and bitter even though she won't admit it! One second she's saying that her feelings had "totally changed" for me (for the worst), the next second telling me that I would "HAVE TO move" to be with her! (Strange if she eludes to NOT loving me anymore! YES????)

This was triggered as I spoke in a non-threatening and non- judgmental, Christlike manner. (I prayed at great lengths before calling her..for the Holy Spirit to lead me and control my thoughts and words as I was about to speak with my wife!)The more at peace that I was, and when I began speaking of the Lord God, His will for our lives and my desire to put him first in our marriage (What we BOTH used to be totally committed to the desire/plans of!) and reconciliation, It is as though I had 'spit' in Satan's face personally! The 'hounds-of- hell' were unleashed I SWEAR!~ (Not really swearin' tho! LOL)

There were conflicting messages being sent left and right! Cynthia was really struggling with 'demanding' her will and it seemed to tear her up when I suggested that We pray for the Lord's WILL!!!! Cynthia IS a Born-Again Christian (Who is off of God's path sadly) so I can see why there was such turmoil inside! The Holy Spirit was truly at work here people!!!! Satan doesn't want God's will or peace for HIS children! PRAISE THE HOLY NAME OF JESUS CHRIST FOR REVEALING HIS PRESENCE!!!!I really am receiving a total peace and comfort after such a 'heated' conversation from my beloved wife! I sense completely that the Holy Spirit is calling us to RISE UP and FIGHT (on our knees) against the Enemy!!! I have no doubt that this IS the violent STORM before the Victory that is mine in the Name of Jesus Christ. Pray my strength in the Lord!"

Ronald continued to send these kinds of delusional self-help pep talks by a plethora of emails sent to hundreds of Christians unknown to him, seeking their prayer support. As I continued to read them, Ronald's life unfolded, exposing a personality filled with contradictions. Attempting to appear spiritually strong, his weaknesses became glaring. He is stoical and yet seeks love, he is erratic and spasmodic in his action, yet extremely legalistic and dogmatic in his beliefs,--- utterly illogical in his rationalizations and continued profession of counterfeit faith that "he and Cynthia would serve the Lord together in ministry." Eventually, I began to commensurate with Cynthia, suspecting that there was a major piece of this puzzle that Ronald was hiding, perceived from one of his many emails:

"Cynthia is pushing for a divorce quickly with 2 different attorneys already hired! There is still some real bitterness, rage, resentment and cruel behavior (towards me) inside of her. What this stems from in her past, and is triggered by I do not know. This is a matter that only our Heavenly Father can utilize the Holy Spirit to correct, and to turn her heart towards Him once again and then the marriage will have the opportunity to repair with the Lord's forgiveness, tender mercies and blessings upon us. Please ask the Lord God to take the 'wind' out of her sails in all of this! The attorney fees, etc.... are going to eat me alive! Finances are already in turmoil.

I have been in deep prayer every day about this. The Lord has showed me in His holy Word and with the touch of the Holy Spirit on me, that He IS in fact revealing to me (inaudibly) that He IS restoring this marriage and Sara's heart and mind for us to be together and serve Him in some form of ministry.
I have had the ministry images in my mind since I was about 10 years old! Sara had expressed very similar desires in ministry with young ladies and

women."

Out of the abundance of the heart, the mouth speaks through Ronald's email. The religious demon had begun to set Ronald up for this fall since he was ten years old! It requires a very deep devotion to the truth which the Lord has declared will set the captives free, for a believer like Ronald and others so affected to be set free---a truth which cuts, breaks and ultimately humbles. To experience spiritual manifestations and to express religious platitudes does not make a believer "spiritual." In fact, captives who have a false spirituality are vulnerable to "going off the deep end" by assuming that every supernatural inclination is from the Lord. A spiritual person is one who is prepared to admit the possibility of deception. Ironically, Ronald will have advanced in spirituality if he did not resist the humiliation that I am sure followed after the he has to accept the fact that the Lord did not restore his marriage. If Ronald admitted that he believed a lie, then he will have opened himself to be set free by the truth.

A spiritual nugget of gold for me was to overcome the humiliation that the religious demon tried to inflict upon me, not by one husband only, but by two. Where demonic soul ties are concerned, I have found that the key to true humility and meekness is to be capable of baring the humiliation that inevitably accompanies the truth that declares "I have been deceived." When a captive can become diminished or lowered in his own estimation of his spirituality and yields to it without explanation or defense, then he is on his way to becoming a truly spiritual person, who may not need a soul mate to fulfill his calling in Christ Jesus. I have evolved into such a woman. Some might contend that I am in denial of my needs for companionship because I have failed at love and marriage three times. I must disagree. I am not in denial of my needs. In fact, as my heart has grieved and mourned over unrequited love, I have found the blessing of comfort that Jesus has promised. Therefore, without bitterness or shame, I have turned my back on what is behind, as I stretch forward toward the mark of my high calling in Christ Jesus---that is---to set the captives free!!!!

Endnotes

1. See "To Curse the Root." This counterfeit mission is presented in the dedication.

2.bethelministries.com/divorce.htm I disagree with Harry Bethel regarding any and all of his teachings about the role of Christian women. However, he has provided some excellent Christian scholarship regarding marriage and divorce and though considered a bit radical by most Christians, Bethel seems to "know what time it is" for America in general and the church in particular.

CHAPTER 14: SWIMMING BEYOND THE ROPE

By now, hopefully the eyes of each reader have been opened to the intensity of what the elect face in this hour of human history. Whatever the pivotal point and however tortuous the journey, if you have digested the impact of this book, then you have awakened to the reality of a need for readiness to do battle. If true believers everywhere seriously understood the magnitude of spiritual deception, they would scrupulously   prepare themselves for the final onslaught that the enemy has masterminded. In this regard, the fivefold ministry within the true Body of Christ must be equipped for the challenges of living in a supernatural age that may be very close to "the end." It has been difficult for me to bring an end to this book because as I write, more faces are continuing to be revealed. Therefore, I believe that I have but touched the tip of the iceberg, since much of the spiritual activity of these times emanates from the powers of darkness.

Since the faces and profiles in this book are in no way exhaustive, I myself must remain consistently on guard. Consequently,   I continue to confront each new demonic face with the knowledge that I have previously obtained, yet expectant to consider new understandings and peculiarities that may even challenge what has already been revealed. In this regard, flexibility and objectivity are essential. To do this work takes time; the more entangled and the more barricaded a captive has become, the more time is required. With the ever increasing specialization of the enemy, particularly the witchcraft demon and the religious spirit, we must earnestly seek the wisdom of God. As Satan would sift Peter like wheat, no believer is exempt. As the Lord prayed that Peter's faith would fail not, this is my prayer for you the reader as well as for myself.

A true and a living faith is demonstrated by a Christian who not only preaches, teaches and counsels, but who also demonstrates the power of God. The hour is at hand when like Moses, we will need "the rod in the hand." (Exodus 7:8-13) Divine miracles will be crucial to combat the supernatural magic and trickery of present day false prophets. Miracles from the Holy Ghost will be so awesome that no one will have to defend or prove them to be divine. Yet be warned that if your motivation for seeking signs, wonders and miracles is to prove that you are anointed, you will become susceptible to the religious demon. Therefore, walking in meekness and with a contrite heart is essential. Jesus Christ will cause definitely anoint His own to move in supernatural power.

I believe that as in the days of Moses, the Lord will use miracles as a means to draw people to Him, particularly those whose minds have been seriously blinded by the enemy. By now, you realize that one of the most outstanding revelations of "Faces of the Religious Demon" is an important warning that not every supernatural manifestation is from the Holy Spirit. As Satan uses his power to attempt to qualify the false prophets, the Holy Ghost will use His miracles to legitimize His ministers on His own, without our help to prove anything. Consequently, our prayer today should be this. "Lord, give me the rod and I commit myself to walk in the meekness of Moses, the meekness of the Lord Jesus Christ. I submit myself to you to be broken anywhere in my character that is an open door to the enemy. As you give me discernment, please give me the ability not to be fooled by a false sign." So Beloved, if you do not have the faith to walk the supernatural walk, then you ought not challenge any demons.

Those who have sought after signs, wonders and the gifts of the Spirit in the Charismatic church, the word of faith assemblies, and the Catholic faith have not only been infested by the religious demon, but through their idolatry have also given place to the spirit of Jezebel. Therefore, the servants in this season should also be very patient, deliberate and careful in our preparation of each captive for deliverance. In unbelievers, rarely does the witchcraft demon leave of its own accord without being cast out. As stated throughout this book, I am personally an example of a person who had a spirit of divination, that the Holy Spirit sovereignly cast from me at the moment of rebirth. Once I was saved, demons could no longer enter my soul and speak through my larynx according to their own will. Twenty nine years have past and I have not had one such experience, wherein it was a constant occurrence prior to my salvation.

However, my experience has shown that this is not really the way the Lord chooses to contend with this or any other demon. I believe that the Lord delivered me sovereignly because 29 years ago, there were no believers available in my locality bold enough and wise enough to stand face to face and contend with the spirit of witchcraft and my time for deliverance had come. Today the Lord is seeking "a Moses" with a rod in his hand to set his people free. The witchcraft demon in the Egyptian sorcerer was able to turn a rod into a snake. However, Moses' snake devoured the sorcerer's snake. Furthermore, as Elijah challenged and defeated the supernatural power of Baal with the power of the Holy Spirit, I believe that we shall be called to do the same very shortly.

As a foreshadow of what lies ahead, a few years ago, a woman sent me an email seeking to understand why she could hear fearful voices in her head screaming and cursing and saying "Get off of this website.!" This happened twice while she was on line at www.healingwaterscc.com., as she looked into a picture of my face. I informed her that the demons in her apparently respected my anointing to cast them out. Determined not to leave, I believe that the demons IN her were trying to frighten her from contact with me. Since then, others have contacted me with similar reports, which I consider to be a good sign. For most assuredly, in order to stand against the religious demon and the spirits of witchcraft, these demons must respect the fact that you are anointed to cast them out and that your faith in the name of Jesus is greater than their faith in the name of Satan. Without their respect, you will not be victorious because the witchcraft demon is the strongest fighter in the enemy's army.

Even so, it is easier to cast out a spirit of witchcraft than a religious demon because of one thing: the freewill of the captive. To be quite honest, I have often believed that if a captive were to receive truth, pray and simply repent, the religious demon would leave them of its own accord without anyone having to cast it out. Proceeding with hopeful discretion, I believe that I have just witnessed such a case. As I bring this book to a close, what a great blessing to be able to present a potentially successful case. Just yesterday, an African woman whose name I have changed to "Celie" contacted me by email with this request.:

> "I believe that there is a spirit of confusion sent to my home to bring
> confusion between my husband and I. I live in Africa now. This family has a
> history of dabbling in things of the occult. This sort of thing is very
> prevalent here. I myself as a child was sent by my mother to see various

fetish priests. When I received Jesus as my Saviour I denounced all these things. My husband is also born-again."

I responded to Celie's email, interpreted some of her dreams and suggested that in a month, when this book has been published, that she obtain a copy. Well, apparently, she did not need to wait for this book. Celie simply visited my website at www.healingwaterscc.com , read some of my articles about the religious demon and the prosperity doctrine, and the Holy Spirit apparently used her to cast out demons from herself!!!! The Lord Jesus Christ be praised! The Healing Waters are flowing , from city to city, nation to nation! Note the cultural witchcraft, the generational curse of anger, the dysfunctional family themes, the sexual abuse, and the charismatic witchcraft of the late grandmother and the prosperity preaching church. Celie's words in this email demonstrate a heart of repentance. Here is her remarkable testimony of deliverance from a religious demon, in her own words:

"Thank you for your message. It is a confirmation of what the Lord has been ministering to me. I think a lot of change is coming into my life and I think that God is preparing me for this. I would also like to take this opportunity to thank you for something else. I only logged onto your website for the first time yesterday. I was looking to ministries that dealt with dream interpretation and I read your message about religious demons with great interest. I have been born again for as long as I could remember but I really suffer badly from a spirit of anger and usually directed at my children. I used to direct it towards my husband and as a consequence our marriage suffered greatly. God through his awesome grace dealt with me and after reading "The Power of a Praying Wife" and fasting and steadfast prayer my marriage is abounding in leaps and bounds thanks to the grace of the Lord.

Yet I still have a terrible spirit of anger towards my children. I grew up with a strict father, was sexually abused when I was about five. Anyway to get back to the religious spirit, I grew up with my grandmother and she was the one who really introduced me to Christianity because my parents are catholic and she used to worship in a church called Zaoga. This church is one of those that focus on prosperity big time and tithing (another of your articles I read).
To cut a very long story short, lately I have been dreaming of my grandmother in very negative ways (although she passed away a year or so ago). Although prayerful, she was really not a very nice person and was accused more than once of witchcraft by family members. I have been praying and praying about this and after reading your article the Lord revealed to me that although having been saved, I have worshiped in a church dominated by religion and false doctrines. I also had a mentor (my grandmother) who proclaimed to have been saved but had not put away the old man for the new, I had a stronghold in my life. I went home and prayed for deliverance and a powerful demon came out and I later dreamed of swimming in clear blue waters. I feel good and wait to see whether this was where the stronghold of anger was coming from. If you have any advice you can give me I would be grateful to have it. Previous to yesterday I have had several dreams where I go into a shower to shower and cannot because the

shower is surrounded by feces or it is so unclean I cannot go in. This usually happens when I dream I am with old school friends and am in a dorm and wanting to go to shower. I will see after my deliverance of yesterday if this will continue to occur.

Thank you so much for your website. I found it an inspiration yesterday."

Once Celie was apparently set free, It seems that the Lord used her to send me a personal prophecy, even though she does not realize that this word may have been specifically meant for me. Such an occurrence is reminiscent of how through the mouth of Laura, I received the prophecy previously mentioned of "The Seven Walls." Like Celie, Laura had just been delivered from a demon---the very first demon that Zonnita and I ever confronted. Immediately thereafter, Laura prophesied one of the most significant words that I myself have received since being called to preach. Taking my own advice and counsel, I will remain cautious, as even this word could be the underhanded work of a religious demon.

I particularly move with discretion in this matter because this dream has a supernatural bent to it. Celie herself has no idea that in "The Making of a Prophet: A Spiritual Indictment to the Organized Church", as a virtual unknown, I confronted an entire denomination and those like the AME Zion Church. An historic black church that is over 200 years old, I call the AME Zion Church and its counterparts: "the church at Sardis." Furthermore, I believe that Celie's dream of "clear blue waters" is symbolic of my ministerial name, "Healing Waters." Here are her prophetic words that she received almost immediately after she was set free from a demon after visiting the Beware Christian website:

"Lastly I have something to share that the Lord gave me yesterday:-"

This prophecy is based upon Revelation 3 v 1-12 - This means that the Lord is going to open doors for those who are unknown to come in His name and overcome those from "Sardis". The Lord does not tolerate the rubbish and utter filth that is going on in churches. A satanic religion is taking over churches. No- one is safe except those that stay in the Vine. Things are going to happen extremely shortly that no eye has seen nor any ear heard. Deaths are going to rock the world. Hence my husband and I (and all those sheep of the Lord) have to stand firm. The Lord promises to open doors that we least believed could be opened. This is the word of the Lord on the night of 27th April 2006 at 23:25pm (GMT time).

If Celie has truly been delivered from a religious demon just by reading a few articles on my website, this book is truly a swim "beyond the rope." I have offered to counsel with her so as to ensure that the issue of cultural anger and others have been sufficiently addressed, so that she will take hold and maintain a lasting and enduring deliverance. I will certainly have the opportunity to utilize the strategies that are outlined in Chapter 11, "The Dysfunctional Family." Nevertheless, it has been my experience that the spirit of witchcraft is much easier to cast out than the religious demon. In fact, I have never actually cast out a religious demon, other than from myself. Considering both the religious and the witchcraft faces of the spirit of Jezebel as separate entities, I have found that the repeated cycle of torment characterized by witchcraft necessitates the captive to be more prone to participate in his own struggle to be set free. Without the element of torment, those in the grips of religiosity are not as willing to deny the gratification that religiosity brings to their flesh.

In addition, while the religious demon will pretend to the end that the captive is a faithful follower of the Lord Jesus Christ, the witchcraft demon is less "faithful." It has been my experience that the witchcraft demon will pretend to follow Jesus up until it has been exposed. Once unmasked, it will use the captive to scream obscenities, and the demon will speak out and openly confess Satan and deny that Jesus is Lord. Since any face of Jezebel is dangerous, the counselor must realize that he himself must walk in the power of God, or he will be defeated. Where the conflict between the kingdom of God and the religious demon focuses on truth and error, the conflict between the Lord's followers and the witchcraft demon is a struggle between counterfeit power and the supernatural power of the Holy Spirit. Jesus said these words to those who had accused Him of casting out devils in the power of the devil. He said to them: If I cast out devils by the Spirit of God, then the kingdom of God has come upon you. Or else how can one enter a strong man's house, and spoil his goods, except he first bind the strong man? And then he will spoil his house." (Matthew 12:28,29)

What I glean from this word is that as a pastor or counselor, my goal is to "examine the captive's house." If a Christian, the captive is really a strong man that has been bound--spirit, soul and body. Therefore, it is my job to discover how did he get bound. It most definitely was a demon or demons that "entered the captive's house, bound him and spoiled his goods: his family, his job, his peace of mind, even his sanity. However, if I am bound myself, how can I unbind the captive? Good question. The answer is "I cannot!"

To make a spiritual point, consider my experience as a long distance swimmer. I swim in many different public places that include pools and lakes. All of these bodies of water are bound by a rope or ropes that define and limit my space. Since there are others on each side of me when I am swimming laps in a pool with roped in lanes, I can be distracted when someone jumps into the pool on each side of the rope and swims faster than I do. At both ends of the pool are walls that can cause me to break my stride before I turn around and swim back down the lane. I always feel better, more free, when I swim at a time when no one else is in the water. Regardless, I swim for an hour, at least 30 minutes longer than the average lap swimmer.

When I swim in a backyard pool, I am even more restrained. There are all kinds of floating tubes and balls in the water. I have to swim around them. Since the space is very small in comparison to the Olympic pool of the YMCA, I must now go around and around in circles. I cannot stay there long. It becomes boring to me and I don't usually swim there for more than 30 minutes. However at my favorite lake, I enjoy swimming the most.--- Why? Because lap swimmers are permitted to go beyond the rope. Beyond the rope, there are no collisions with those who are frolicking and playing in the water. Even though there is a rope on one side of me and I have to make sure that I don't go too far "out there," I feel free. I truly enjoy my swim. If I don't look at the rope on the side of me, I can see the landscape and the beauty of the sun hitting the water. No one is out there with me and so I am not distracted by any other human being or sound. The water feels like silk, and I can glide in it for two hours or even more.

I use this natural example to present a spiritual truth to the one who is called to deliverance, and that is--- YOU MUST GO BEYOND THE ROPE. Going beyond the rope is to lose all fear in your own quest for personal freedom. There are occasions when I learned five years of lessons in one year but most of the time, it took five years or more to learn one lesson. In fact, I have been learning spiritual things for more three decades: Three years completely on the dark side and 29 years in Christ, of which almost 25 of those years have been in ministry. If you read in my first book "To Curse the Root", you will find out that I have been broken several times. I have been broken even more since I finished the book in 1996. I was broken again less than a week ago.

Even though I have been serving in ministry since Oct. 25, 1981, experiential learning has been more a part of my serving than preaching, pastoring or any other ministerial function. What I have been learning for the most part is how to be "spiritually sensitive." At first I thought that spiritual sensitivity could only be attained through the 9 supernatural gifts of the Holy Ghost, particularly the discerning of spirits. Yet the word of God makes it plain that these 9 gifts only operate "as the Spirit wills" and not simply because we either desire them or seek them. We are told to seek them and to desire them, yet one of the purposes of this book is to warn the elect that Satan has some very clever counterfeits. In summary, here are some biblical truths to remember:

1.Anyone who is truly saved cannot be touched by the devil without God's permission. (Job Ch. 1)

2.The plan of God is to lead the demons to reveal their own folly. (II Timothy 2:26)

3.The devil believes that the only thing that keeps the believer faithful to the Lord is the fact that he or she is protected by the hedge. In other words, we are in it for the blessings and protection from demons. Demons are convinced that when the pressure is placed upon us, we will not stand. (Read Job)

4.When a demon has been able to have place in a Christian's life, we should examine the situation based upon points 1-3.

5.When the battle comes in a believer's life, the Lord will make a way of escape. Very often, you as a counselor, shall be the "way" that the Lord has made for a particular captive to escape.

6.Sometimes the Lord will permit a believer to be deceived because there is a valuable lesson to be learned from the experience.

7.We must all accept being vulnerable to demonic deception and attack.

8.We will never be smart enough to discern the trap that has been set before us. However, if we remain lovers of the truth, the unction of the Holy Spirit that we have received will reveal all truth to us. (John 16:13)

9.Deliverance counselors must simply trust God to open our spiritual eyes and reveal demonic devices to us, as long as we continue to walk by faith with complete and total trust in Jesus Christ.

10.Anyone who is not saved, is in the hands of the devil because the devil has rule and authority over him. Any unsaved person who seeks deliverance must first come under the authority of Jesus Christ of Nazareth, who is the Deliverer.

Although I may not be able to walk in a supernatural gift according to my own will like the false prophets and psychics do with Satan's power, I leave supernatural manifestations in the hands of God. In fact, I no longer actively seek the supernatural, as it is definitely a weakness of my flesh. For example, if the testimony of Celie in Africa is of the Lord, then He will move miraculously when He chooses, without even my personal knowledge. What I have learned is that I can become "spiritually sensitive" to the extent that I can discern the Lord from what is emanates from my own soul, or from what is demonic in nature. As you can ascertain from the profiles that have been presented in this book, the bulk of this kind of discernment has come to me by learning through experience. For everyone who partakes only of milk is unskilled in the word of righteousness, for he is a babe. But solid food belongs to those who are of full age, that is, those who by reason of use have their sense exercised to discern both good and evil. (James 5:12-14) The "exercise" to which James is referring will produce true "LEARNING!" The more you and I learn, the more we can discern. Hopefully, you too can learn from my trial, errors and failures.

How does "learning to discern come?" Many study all the time by learning facts but they cannot discern truth in the spirit. I have found that the most important aspect of learning how to discern is to experience the Lord's hand upon me as I myself am broken. When I am broken, then I become sensitive and discerning. Here is an example. I am acquainted with preachers who have studied all the scriptures on pride and can quote them, even preach a good message about pride, yet not really be able to sense the sinfulness of pride in their own spirits. Therefore, when pride appears in the captive, such a minister will not be able to sense it. His spirit will not be distressed. He may even feel sympathetic to the captive when what he should be feeling is a sense of distress within his own spirit.

When the Lord deals with me through the work of the Holy Spirit by breaking me, then when I come across a sinful situation, I feel distressed because my senses have been exercised to discern evil and to feel what God Himself feels about that evil. Once I have discerned the ailment or weakness that opened the door to demonic oppression, then I can serve my brother in the area of pride, if pride was the problem. The more my own soul is renewed, the better I can serve. The more I myself have been dealt with, the better I am able to make an assessment based on spiritual truth. Once The Holy Spirit has broken me in a particular area, I find that I am better equipped to pinpoint the real condition of others.

A previously indicated, just as the mouth speaks what is in the heart, so too does the mouth speak through an email. To make a good assessment of a person's soul, we listen to his mouth. One of the benefits of using emails in counseling is that I can examine every written word and phrase, even the ordering of a captive's thoughts by the way he puts forth his inner man in his sentences. Since both the religious demon and the witchcraft demon are rooted in the pride of its captive, pride uncovers the nature of the soul. In the scriptures, rebellion,--- a form of pride---, is comparable to witchcraft. However, since the captive to the witchcraft demon will invariably suffer loss, or some other negative outcome to his physical and emotional well being, its captive will ultimately desire freedom. I repeat again that the relief from torment by an apparently passive captive will often reveal a rebellious heart, filled with pride.

Therefore, it is important for you to know that once you move beyond the rope of infancy in Christ in the first stage of your spiritual walk, the Lord will not stop you from making bad decisions. If you the reader have learned nothing else, I believe that my testimony is a living witness of this spiritual truth. If you do not heed conviction that emanates from within your spirit by the Holy Ghost, you will grieve and quench Him. When He warns you within your spirit, His conviction will often feel like a knife is stuck in your chest. Once the Holy Ghost is grieved and quenched, you as a Christian shall be very vulnerable to deception because you could be turned over to a reprobate mind. A reprobate mind is susceptible to delusions and illusions. I have found that once the conscience of a saint is shut down, he or she will be subject to charismatic witchcraft which I have defined as a co-working of the religious demon and the spirit of witchcraft--- manifested through divination, necromancy and sorcery, a counterfeit of the gifts of the Holy Ghost. This is the domain of the Jezebel spirit.

The SEW Program is the training grounds for those who would become deliverance counselors within the framework of Spiritual Bootcamp Sessions (SBS) Designed according to a brief problem solving approach, my goal in creating both the training and the counseling models is to prepare captives for deliverance, both to stand and to maintain against the unseen enemy. In some of the most difficult cases, the objective is to take territory from the the the demons, inch by inch. If the captive can gain an in improvement in his relationships with others and with himself, so that he becomes less isolated, less hostile, less self pitying, where the captives comes to terms with the fact that "we wrestle not against flesh and blood but against principalities and powers, then I have helped the captive to regain his own soul. In fact, anytime that a captive is able to internalize a spiritual truth, if he can cease to see others around him as a menace to be fought, manipulated or avoided, then I have gained significant ground.

The Lord declared that the truth shall set us free. Therefore, spiritual freedom is my overall goal of deliverance. For until the captive is free from religiosity, he will never experience the freedom that truth brings. Therefore, the SEW Program and SBS are geared toward helping a captive to take a stand for his own well being and ultimate survival. Fro why should a believer in Jesus Christ religiously misapply "turning the other cheek" to a demon who is hell bent on destroying him? Why should he continue to sacrifice himself for those who abuse him in the church? Why should a disciple of Jesus have an insatiable desire to manipulate and control others with religiosity, simply because he has an unhealthy striving for recognition, position and power? Why should a saint live with a constant fear of being submerged by others, so that he is compelled to ascend himself above them, just to survive? Why should an overcomer in Christ Jesus be a mealy mouthed, passive person, who breaks those in his immediate environment with his legalistic restrictions and complaints? Why must a prophet think that he must speak words into the lives of the brethren like he was a psychic, just for the sake of power and manipulation? Therefore, where deliverance is concerned, I go the extra mile for Jesus by creating liberating conditions within a captive's soul---a spiritual blockade to the re-infestation by the religious demon.

It is important to note that the creation of a flawless disciple is not within my domain. As a counselor, I can only help a captive to become free by providing an opportunity for spiritual insight. For me, perfection is to be demon free and to face truth every day. It should be clear from every insight presented in this book that where the religious demon is concerned, we can never exhaust spiritual warfare by a single approach. This demon must be combated over and over again from various angles and perspectives. It is so difficult to end this book because I see a new face everyday and I am tempted to sit down and write about it. Every new face springs from a variety of sources and factors and thereby I have to assume new strategies. I am committed to each and every captive that comes my way to examine his attitudes, his personality and his issues.

Even though I believe that "the house is burning,", in spite of the spiritual damage that may have occurred within an organized church, recovery in Christ is inevitable because of the words of the Lord, "My sheep KNOW my voice and the voice of a stranger they will not follow." No one will be able to pluck the Lord's sheep out of His hand. He will ALWAYS prepare a way of escape. If a way of escape cannot be found, I personally believe that most of those who seem to have suffered irreparable damage are among those whom our Lord never knew. Among the saints, there are also the lukewarm ones, whom the Lord shall spit out of His mouth. Every good and perfect gift comes down from the Father of lights. God is light and in Him there is no darkness at all. The Lord Jesus said that what is covered shall be uncovered and what is hid shall be made known. He also said that you "shall know them by their fruit."

My personal testimony stands as a beacon of light in the midst of darkness in the church. Darkness surrounded me on all sides but the Lord saw to it that darkness did not overcome me by smothering my light. Furthermore, I believe that the Father of lights has an appointed time when the false religious demon that has mixed itself with the children of light shall be exposed in each and every situation. I believe that the appointed time for exposure is at hand today. In Isaiah 49, the Lord speaks through the prophet and says that in an acceptable time, He has heard us and in the day of salvation, He helps us. In an acceptable time, He heard me, and in the day of my salvation, the Lord Jesus Christ helped me by empowering me to set many captives free.

In the day of exposure, the children of darkness are stumbling everywhere, causing them to reveal themselves of their own accord. Even though the wheat and the tare will continue to grow together until the second coming of our Lord of the Harvest, this does not mean that we will not be able to discern the tares. There are times when the tares and the wheat are almost identical in appearance. To break it down further, those who profess to be saved and who are not will be used by demons to hinder you. However, if you walk in the light as Jesus is the light, you will have the victory.

Yes, this is the time of exposure. Lately, people who I have believed were truly saved have themselves looked me in the face and declared "I never believed." From the Internet to my own community and even significant people among my family and friends---people who have professed the faith for years---are now revealing from their own hearts that they are still children of darkness. As I continue to walk in the light, darkness backs up. How does such a thing happen? Well, invariably some do have faith in His name, but they anchor their faith in a delusion, an illusion or an obsession, and end up believing that they are saved when they are not.

Each case that I have presented involved different factors. I cannot over-emphasize that the wiles of the religious demon are countless, specifically fitted to the ways, personality and circumstances of each of its captives as well as to the one who is standing in the gap. As a wile is a strategy by which a demon gains his objective, it is crucial to be familiar with the conditions that need to be in place in order for the enemy to achieve his desired end and conversely, the terms that need to be fulfilled in order for the captive to be set free.

Consider the case in scripture where the apostles were not able to cast out a demon from an epileptic. After rebuking them for a lack of faith, Jesus also pointed to two other conditions for this particular deliverance to be possible----conditions that the apostles had not fulfilled, namely, prayer and fasting. I have personally discovered that where the religious demon is concerned, an essential condition is agreement and respect between the captive and the one who stands in the position of the deliverer. Simply put, those who have continued to challenge my authority and anointing are those who have not been set free. There are several other conditions.

Since all of the demon's wiles and devices are set in motion to keep both the captive and the deliverance counselor in the dark, both parties must maintain the ground of attack by making sure that dominion over sin has been accomplished. For any un-crucified or weak spot in either party is an open target for the enemy to deceive. Moreover, since each deliverance is an education in the spirit that must be patiently mastered, the captive as well as the deliverance counselor must open their minds to all truth, and close them to all error. Discernment requires accuracy in discrimination relative to perceiving the character and motives of those involved, particularly those aspects of a situation that are not clearly evident to the average intelligence.

I believe that it is crucial to point out that I take great care not to be derailed into a necessary search for historical origin of demonic doorways to such an extent that I overlook the captive's responsibility to fight and the Lord's desire that the captive be free, in spite of what his ancestors have done. I encourage the captive to become familiar with his own inner strongholds and how the religious demon may have used his own weaknesses to keep him bound---driven to act in accordance with the religious demons strategies and devices. Once a particular weakness has become visible to me during counseling, it is my job to make the captive aware of its influence upon his captivity.

With each new face of the religious demon exposed, new insights progressively lead to new challenges that neither the captive nor the deliverance worker has encountered before. Yet I have found that in spite of all of the individual variations, the crucial conflicts around which the religious demon thrives are embedded with repetitive factors like competitiveness, hostilities between people, fears, and diminished self esteem. All parties in a deliverance must commit themselves to literally scrutinize everything. Scrutiny is effective when close attention is paid to detailed, precise and objective observation in a search for defects, errors and sins. All parties must press toward enlightenment in an aggressive fight to cast off the works of darkness and put on the armor of light. Although each and every relevant element of the client's bondage must be examined and understood, one thing remains constant. As a deliverance counselor, I must "go beyond the rope" and "work it through."

Nevertheless, in every case, my approach is basically the same---search for the hidden and the obscure; bring what I have found to the captive's awareness; cause him to recognize how he has been working against himself; teach him who he is in Christ; and enable him to stand against all of the fiery darts of the enemy's attack and counterattack. In this regard, I have also found through experience that there are four primary reasons as to how the religious demon obtains ground in a professing believer in Jesus Christ: a lack of understanding of the nature of true repentance and why repentance is absolutely essential to the new birth, a belief in "another Jesus", an extreme seeking after signs and wonders without trying the spirits, and the influx of charismatic witchcraft, the fruit of "out of context" preaching.

As a former witchcraft practitioner, in all humility I confess that I know what it feels like to be caught up in a supernatural deception of false power. Satan and his demons DO have the ability to transform themselves into beings of light. The word of God warns us in more than one scripture that many of the elect shall be deceived in the last days. I believe that there are several seekers today who may be among the elect who are living under the power of a strong delusion. In these last days, it is crucial to repeat the words of Hosea the prophet in this matter: "My people are destroyed for a lack of knowledge." With humble contrition, I thank the Lord that although I myself was almost destroyed for the lack an ability of discerning good from evil, He showed me the way to the truth.

In retrospect, a common thread throughout this book is that the biggest enemy to complete deliverance from religiosity is not the demons, but it is the flesh. As we have seen, the capacity of the captive to recognize the consequences of demonic deception is limited without a commitment to stand against the forces of darkness, regardless of the apparent ruthlessness of the truth. Going beyond the rope embraces several aspects of spiritual warfare including those attributes of deliverance counseling that help the captive translate the messages obtained through learning how to read the subtle messages that the trends, seasons and cycles of his life unfold.

In the final analysis, life itself is a very effective teacher, not within our own control but in the hands of the Holy Spirit. If we do not grieve Him or quench Him with our carnality, we can help Him to set the captives free in the Name of Jesus Christ of Nazareth. For me, this is like swimming beyond the rope of merely commanding a demon to depart, which I will do, as the Holy Spirit leads me. Yet to be truly effective, I must stop the religious demon in its tracks by imparting truth. Jesus Christ has left his disciples with His word, His armor and His name. As long as we do not allow the lust of our flesh for religion to grieve and quench the Holy Ghost, **_we will win!!!!_**

about the author

Formerly a psychic medium and an astrologer from 1974-1977, Rev. Pamela Sheppard LMSW had a Damascus Road type of experience with the Lord Jesus Christ while she was an atheist. Converted in her living room on March 29, 1977, she was sent by the Holy Ghost to the African Methodist Episcopal Zion Church in 1979 where she served as a local preacher, a pastor and an evangelist from 1981-2004. She obtained both a BA and a Masters Degree in Social Work, conferred by the State University in Albany New York, licensed in the state to practice counseling as a social worker.

Pam has worn many hats in the Body of Christ in the last 25 years: Evangelist, teacher, intercessor, pastor, and prophet. A deliverance worker, a spiritual warrior, a healer and an author of 4 books, Pam is an active Christian therapist engaged in private practice. The founder of Healing Waters Counseling Center, Pam has developed a unique pre-deliverance Christ centered training model called Spiritual Empowerment Workshop known as "the SEW Program." Those trained in SEW will be equipped to conduct pre and post deliverance counseling within the unique Spiritual Bootcamp Sessions modality.

To learn more about the diversity of Pam's approach, visit her website at www.healingwaterscc.com or send an email to pastorpam911@yahoo.com If you are interested in seeking deliverance counseling by telephone from any part of the USA or abroad, you should send an email to that effect or call toll free at 1-866-492-2409. Pam is also available to conduct conferences, workshops and seminars anywhere in the world.

Other books by Pam Sheppard: To Curse the Root: A Christian Alternative to 12 Steps, (ISBN 1-4259-0766-0) the Making of a Prophet, A Spiritual Indictment to the Organized Church. (ISBN 1-4208-4725-2) The SEW Program Training Manual is soon to be released.

Other books by the author

COME OUT OF HER, GOD'S PEOPLE: Don't Receive Her Plagues
IBSN 978-0-557-41416-1

THE FAKE JESUS: Fallen Angels Among Us
ISBN 978-0-615-21977-6

TO CURSE THE ROOT: A Christian Alternative to 12 Steps
ISBN: 978-1-425-90766-0

Visit the author at www.pamsheppard.com

On the website, you can make an appointment for telephone counseling, mentoring, or enter any of her online deliverance counseling training programs.

To contact the author, send an email to contact@pamsheppard.com

The author's fifth book concerns a unique counseling population---Christian women who claim to perform a sexual act with invisible entities, ie. demons and/or devils.

Made in the USA
Middletown, DE
21 June 2017